DATE DUE

JE 8'04			

DEMCO 38-296

THE GIFT OF TIME

JONATHAN SCHELL

The Gift of Time

THE CASE FOR ABOLISHING NUCLEAR WEAPONS NOW

Metropolitan Books
Henry Holt and Company
New York

Metropolitan Books
Henry Holt and Company, Inc.
Publishers since 1866
115 West 18th Street
New York, New York 10011

Metropolitan Books™ is an imprint of Henry Holt and Company, Inc.

Library of Congress Cataloging-in-Publication data are available.

ISBN 0-8050-5960-1

Henry Holt books are available for special promotions and premiums.
For details contact: Director, Special Markets.

First Edition 1998

Designed by Kate Nichols

Printed in the United States of America
All first editions are printed on acid-free paper. ∞

10 9 8 7 6 5 4 3 2 1

For Tom, Turner, and Wally,

in friendship

CONTENTS

THE GIFT OF TIME

I

THE GREAT
THRESHOLD

In early December of 1997, a disconcerting piece of news seeped out of the White House. The nation's plans for fighting a nuclear war had been revised by a Presidential Decision Directive (a so-called PDD) for the first time since 1981. No public announcement had been made, but reporters got wind of the change, and the Clinton administration confirmed the news. It was, of course, disturbing in this peaceful time merely to be reminded that the United States still had plans for nuclear war. Just days earlier, on Thanksgiving, President Clinton had proclaimed, "In this new world, our children are growing up free from the shadows of the Cold War and the threat of nuclear holocaust." The PDD appended a decidedly jarring footnote to the president's assurance. If, now that the Cold War was over, we were free of the threat of a nuclear holocaust, then what need was there for nuclear arsenals, or for revised plans for using them?

The jolt was not eased by the few cryptic fragments of explanation that were offered by the administration. In an interview with R. Jeffrey Smith of the *Washington Post*, Robert Bell, who serves on the National Security Council, sought to draw a clear distinction between the new directive and its Reagan-era predecessor. The new one, he proudly stated, "removes from presidential guidance all previous references to being able to wage a nuclear war successfully or to prevail in a nuclear war." That innovation, however, could scarcely qualify as a bold departure from Cold War policy. After all, in 1985 President Reagan and Soviet Communist Party general secretary Mikhail Gorbachev had jointly declared that "nuclear war cannot be won and must never be fought." Was the public now to understand that it had taken twelve years—during five of which Bill Clinton was president—for this high-level affirmation of rudimentary sanity in the nuclear age to travel down the spinal cord of the military machine from the commander in chief to his subordinates at the Pentagon? And was it to understand that this delayed implementation, six years *after* the end of the Cold War, of a policy announced six years *before* the end of the Cold War was the most significant change wrought in U.S. nuclear policy by that revolution in international affairs?

Far more striking than any differences from early Reaganite excesses was the continuity of the new directive with orthodox Cold War nuclear policy. Just as the doctrine of nuclear deterrence had guided U.S. policy toward the Soviet Union, so now it guided our policy toward Russia. Just as the Soviet government and military had been targeted for destruction, so now the civilian and military leadership of Russia was being targeted. In the event of attack, Bell stated, nuclear retaliation "would be certain and overwhelming and devastating." In light of all this, his general conclusion was not surprising: nuclear weapons were to remain the cornerstone of U.S. security for "the indefinite future." There were, it is true, a few modest changes. The directive was to be implemented with a maximum of about eight thousand strategic warheads—the number mandated by the first Strategic Arms Reduction Talks (START I), which was signed in 1991 and went into effect in 1994. The list of targets in China had been expanded (prompting a remonstration from China's foreign minister). And a few new countries—those judged to have "prospective access" to nuclear weapons—were added to the list. (No countries were named, but it seems likely that Iraq, Iran, and North Korea are among them.)

Russia, of course, also retains large nuclear arsenals and has plans for using them. In other words, on both sides of the now-missing Iron

Curtain, the policy of nuclear deterrence remains in force, dictating that each side maintain forces that, in the event of an attack by the other side, can destroy the attacker's society. The question today is, Who wants these reciprocal threats of annihilation, and why? Communism was the issue between the Soviet Union and the United States. The government now in power in Russia overthrew Communism, and today relations between Russia and the United States are cordial. The great nuclear arsenals of the United States and the Soviet Union were created as instruments of the Cold War. Now that that conflict has been dissolved, can't the arsenals, too, be dissolved? Now that the war is over, can't we stand down the arms that were built to fight it? Over a period of years, the peoples of the Soviet empire dismantled the system of totalitarian terror under which they lived. Can't we and they together now dismantle the system of nuclear terror under which we have all been living? Can't we, at long last, abolish nuclear weapons?

This book proposes an affirmative answer to that question. It is a call for the abolition of nuclear arms, not only in the United States and Russia but throughout the world. Or, to be exact, it is a number of such calls, issued in the voices of people who, in many cases, were engaged not so long ago in framing nuclear policy and planning nuclear war. Because the nuclear age and the Cold War were born at almost the same time and developed together at every point, few observers troubled at the time to distinguish clearly between the two. But now that history has unexpectedly untangled them for us, we face the one without the other, and questions in eclipse for half a century have been placed before us again. What we might call the first nuclear era, which lasted from 1945 until 1991, has come to an end, and a second nuclear era has begun. Some thirty-five thousand nuclear weapons remain in the world. Whether these are merely a monstrous leftover from a frightful era that has ended, and will soon follow it into history, or whether they are the seeds of a virulent new nuclear era, in which nuclear weapons are held more widely and rooted more deeply, is not a matter for prediction; it is a matter for choice.

By choosing to call for the elimination of nuclear weapons, the new abolitionists have revived a vision that had all but disappeared since the beginning of the nuclear age, when the United States placed the

Baruch Plan, which called for abolition, before the United Nations. The proposal was vetoed by the Soviet Union, and the United States, the sole possessor of nuclear arms at the time, proceeded with a nuclear buildup that it justified as a desperate, temporary measure to counter the threat that Soviet conventional forces were thought to pose to a ruined Europe. In Western minds, the two evils were soon equated: nuclear weapons, it was admitted, were a horrifying expedient, but so, many said, was the threat they kept at bay—world domination by a totalitarian power.

In the years that followed, the reasons for ruling out abolition multiplied. Once the Soviet Union acquired the bomb, in 1949, proposals for nuclear disarmament were rejected on grounds that the character of the Soviet regime posed an insuperable obstacle. Nuclear disarmament, the Cold War catechism ran, was possible only if the arrangements could be fully inspected; but the Soviet Union, being a closed society, would not permit inspection of its military establishment; therefore, nuclear disarmament was impossible. In other words, the totalitarian character of the Soviet regime became both the justification for building nuclear arsenals and the specific explanation for the impossibility of eliminating them. Even the most ardent opponents of nuclear weapons had to admit that the obstacles in the way of complete nuclear disarmament were towering. Few in the West were ready to rely on trust alone to guarantee disarmament agreements, and even fewer supported unilateral disarmament. The range of proposals considered feasible was sharply restricted. The opponents of nuclear weapons were most successful, they found, when they confined themselves to ameliorative proposals, such as an atmospheric test ban or a freeze on nuclear arsenals. Hopes of ridding the world of nuclear weapons died, and the superpowers embarked on their four-decade-long nuclear arms race.

In the 1950s, the rise in the West of the doctrine of deterrence, which taught that safety from nuclear terror could be found only in threats to unleash that same terror, placed a reassuring gloss on the nuclear peril. Official acceptance of this doctrine, in which nuclear arsenals became their own justification, gave the nuclear buildup a legitimacy and a momentum that at first it had lacked. The horrifying expedient came to be seen as a lasting necessity, even a positive good.

The belief that great benefit could be extracted from nuclear arms perfectly complemented the belief that their abolition was impossible. If you could not eliminate nuclear weapons, it was comforting to discover that you would not want to anyway. Abolition was doubly ruled out. Nuclear terror, at first regarded as intolerable, was declared the new foundation of the world's safety.

The conviction that abolition was impossible became pivotal in moral as well as political thinking about the nuclear question. Nuclear weapons are distinguished above all by their unparalleled destructive power. Their singularity, from a moral point of view, lies in the fact that the use of just a few would carry the user beyond every historical benchmark of indiscriminate mass slaughter. Is it necessary, fifty-three years after Hiroshima, to rehearse the basic facts? Suffice it to recall the old rule of thumb that one bomb can destroy one city. A large nuclear weapon today may possess a thousand times the explosive power of the bomb that destroyed Hiroshima—far more than enough to annihilate any city on earth. A single Trident II submarine has the capacity to deliver nearly two hundred warheads, which could lay waste any nation, giving another rule of thumb: one boat, one nation. The use of a mere dozen nuclear weapons against, say, the dozen largest cities of the United States, Russia, or China, causing tens of millions of deaths, would be a human catastrophe without parallel. The use of a few hundred nuclear weapons, not to speak of a thousand, would raise these already incomprehensible losses by an order of magnitude, leaving the imagination in the dust. Because so few weapons can kill so many people, even far-reaching disarmament proposals would leave us implicated in plans for unprecedented slaughter of innocent people. The sole measure that could have freed us from this burden was abolition. But abolition, as long as the Cold War lasted, was ruled out.

The moral crisis created by the invention of nuclear weapons, then, lay in the fact that politically realistic people felt themselves virtually barred from championing the only measure that would have returned governments and their peoples to the realm of minimal moral sense.

The resulting gap between political and moral requirements left us for almost fifty years with a fracture down the center of our beings. In the words of James Agee, in August 1945, just a few weeks after

Hiroshima, "All thoughts and things were split." Rudimentary moral principle taught that we must never, even in "retaliation," threaten to kill millions of innocent people, but nuclear strategy required us to do so. Common sense rebelled against offering up every person in our country as a hostage to a hostile power and seizing every person on the territory of that power as a counterhostage, meanwhile placing the whole arrangement on a hair trigger; yet policy called this logically necessary. The experience of our century taught us that genocide was the worst of all crimes, but a nuclear "priesthood" taught us that to threaten it, and even to carry it out, not only was justifiable but was our inescapable duty. Every scruple in the human conscience declared that we must never risk extinguishing our species—the supreme crime against humanity, and the only crime greater than genocide—but solemn doctrine declared that it was essential to threaten this act. All thoughts that led toward other conclusions had to go unthought—and unacted upon. These were the truly "unthinkable" thoughts of the Cold War period. The morbidity of the era consisted of more than the threat of universal death with which it was overhung; it consisted also of the prohibition, so humiliating to the human spirit, against taking action to remove the threat. Thus did the reasoning of the age seemingly compel not only totalitarian regimes but great democracies to enter, against all their better instincts and understanding, into a hated complicity in potentially limitless killing.

Today, the terms of the nuclear predicament have been altered fundamentally. The barrier of impossibility has fallen. The Soviet Union has unexpectedly—almost magically—cleared itself out of the way. Gone is the murderous, implacable hostility between global rivals, which just a few years ago seemed destined to last forever; gone the totalitarian empire; and gone the obstacles to inspection that have been considered the main brake on nuclear disarmament. The elimination of nuclear weapons has always been much to be desired. What distinguishes our moment is that, for the first time since the invention of the weapons, it is entirely reasonable to believe that the goal actually can be reached. The opportunity for action that has now opened up is, above all else, an opportunity to heal our fractured selves. It is an opportunity to end the forced cohabitation with horror, the shotgun marriage with final absurdity—to snap out of the trance of the Cold War, annul the suicide pact dictated by the doctrine of deterrence, and take the step that alone can free us from nuclear danger and corruption—namely, the abolition of nuclear weapons. Abolition is the great threshold. It is the logical and necessary destination because only abolition gets us out of the zone of mass slaughter, both as perpetrators and as victims.

Since the beginning of the nuclear age, it has been a commonplace to say that humanity's technical achievements have outstripped its political achievements. Now the situation is reversed. The world's political achievements have raced ahead of its technical achievements. In the political realm, peace reigns, but in the technical realm, hostility—indeed, the threat of "mutual assured destruction"—remains the order of the day. Today, we require a technical event as great as the political event that was the end of the Cold War. To use a homely metaphor, the West in the wake of the Soviet collapse is like a person who has won fifty million dollars in the lottery and then declares, "Wonderful—now I can redecorate my living room." Why not buy a whole new house? History has handed us a political windfall. Why do we refuse to spend it? Political assets, unlike financial ones, are not apt to increase over time. If not made use of, they can, in an instant of crisis or war, evaporate.

The questions that need to be addressed are moral, political, and strategic. The moral question for the United States is whether, during the Cold War, we so accustomed ourselves to threatening nuclear annihilation that it became second nature to us. It is often said to be the prime duty of a government to protect its citizens. Why shouldn't America's leaders, by agreeing together with Russia's leaders to abolish both countries' nuclear arsenals, rescue our people and theirs from the threat of annihilation? Was the Cold War not, as we first hoped, the apogee of the era of nuclear weapons, to be succeeded by an era of disarmament and peace, but instead a period of initiation, in which not only Americans and Russians but Chinese, Indians, Pakistanis, Israelis, Koreans, Iraqis, Iranians, and others were unlearning their horror of nuclear destruction—were learning to think the unthinkable? Was the Cold War a sort of Trojan horse whereby nuclear weapons were being smuggled into the moral and political life of the world? Have we, in a silent but deep moral revolution in which the United States has played the leading role, come to regard threats of mass destruction as normal—as the proper and ordinary procedure of any self-respecting nation, whether or not it faces an extraordinary danger from without? Can we still remember that to destroy hundreds of millions of human beings is an atrocity beyond all history? Or have we, so to speak, forgotten this before we had ever quite learned it? And have we, accordingly, adopted the strange vocation—so deeply at odds with the principles on which our nation was founded—of salesman of terror to the world?

The chief political question is whether nuclear proliferation can be stopped and reversed if the current nuclear powers declare by their actions as well as their words that nuclear bombs are indispensable instruments of national power. Or should proliferation perhaps be reluctantly accepted, or even enthusiastically embraced?

The development that sets the stage for proliferation is, of course, the spread of nuclear technology. Although politically speaking it may in a sense be 1945 again, technically speaking it is much later than that. While the world was understandably transfixed by the mortal rivalry between the two superpowers, the knowledge underlying the bomb and the technical wherewithal for building it were becoming increasingly available. During the Cold War, the "secret" of the bomb was held by a few governments. Now it is published in magazines. Back then, the nuclear club was exclusive. Now just about anyone can join. Then, the necessary scientific knowledge was centralized in a few places. Now it is ubiquitous, protean, osmotic—fully up- and downloadable, just like any other information in the information age.

The principal strategic question is whether the doctrine of deterrence, having been framed during the Cold War, will now be discredited as logically absurd and morally bankrupt or, on the contrary, recommended to nations all over the world as the soundest and most sensible solution to the nuclear dilemma. The question then will not be whether a particular quarreling pair of nations (the United States and the Soviet Union during the Cold War) is better off with nuclear arsenals but whether any and all such pairs (India and Pakistan, Greece and Turkey, Iraq and Israel, or Iran and Iraq will do as examples) are better off. If, as many analysts say, deterrence was a successful answer to the dangers of the Cold War, then why should it not be adopted by all nations prone to conflict? Why resist proliferation? Wouldn't it be better to step it up— to proceed knowingly and deliberately to an increasingly nuclearized world? This is the direction in which events now appear to be drifting, and a few theorists are honest and unflinching enough to champion the goal. For example, John Mearsheimer, of the University of Chicago, has called nuclear weapons a "powerful force for peace" and advocates "well-managed proliferation." He hopes that Germany will acquire nuclear weapons and advises the world to "let proliferation occur in Eastern Europe." In statements like his, we can see the elements of a possible new conventional wisdom, in which nuclear weapons become entrenched in the plans and policies not just of a few great powers but of the world at large.

It's plain that the moral, political, and strategic aspects of the question are in practice tightly linked. The fundamental choice in all three areas is between, on the one hand, condemnation of nuclear weapons and their abolition and, on the other, their full normalization and universalization. Normalization and universalization go naturally together. Normalization will be complete when no extraordinary external threat—and perhaps no threat at all—is thought necessary to justify building nuclear arsenals. Universalization is its natural consequence, because if possession of nuclear weapons requires no special justification, then almost any nation would be justified in having them. The implications for U.S. policy of the resulting "new deterrent framework" (in the phrase of Robert Joseph, director of the Center for Counter-Proliferation Research) would be deterrence *à tous azimuts*, in the official French phrase, which is to say a policy of nuclear deterrence aimed at forestalling threats that might arise at any point on the globe. (And, in fact, the new Presidential Decision Directive takes a few steps in that direction.) The question today is: Will the *world* be better off with or without nuclear weapons? This is the debate that has now begun.

It's plain, too, that in addressing the new issues our assessment of the nuclear policies of the Cold War will be of the first importance. Was the nuclear buildup a story of wise management of a terrible dilemma that had no other solution? And was it, further, a fortuitous training session, in which the world was introduced to the previously unsuspected virtues of nuclear arms? Or was it a tale of the reckless endangerment of mankind? If the first is true, then nuclear weapons are a marvelous gift of proven worth to the world. If the latter is true, then abolishing nuclear weapons is the unfinished business of the end of the Cold War. In the first case, we *cannot* do without them. In the second, we *must* get rid of them.

In the face of these questions, the citizens who oppose nuclear arms are as sorely in need of fresh thinking as the governments that possess them. The starting point of this thinking must be recognition that even as the main obstacles to abolition have been removed the main goad to getting there—the immediate danger of a full-scale nuclear holocaust—has been greatly reduced. The fact is that the public at large, enjoying a reprieve from immediate, universal terror bestowed by the end of the Cold War, is not paying much attention to the nuclear question. It's also true that the public is actively worried—and with good reason—that a terrorist group or government will use one or more nuclear weapons somewhere in the world. But the feeling of relief dominates.

During the Cold War, abolition, though perhaps highly desired, was found impossible. Now it appears possible but is not so urgently desired. Then, opposition to nuclear arms was driven by immediate, overwhelming fear—fear that ran headlong into the wall of political impossibility. Today, in sharp contrast, fear has been radically reduced. The combination of only moderate fear of nuclear danger and high opportunity to solve the nuclear dilemma is new. Our primary inspiration for attending to the nuclear question, accordingly, should not be fear but fear's opposites, hope and faith—hope that, in the transformed and brightened political scene, the goal of abolition is achievable, and faith that we possess the nerve, stamina, and wisdom to reach it. At the very least, all who, at one terror-stricken moment or another of the Cold War, picked up a sign or shouted a slogan or organized to protest nuclear danger should now stir themselves again to seize the present opportunity actually to rid the world of the weapons. Protest is not something undertaken for its own sake; it is supposed to inspire constructive action. And the time for action has come.

It may be that the initiative for such a radical challenge to the status quo must be taken by the public, as has happened so often in the past, and especially in the United States. But there are no rules in such matters, and the initiative could also come from the political class. Rarely in history has a riper opportunity for political leadership presented itself. An achievement that, soberly speaking, is of measureless value is within reach, if only the will to act can be found. This leadership might come from some unexpected quarter, but the obvious candidate is a president of the United States. It could be—it *should be*—Bill Clinton. If it is not Clinton, it could and should be Vice President Al Gore, whose concern for the earth's environment ought to inspire from him efforts to preserve it from the greatest by far of the perils that threaten it. No cause is greener than the abolition of nuclear weapons. But the abolition movement need be no respecter of the political or party divisions of the Cold War. In the contest that is about to begin, we can be sure, lines will be drawn, ambitions and interests will clash, and political battles will be fought. But it is by no means clear yet that these will occur along the familiar fault lines of left and right, liberal and conservative. A Republican may step forward. The most fervently abolitionist president of the Cold War period, let us recall, was Ronald Reagan, who regarded his scheme for antinuclear defenses as a path to abolition. On many occasions, he described the system of mutual assured destruction as "immoral" and asked, "Wouldn't it be better to save lives than avenge them?" His meeting in 1986 at Reykjavik with another abolitionist, Mikhail Gorbachev, was the only occasion on which the heads of the two superpowers seriously discussed abolition. There may well be a successor in his party who will take up the forsaken cause.

If the United States defaults on its responsibilities, other countries may assume leadership. (If the movement is not American, it can easily turn out to be anti-American.) No country is *un*qualified to lead a movement for the abolition of nuclear arms, since all are threatened by them. In Australia and New Zealand, to give just two examples, the antinuclear movement has been especially vigorous and effective recently.

In the meantime, a new generation, innocent of the divisions of the Cold War, is coming of age. Its thoughts and feelings, which have yet to make their weight felt on any great issue of public concern, are largely unknown. If its members do not feel the urgency to escape the nuclear danger that some of their parents felt, neither have they developed the deep attachment to nuclear arms also often found among their parents, including most of the governing class. The minds of the young, it appears, are open. A call for abolition should therefore be, among other things, a call from an older generation to a younger one. Among the many links between people that this effort would forge is a new link between generations. And since the project, if successful, would save the lives of future generations, that link would be the first in an everlasting chain.

The task is of course immense. But history has given us the gift of time—a limited time, perhaps, but enough to proceed, without haste, to scout the obstacles in our path, to weigh carefully and thoroughly the course to be followed, and then to create the structures that will carry us to the goal and keep us there. If we use the gift properly and rid the species for good of nuclear danger, we will secure the greatest of time's gifts, assurance of a human future. Of course, some will say the goal is a utopian dream of human perfection. We needn't worry. There will be more than enough sins left for everyone to commit after we have taken nuclear bombs away from ourselves. Others will say the obstacles are too great. We can answer, as George Washington once did, "Let us raise a standard to which the wise and the honest can repair. The event is in the hand of God."

If it seems paradoxical to call for the greatest exertions at a time of relaxed fear, we should remind ourselves that the opportunity is greater for the same reason that the danger is smaller: the end of the Cold War. That people can be inspired to act as much by the appeal of reaching a great goal in a time of peace as by immediate and overwhelming terror in a time of conflict is admittedly an unproven proposition. Terror, unquestionably, is a powerful spur to action. If we wait for terror to revive, however, what price will we pay? Will it be New York City? Teheran? Berlin? Beijing? And are we sure that after such a catastrophe we would act wisely? Our reasons for acting are bound to shape the character of our action. Measures taken abruptly, after the sudden end of fifty years of nuclear peace, possibly in an atmosphere of global suspicion, bewilderment, panic, and calls for revenge, seem unlikely to be as sensible as measures adopted now, in an atmosphere of cooperation, after thorough and careful discussion.

The nuclear crises of the Cold War called for the swift, sharp shock of protest. On June 12, 1982, a million people, dismayed by a renewed acceleration of the arms race, gathered in New York City to call for a freeze on nuclear arms. In the years that followed, their wishes were more than granted: nuclear arsenals were not merely frozen, they were reduced. The million never gathered again. In our new circumstances, what is needed is not just a moment of protest but the steady engagement of citizens and their representatives over many years of constructive effort. Can a movement based on hope, confidence in the concerted powers of human beings, and faith in the human future be as great as one based on terror? It must, in fact, be greater. In the words of Jody Williams, on the day her campaign to ban land mines became a treaty signed by 121 nations, "Together we are a superpower. It's a new definition of superpower. It's not one of us; it's all of us." The abolition of nuclear arms—to cite a chapter from American history—would be to the end of the Cold War what the Constitutional Convention was to the War of Independence. The end of the Cold War was a liberation. Abolition is the act of foundation toward which that liberation points as its natural consequence and completion.

To succeed in the task would, by securing human survival through human resolve and action, go far toward restoring our faith, so badly shaken in this century, in our capacity to make use of the amazing products of our hands and minds for our benefit rather than our destruction. It would bring undying honor to those who carried it to fulfillment and to their generation. It would have the character not of a desperate expedient resorted to under pressure of terror but of a tremendous free act, following upon calm public deliberation in every nation—among all humankind. In a way, it would be the foundation of humankind.

II

THE
UNITED STATES

1   THE STATUS QUO

In the years since the end of the Cold War, a striking number of the men (there were almost no women among them) who had responsibility for nuclear policy in the United States, Russia, and Europe have undergone changes of heart about nuclear weapons. They now support a position unthinkable for most of them even a decade or so ago—the global elimination of nuclear weapons—and many have come to question the Cold War strategies they once devised. In the pages that follow, I present the results of conversations I have had with these men and several other people now committed to abolition. All have thought long and hard about the questions involved, which are technically elaborate, intellectually complex, and ethically daunting. Although almost all of them favor abolition, they disagree on many points. It quickly became clear to me that a debate has begun not only between abolitionists and their opponents but among different schools of abolitionism. Both the post–Cold War political situation and the dilemmas it poses are radically new, and so, in many cases, are the positions taken. Some of the abolitionists have been on the political right, some on the political left, and some in the center. Some favor antinuclear defenses in a nuclear-weapon-free world, some oppose them. Some believe that all the functions now served by nuclear weapons in U.S. military planning could be better served by high-technology conventional arms; others think these weapons are not as effective as advertised or wouldn't want them used even if they were that effective. Some wish to retain a right to nuclear armament if a nation violates an abolition agreement; others are dismayed by the idea. Some want to embrace the goal of abolition all at once; others prefer to proceed step by step. I have tried to present all these shades of opinion and more, in the belief that we are at the beginning, not the end, of a great debate and that a variety of views, even among the champions of abolition, need to be heard. I have also recorded my own views, arrived at in the course of what, for me, was a protracted and intense education in the subject.

Two other groups, broadly speaking, have begun to call for nuclear abolition. One consists of traditional antinuclear and antiwar groups, working at the grassroots level. The other consists of politicians and diplomats from states without nuclear weapons. For both groups, which have cooperated extensively, the United Nations has been a center of activity. The spark that ignited the fledgling movement was struck in April 1995, at the Nuclear Weapons Non-Proliferation Treaty review conference, where a gathering of representatives of nongovernmental organizations founded a group called Abolition 2000, which issued an appeal for abolition over the Internet. (Under the NPT, which was signed in 1968 and extended indefinitely in 1995, nonnuclear nations agree not to build nuclear weapons in exchange for a promise by the nuclear powers to work to eliminate their nuclear arsenals.) In the next few days, three hundred groups from around the world joined, and within a year the number was more than one thousand. Most of the groups were veterans of the antinuclear cause. Among them were the International Network of Engineers and Scientists Against Proliferation, which is based in Europe; the International Physicians for Prevention of Nuclear War; the Lawyers' Committee on Nuclear Policy; and the American Friends Service Committee. According to Alyn Ware, executive director of the Lawyers' Committee, Abolition 2000 is not a full-fledged organization; it is a "network" of groups that coordinate their activities without pursuing any single agenda. "It's a linking type of thing," he said, "that uses existing organizations without creating too much new structure."

A decision by the World Court sharply restricting the legal use of nuclear weapons has aided the activist groups. The decision, taken in response to a request from the World Health Organization and the U.N. General Assembly, found that "the threat and use of nuclear weapons would generally be contrary to the rules of international law applicable in armed conflict, and particularly the principles and rules of humanitarian law"—except, possibly, in "an extreme circumstance of self-defense, in which the very survival of the state would be at stake." It enjoined the nuclear powers to move expeditiously to fulfill their agreement in Article VI of the Non-Proliferation Treaty (NPT) to eliminate nuclear weapons. According to Peter Weiss, a leading figure in the World Court Project, which played a central role in the campaign to bring the issue of the legality of nuclear weapons before the Court, the greatest importance of the ruling lies in "the foundation it supplies for organizing." Ware added, "It brings in organizations that previously may not have been involved in nuclear disarmament. The field is no longer the prerogative only of the disarmament experts. People from legal departments and other parts of government are intervening in policy decisions. They ask, 'What are you doing—the Court says you have an obligation.' "

The review process agreed to as a condition for the extension of the Non-Proliferation Treaty has also been an important tool for the new movement by providing a forum at which the nuclear powers can be called to account for failure to progress toward the elimination of nuclear weapons. In December of 1996 the U.N General Assembly appealed to all states "to fulfill that obligation" outlined by the World Court "by commencing multilateral negotiations in 1997 leading to an early conclusion of a nuclear weapons convention prohibiting the development, production, testing, deployment, stockpiling, transfer, threat or use of nuclear weapons and providing for their elimination." One hundred fifteen nations voted in favor, thirty-two abstained, and twenty-two (including the United States) were against. This past December the assembly repeated the call.

At present, the nuclear future lies open. Public opinion polls suggest, first, that the public is friendly to abolition; but, second, that it doesn't take much interest in the subject. A recent poll conducted by Lake Sosin Snell & Associates showed that a full 87 percent of the American public favor an international treaty eliminating nuclear weapons. However, few of the respondents have as yet shown any enthusiasm for acting on that belief. Strategic nuclear arms have, it is true, followed a downward curve initiated by START I and continued by START II, which has been signed by the presidents of the United States and Russia and ratified by the U.S. Senate but remains unratified by the Russian Duma. START II, if implemented, will reduce the strategic arsenals to some three thousand warheads on each side. ("Tactical" warheads, which are mounted on short-range delivery vehicles, are incompletely covered by existing agreements. The United States has nevertheless reduced its tactical warheads to about one thousand. Russian figures, though unknown, are believed to be much higher.) At the Russian-American summit meeting in the spring of 1997, Presidents Clinton and Yeltsin discussed further reductions to about twenty-five hundred strategic weapons on each side. Hence, even within the START framework, the two powers plan to retain thousands of nuclear weapons into the indefinite future. Neither wholeheartedly embraced nor rejected, the weapons seem to have drifted into a limbo, like a becalmed navy waiting for a breeze to carry it somewhere.

Meanwhile, the chronicle of the nuclear age is crowded with events that make clear the capacity and will of nations to acquire nuclear weapons and that seem to point the way to accelerated nuclear proliferation. In 1990, according to an article in the *New Yorker* by Seymour Hersh, Pakistan and India came closer to embarking on a nuclear war than any two nations since the Cuban missile crisis of 1962. In 1991, the discovery that Iraq had, in violation of its commitment as a signatory of the Non-Proliferation Treaty, created a secret program to build the bomb and, at the moment of its defeat in the Gulf War, had been within perhaps a year of success, shocked the intelligence agencies of the world. The United Nations' program to dismantle Iraq's weapons of mass destruction is still in progress. Israel's untested nuclear arsenal is an old but continuing story, as are reported efforts by Iran to build nuclear weapons. In 1994, evidence was discovered of a nuclear weapons program in North Korea, whose leaders, after a bout of tense and tortuous diplomacy, agreed in effect to abandon it in exchange for an international commitment to build two nuclear reactors of a relatively safe kind. In 1995, France embarked on a series of nuclear tests in the South Pacific, cut short only in the face of widespread international protest.

Other events, however, indicate the readiness of nations to renounce nuclear weapons. Though little noticed in this country, a series of steps have been taken that, together, represent sweeping progress toward the goal of a world without nuclear weapons. In 1986, much of the South Pacific, including Australia, New Zealand, and Papua New Guinea, established itself as a nuclear-weapon-free zone with the Treaty of Rarotonga. Six years later, in May 1992, Ukraine, Belarus, and Kazakhstan, all of which had inherited nuclear arms when the Soviet Union broke up, agreed to surrender them to Russia for dismantling and to sign the Non-Proliferation Treaty. In 1993, South Africa revealed, first, that it had built six nuclear bombs and, second, that it had dismantled them by 1991—thus becoming the first state in the world to abolish a nuclear arsenal. Two entire continents—South America and Africa—then formally declared themselves nuclear-weapon-free zones: South America in 1994, when Brazil and Argentina, both of which had once had extensive nuclear programs, finally ratified the 1967 Treaty of Tlatelolco; and Africa in 1996, when all its nations signed the Treaty of Pelindaba. In May 1995, the Non-Proliferation Treaty, signed by 185 nations, was renewed indefinitely, and a strengthened review process was established. In September 1996, the Comprehensive Test-Ban Treaty was voted on in the General Assembly and opened for signature, over the dissent of India, which demanded as the price for its agreement a commitment by the nuclear powers to abolition by some fixed date.

In the United States, official voices have persisted, for the most part, in the message of the Cold War: nuclear deterrence works; only nuclear weapons can protect us from nuclear weapons; full nuclear disarmament is dangerous; nuclear arsenals are necessary indefinitely. However, before reviewing the current state of official policy, a prefatory word may be in order about the role of the United States in the decisions that lie ahead.

The nuclear dilemma is in its essence a global human dilemma, but in several ways the role of the United States in nuclear matters has been outsized. In the words of George Kennan, it was we "who first produced and tested" the bomb, we who were "the first to raise its destructiveness to a new level with the hydrogen bomb . . . and we alone, so help us God, who have used the weapon in anger against others, and against tens of thousands of helpless noncombatants at that." This history suggests that we have a large role to play in finding a solution to the dilemma and special reasons for doing so.

First, there is the simple fact that our arsenals are such a large part of the problem—a little under 50 percent of it, if we reckon in numbers of strategic warheads.

Second, Americans have had, for fifty-three years, both occasion and cause to think deeply about the nuclear question. Hiroshima and Nagasaki lie uneasy on the American conscience. It seems safe to say that, whether we have thought soundly or not, no other people has thought as much about the bomb. (There is also a sense in which no other people has strained harder not to think about it.) America needed a bridge between the humane ideals it professed and the reality of unlimited slaughter it was now threatening. The doctrine of nuclear deterrence, which teaches that nuclear armament is not only justified but ineluctable, provided such a bridge. Now we should ask, do we need that bridge any longer? It would be fitting if the United States, which led the nuclear powers at each step up the slope to the nuclear precipice, were to help lead the world back down again.

Third, the United States has a particular interest in abolition, owing to its prominence as a potential target of nuclear destruction. Can we fail to see that, with nuclear technology spreading rapidly and probably unstoppably around the world, the destruction we once visited on others may, sooner or later, visit our shores? In the words of Seneca, used by Robert Jay Lifton and Greg Mitchell as an epigram for their fine, meditative work *Hiroshima in America*, "Power over life and death—don't be proud of it. Whatever they fear from you, you'll be threatened with." Weren't the bombings of the World Trade Center and the federal building in Oklahoma City warning enough?

Fourth, as a practical matter, the United States seems destined to play a disproportionately large role in the world's decisions regarding nuclear weapons. If the United States were, after a period of national deliberation, to decide in favor of a world without nuclear weapons (as it did, briefly, in 1946), there is good reason to assume that the other nuclear powers would follow suit. At the very least, it is scarcely conceivable that nuclear weapons can be abolished without the energetic and willing participation of this country.

The 180 nations that have, under the terms of the Non-Proliferation Treaty, renounced nuclear weapons manage very well without fission bombs, fusion bombs, nuclear-powered submarines, or multiple independently targetable reentry vehicles and give no thought to nuclear deterrence, mutual assured destruction, flexible response, or any of the rest of it. If we say that we seek a nuclear-weapon-free world, the goal seems ambitious. But if we note that all we need to achieve is a nuclear-free United States, Russia, China, France, England, India, Pakistan, and Israel, the problem suddenly looks more manageable.

Fifth and finally, in the nuclear age, as long as the United States believed itself menaced by great, malevolent powers bent on its defeat or destruction, a degree of separation could be maintained between the country's underlying principles and the dread means we were employing, temporarily, in their name. From the moment of the founding of the Manhattan Project, such enemies—first Hitler's Germany, then Imperial Japan, then the Soviet Union—were in the field. Now the United States is left with the dread means but without any extraordinary threat. In these circumstances, if we keep nuclear weapons, they will become as much a part of what we are and stand for as the Constitution.

The nuclear policies of the Clinton administration have been both tentative and vague, and their articulation mainly left to lower-level officials. Twice, the administration has proposed "bottom up" reviews—first for military policy as a whole and second for nuclear policy in particular. Each time it has advocated nothing more than modest adjustments of the Cold War status quo. The United States and Russia have formally de-targeted each other's forces and territory; however, re-targeting can occur in seconds.

In the words of Bruce Blair, of the Brookings Institution, "No major change in the U.S.–Russian nuclear equation has occurred—not in war planning, not in daily alert practices, not in strategic arms control, and maybe not even in core attitudes." More important is the fact that the doctrine of deterrence has remained in place, as the Presidential Decision Directive makes plain. No issue that could justify even the smallest of conventional wars divides the two former superpowers, yet each nation's nuclear arsenal is still poised on a hair trigger to blow the other to kingdom come several times over, and no plan that would fundamentally alter this state of affairs is even on the drawing boards.

The principal formulation of the Clinton administration's underlying policy for the post–Cold War era has been the Nuclear Posture Review. The text of the review is classified. The president, who reportedly did not take an active role in its conception, has had little to say about it. Its contents were made known in a hardly noted press conference in September 1994 by Secretary of Defense William Perry, Chairman of the Joint Chiefs of Staff John Shalikashvili, and Deputy Defense Secretary John Deutsch. On the one hand, Perry pejoratively likened the policy of mutual assured destruction to "two men holding revolvers and standing about ten yards away and pointing their revolvers at each other's head, [while] shouting insults at each other" and called the administration's new policy "mutual assured safety." On the other hand, he confusingly added that the policy "remains the same." The new policy, he said, struck a balance between "leading" and "hedging." "Leading" meant leading toward modest further reductions in the number of nuclear weapons on both sides—a policy, said Perry, that would continue "on into the next century." "Hedging" meant hedging against a potential "reversal of reform in Russia"—an idea that introduced the notion that nuclear arms were needed to deal not with any present threat but with merely potential threats.

The feeling that little had changed but words was reinforced by Deputy Secretary Deutsch's comments. His chief theme was that deterrence remains necessary—that the United States still must assure "the ability of our forces to withstand a postulated first attack so that we know that we were able to retaliate and, thereby, that ability to retaliate deterring the probability of a first strike initially." Plainly, here again were the two men pointing revolvers at each other's heads at ten yards.

If these remarks didn't demonstrate that Cold War nuclear policies toward the Soviet empire were now being transferred to the Russian nation, Deutsch's further comment that "we're not looking for abrupt changes; we're looking for adaption to change" made the point clear. He added, indeed, that mere hedging might not be enough, and that if Russia does "not develop as we hope," then the United States might have to return to a more "robust" nuclear posture.

It was not until two years later that a spokesman for the administration spelled out the U.S. position on the limits of negotiated reductions. The clarification came in testimony by Under Secretary of Defense for Policy Walter B. Slocombe before the Senate Governmental Affairs Sub-Committee on International Security. Slocombe embraced the abolition of nuclear weapons as a goal of American policy. To do otherwise would have been embarrassing, for the United States had committed itself to this goal when it signed the Non-Proliferation Treaty. The commitment had been exacted by the nonnuclear nations as the price for their signatures: they agreed to forgo building nuclear weapons as long as the nuclear powers agreed to commit themselves to abolishing theirs. Slocombe, however, placed abolition on the far side of the political horizon. For one thing, he repeatedly linked complete nuclear disarmament with "general and complete disarmament"—a goal that few abolitionists call for and virtually none see as a *precondition* for nuclear disarmament. "The U.S. is committed," Slocombe said, "to Article VI of the NPT, which calls for the complete elimination of nuclear weapons in the context of general and complete disarmament"—a formulation that links nuclear abolition much more tightly to general and complete disarmament than does the language of the Non-Proliferation Treaty, which places the two goals in sequence. (Its language calls for the nuclear powers "to pursue negotiations in good faith relating to cessation of the nuclear arms race at an early date and to nuclear disarmament, and on a treaty on general and complete disarmament under strict and effective international control.")

Having shunted abolition off to the unforeseeable future, Slocombe proceeded to the burden of his argument, which was to make the case against abolition as a goal of present policy. After taking note of "radical" proposals for abolition, he reiterated the arguments presented by Perry and Deutsch at their press conference: The United States, he said, needed thousands of nuclear weapons as a hedge against a collapse of Soviet democracy and to deter "rogue states" that might obtain nuclear weapons. First, he generalized the potential threats mentioned by Perry. "We will need [a survivable deterrent] force," he said, "because nuclear deterrence—far from being made wholly obsolete—remains an essential ultimate assurance against the gravest of threats. A key conclusion of the Administration's National Security Strategy is that the United States will retain strategic nuclear forces sufficient to deter any future hostile foreign leadership with access to strategic nuclear forces from action against our vital interests and to convince it that seeking nuclear advantage would be *futile*." In the phrase "any foreign leadership" we see the replacement of the specific, present Soviet threat in the Cold War period by merely possible threats from any quarter whatever in the post–Cold War period. (In July of 1994, President Clinton had sounded a vaguely global note. After reciting his administration's strategy he added, "We will retain strategic nuclear forces sufficient to deter any future hostile leadership with access to strategic nuclear forces from acting against our vital interest. Therefore we will continue to maintain nuclear forces of sufficient size and capability to hold at risk a broad range of assets valued by such political and military leaders.")

Slocombe then enumerated the reasons why "abolition, if understood as a near-term policy, rather than, as President Clinton has stated, an ultimate goal, is not a wise and surely not a feasible focus of policy." The first reason was that nuclear weapons had proved their value. "It is a remarkable fact," he stated, "that for almost half a century, the U.S. and its allies faced the U.S.S.R. and its coerced auxiliaries in the division over ideology, power, culture, and the very definition of man, the state, and the world, and did so armed to the greatest extent huge sacrifice would afford, and yet did not fight a large-scale war. No one can say for sure why that success was achieved for long enough for Communism to collapse of its own internal weakness. But does anyone really doubt that nuclear weapons had a role?" In other words, deterrence worked. And if it worked during the Cold War, why not now? And in any case, "There is no reasonable prospect that all the declared and *de facto* nuclear powers will agree in the near term to give up all their nuclear weapons. And as long as one such state refuses to do so, it will be necessary for us to retain a nuclear force of our own."

None of these arguments broke new ground. But Slocombe then went on to tackle the fundamental question left unaddressed by Perry and Deutsch—how far a *negotiated* reduction of nuclear arms might properly go. Slocombe, goaded by the "radical" proposals he had mentioned, addressed it. His observation that *other* countries might be unlikely to embrace zero as a goal left open the possibility that the United States would like to but was being held back by this foot-dragging elsewhere. Was the United States eager to get to zero—only to be thwarted by other, benighted powers? Now Slocombe, proceeding to the heart of the debate, observed that even if, surprisingly, all powers *were* to sign an abolition treaty, the goal itself would in fact be undesirable. In other words, his deepest objection to a world without nuclear weapons was not that you couldn't get there (true as that might be) but that you wouldn't want to be there. Owing to the fundamental importance of the point, Slocombe's words deserve quotation in full:

> If the nuclear powers were, nevertheless, to accept abolition, then we would require—and the Congress would rightly demand—a verification regime of extraordinary rigor and intrusiveness. This would have to go far beyond any currently in existence or even under contemplation. It would have to include not merely a system of verification, but . . . "an agreed procedure for forcible international intervention and interruption of current efforts in certain and timely fashion." The difficulties with setting up such a system under current world conditions are obvious. Such a regime would have to continue

to be effective in the midst of a prolonged and grave crisis—
even during a war—between potentially nuclear-capable powers. For in such a crisis, the first question for all involved would
be that of whether—or when—to start a clandestine nuclear
program. For the knowledge of how to build nuclear weapons
cannot be abolished.

Finally, we who are charged with responsibility for national
security and national defense must recall that we are not only
seeking to avert nuclear war—we are seeking to avert a major
conventional war as well. Our objective is a safe, stable world.
But we must develop our national security policy with the
understanding that nuclear weapons and the underlying technical knowledge cannot be disinvented, whether or not the
U.S. retains its weapons.

In these paragraphs, Slocombe refers, if only briefly, to most of the
central arguments against a negotiated abolition of nuclear weapons.
They are, first, that nuclear weapons are the only way to deter other
nuclear weapons, as the Cold War has shown; second, that, in addition,
they deter conventional war, as the Cold War has also shown; third,
that inspection of an abolition agreement can never be rigorous enough
to guarantee against fatal cheating; fourth, that possession of large arsenals by a great power prevents proliferation because its allies, feeling
protected, forgo nuclear arsenals of their own; and, fifth, that although
one may destroy the hardware of nuclear weapons, knowledge of how to
build them will remain, and therefore the abolition of nuclear weapons
is a sham, inasmuch as nations can rebuild them in short order when-
ever they like. The essence of these arguments is summed up in a single word—"breakout." Breakout refers to the violation, either covertly
(through cheating) or overtly, of an abolition agreement by an aggressor
that then proceeds, as the sole possessor of nuclear arms, to give orders
to a defenseless world.

The fear of breakout animates all those who wish to retain nuclear
weapons indefinitely. By analogy with the phrase *nuclear abolitionists*,
perhaps we can call them nuclear possessionists. Slocombe, who was
compelled by the United States' obligations under the Non-Proliferation

Treaty to make his case in the context of a long-term dedication to full nuclear disarmament, surrounded his opposition to abolition with many qualifications and evasions. We might call him a moderate nuclear possessionist. As it happened, however, at around that time two former officials gave an unvarnished presentation of the possessionist point of view. We might call them extreme possessionists, or, in view of the immense benefit that they belive will flow, more or less forever, from nuclear weapons, nuclear idealists. The first was James Schlesinger, secretary of defense under Richard Nixon, who set forth his views on the *Lehrer Newshour.* "We ought not and we cannot totally achieve the abolition of nuclear weapons," he said. "Happily, it is unachievable, because if it were not, it would be quite dangerous to the country." Abolition would dissolve deterrence, for "the chief inhibition on the use of nuclear weapons today is the knowledge that there are powers—most notably the United States—that are in a position to retaliate if weapons are used." The chief danger, of course, would be breakout. "The smaller [the number] of nuclear weapons," he explained, "the greater is the premium on having just a few nuclear weapons." Michael May, the codirector of the Center for International Security and Arms Control at Stanford University, recently summed up this important strain of expert possessionist opinion when he wrote, "Nuclear weapons are not all that is needed to make war obsolete, but they have no real substitute."

The second defender of an unadulterated possessionist position was Richard Perle, the former assistant secretary of defense under Ronald Reagan. He spoke at the hearing at which Slocombe had testified. Like Schlesinger, Perle opposed elimination even as a final goal. "I believe . . ." he asserted, "that our security would be profoundly undermined by the elimination of all nuclear weapons, even if agreements providing for this could be negotiated and universally ratified." He, too, expressed delight that "in the real world, there is no serious possibility" of reaching the treacherous goal. Referring slightingly to newly abolitionist-minded generals whose "stars are not on their uniforms but in their eyes," Perle broke down the argument against abolition of any sort at any time into several parts, which, taken together, amounted to a pungent, succinct warning of the dangers of breakout in the event of an abolition agreement.

He began by arguing that the agreement could not be verified—
"not now, not tomorrow, not ever." Therefore, some nations, fearing
cheating by others, would themselves cheat. Indeed, "every state able
to do so would cheat." In the face of this likelihood, elimination "of
our last remaining nuclear weapon" would be an act of "supreme folly."
Since the United States, perhaps alone among nations, might actually
honor its agreement to disarm, "the actual, real-world result would be
the unilateral nuclear disarmament of the country." Even if the impossible occurred, and every nation did in fact live up to the agreement, it
would all be for nothing; for "how long would it be before the continuing technical and scientific know-how and industrial capacity in the
former nuclear-weapon states was mobilized to re-establish one or more
nuclear powers?"

Next, he made the argument that abolition would encourage, not
discourage, proliferation. Nuclear disarmament, by raising the value of
just a few weapons, would create new temptations for proliferation.
"The mere handful that a successful proliferator might manage to
acquire suddenly looks like an arsenal bestowing Great Power status,"
he said. "Is that a situation we would wish to create?" Moreover,
America's arsenal discourages proliferation by its allies, who feel reas-
sured that "the protection we afford them is ultimately backed up by
nuclear weapons."

Finally, he argued that just as nuclear weapons had prevented
war among the nuclear powers during the Cold War, so now they
would "exert a sobering influence that cannot be achieved by any other
means."

Schlesinger's and Perle's arguments against abolition did not break
new ground any more than Slocombe's had. The main points had all
been developed by the proponents of nuclear armament even during
the Cold War. Indeed, mere mention of the fact that nuclear weapons
cannot be disinvented has often been considered adequate rebuttal
of the case for abolition. For example, Richard Haass, the director of
the Foreign Policy Studies Program at the Brookings Institution, concluded his dismissal of abolition in a *New York Times* op-ed piece with
the remark, "Besides, the abolition of nuclear weapons is impractical.
You cannot disinvent an idea." Then, however, these arguments, which

had to do with the general nature of the nuclear threat and not with the Cold War per se, remained in the background, overshadowed by the Soviet Union's refusal, from 1946 onward, to allow onsite inspection of its nuclear equipment.

Recently, however, voices have been raised suggesting that abolition is possible. In 1997, the Henry L. Stimson Center, a nonprofit public policy research institution, published a report advocating the elimination of nuclear weapons at the end of a four-stage process. The report was surprising not only because of its conclusions but because it had been signed by, among others, former defense secretary Robert McNamara; General Charles Horner, commander of the allied air forces in the Gulf War; and Paul Nitze, President Regan's chief arms control negotiator. It was the first U.S. proposal for abolition since the Baruch Plan to enjoy widespread support among established Washington figures. Although the report placed elimination in a quite distant future, it embraced the goal without qualification. "Regardless of the amount of time required," it stated in its closing words, "it is virtually certain that the world will never be rid of nuclear risks without a serious political commitment to the objective of progressively eliminating weapons of mass destruction from all countries. The time to start is now."

In August 1996, the Canberra Commission on the Elimination of Nuclear Weapons, a group established by the Australian government to consider abolition, presented its report. It, too, was notable for the distinction of its signatories, who included General George Lee Butler, a former commander of the U.S. Strategic Air Command; Field Marshal Lord Michael Carver, former chief of the British Defense Staff; Michel Rocard, a former prime minister of France; and Joseph Rotblat, the winner of the 1995 Nobel Peace Prize for his work as president of the Pugwash Conference on Science and World Affairs. The tone of the Canberra report was more urgent and impassioned than that of the Stimson Center, and its prescriptions for action more detailed. Asserting that "the proposition that nuclear weapons can be retained in perpetuity and never used—accidentally or by decision—defies credibility," it declared that "the only complete defence is the elimination of nuclear weapons [and] assurance that they will never be produced again." The report supported this conclusion with closely reasoned advocacy of ways to achieve a nuclear-weapon-free world and rebuttal of the principal arguments opposing this goal. The commission also specified some immediate steps. They were: taking nuclear forces off alert, removing warheads from delivery vehicles, ending deployment of tactical nuclear weapons, ending nuclear testing, pursuing reductions in U.S. and Russian arsenals, and the global adoption of a no-first-use policy.

Voices from surprising quarters in favor of abolition were heard for a third time when a statement in favor of abolition was issued by sixty-three active and retired military men from seventeen countries. Among them were Admiral Andrew Goodpaster, former supreme allied commander of Europe; General Butler; and General Aleksandr Lebed, the former national security adviser to President Yeltsin. In February of 1996, more than one hundred and forty civilian leaders, including former president Jimmy Carter, President Eduoard Schevardnadze of Georgia, and former chancellor Schmidt of Germany, signed an appeal calling for abolition.

The gulf between the possessionist and abolitionist positions could scarcely be wider. The antiabolitionist Richard Haass commented recently that conceptual issues raised by arms control have been resolved, leaving only "implementation," which he called "insider work." It seems more likely, however, that we are on the verge of a debate on nuclear disarmament that, in its depth, scope, intensity, complexity, and importance is destined to be the greatest that has ever occurred.

2 CALLS FOR ABOLITION

CHARLES HORNER

General Charles Horner, a man who combines a blunt, often humorous manner with a shrewd, active intellect, has spent a lifetime in the air force. In 1991, he was the allied air forces commander in the Gulf War and, from 1992 to 1994, commander of the U.S. Air Force Space Command. In July of 1994, he surprised official Washington when, seemingly off the cuff, he declared, "The nuclear weapon is obsolete; I want to get rid of them all." Some observers at the time speculated that his comments were only an impulsive outburst. It turned out, however, that they represented his deeply considered opinion. Today, in retirement from military service, he has become a dedicated advocate of the abolition of nuclear weapons. He is a member of the steering committee of the Stimson Center's Project on Eliminating Weapons of Mass Destruction.

I began my interview with him by asking what first led him to reflect on the nuclear question.

"When I was a young guy, a lieutenant in the air force stationed in England, I'd go out and sit alert with nuclear weapons. I didn't like it. It was the Cold War—the idea was: defeat the Russian horde coming through Germany by putting nuclear weapons down. I understood the deterrent aspect of it. Certainly that seemed reasonable, given how the world was at the time. On the other hand, if I'd actually had to execute, it seemed most unreasonable. The targeting didn't make a hell of a lot of sense. So to the practical person, it seemed like a very unfortunate situation to be in. I never wondered whether I'd execute or not, because, quite frankly, I never believed they would be launched. But when the Berlin Wall went up, I was down in a gunnery camp in Libya and the only way they could recall us was by using the code words for the outbreak of general war. Now that situation never, in fact, posed any threat of the use of nuclear weapons. But we flew back across France, with our guns armed.

"And then when I was in Space Command, I would visit all the ballistic missiles guys. I could relate to them. They had the same feelings I had. They were doing a magnificent job, professional 100 percent, but there they were, sitting in these silos with their fingers on the nuclear button, and not particularly *comfortable* about it.

"The other thing that occurred to me was the lack of military utility of nuclear weapons. In the Gulf War, we took inordinate measures to preclude unnecessary casualties. Nuclear weapons are such a gross instrument of power that they really have no utility. They work against you, in that they are best used to destroy cities, and kill women and children. Now, first, that's morally wrong; second, it doesn't make sense; and then, of course, there is the real threat of nuclear weapons in the hands of irresponsible or desperate powers.

"If you own them, you legitimize them just by your ownership. Now, I'm not so naive as to think we're not going to face a future in which people have, or are seeking, ownership of nuclear weapons. And it's highly likely that they will be used in the future by somebody. But that doesn't mean that we can ignore the problem."

"Did you wonder at the time of the Gulf War whether Saddam Hussein had nuclear weapons?" I asked.

"I think we were all concerned about chemical attacks against our ground forces as well as about Frog rockets and artillery. We were also concerned about biological weapons. But we were pretty well convinced that he didn't have nuclear weapons. Obviously, the surprise later was that he was a lot further along than anybody thought.

"My personal concern, though, was that Israel might use nuclear weapons. I could understand their desperation. When you're in charge of a country like Israel, you're expected to take significant action—an eye-for-an-eye type of thing. Say Saddam Hussein puts a chemical Scud into Tel Aviv. You could understand the motive for nuclear retaliation, but you would also hope that the Israelis would realize how harmful that would be to the best interests of their country and the whole world. First, they'd lose all legitimacy as a nation. I mean, they'd be a pariah. And Saddam Hussein would have emerged the hero."

"Do you think the world as a whole should adopt the elimination of nuclear weapons as a goal?" I asked.

"I think countries should realize that ownership of nuclear weapons has costs far in excess of the benefits. Any country that thinks the benefits of possession are greater than the cost, you've got to suspect that country's reason for being in the family of nations."

"Could you explain what you mean by the benefits and costs?"

"The primary justification for having nuclear weapons is that you deter other states from using nuclear weapons against you. But in a situation in which there is an international agreement to eliminate nuclear weapons—and there is movement toward the goal, as we've seen recently with chemical weapons and biological weapons—I think it's reasonable to hope that countries would come to understand that the possession of nuclear weapons has costs far exceeding any benefits.

"Signing up should confer benefits. It should confer legitimacy. It should not be construed as weakness. We have to create an environment in which not having nuclear weapons puts you in a position of strength, not weakness. The important thing is to get it into people's minds that these devices are illegitimate, so that anybody who decides to build one has to do it in a closet. It should become a commonly held belief that it is dysfunctional for any one nation to have them, so that you release the force of moral outrage, in addition to self-interest. Those are the things that are going to work. It's going to require leadership, and the nations that can provide that leadership are the big ones. Nations will need armed forces, though. You wish it were otherwise, but I don't think that you can eliminate armed forces.

"They say nuclear weapons make the world unsafe for war. I just think that's a bogus argument. At the height of the Cold War we had wars—in Korea and Vietnam, in our case. Russia had Afghanistan, and France had Algeria. I mean, war goes on. It's a failure of mankind; it's an endemic thing with us."

I mentioned the common objection that a larger nation might suddenly and openly violate an abolition agreement, thereby placing itself in a position of overwhelming military strength.

"The danger that after an abolition agreement someone would whip back the curtain and produce nuclear weapons—that's the breakout problem and it's serious," he replied, "but ten nuclear weapons are not going to destroy the United States, Russia, or China. It's going to provoke a very serious response from those nations if they're nuclear-free. Their outrage would be such that nobody would dare whip back the curtain. I guarantee you that if the United States had renounced nuclear weapons and somebody popped a nuke on us, well, it doesn't matter who they were, we would dismantle them militarily or economically.

"So the ownership of these weapons has to have a horrible price associated with it. For example, somebody asked me what we would have done if Saddam Hussein had used them. I said that we wouldn't have nuked him, we would have taken his country apart a brick at a time.

"These dangers are the reason that inspections, control regimes— technical intelligence and human intelligence—are so important. First, the United States and Russia should address their inventories, since they are the mother lode of these weapons. We don't have to like each other. We don't even have to be friends. People ask, 'What if the Russians cheat?' I answer, 'You should at first expect them to cheat.' You should operate as if they are cheating. And they at first should expect us to cheat. I mean, these are the sorts of things you don't take on a handshake. They require inspections, hard work, building confidence over time. But both nations ought to do what's in their own best interest, and that is to get rid of their nuclear arsenals."

Throughout the nuclear age, debate on military defense has been intense, convoluted, and confusing. Within the context of pure deterrence doctrine, antinuclear defenses have been anathema. One of the most unappealing paradoxes of that doctrine has been its conclusion that safety was best assured when each side bared its undefended breast to the offensive nuclear might of its foe. Since each side would then know that if it attacked first, it would be annihilated in return—so the theory ran—neither would attack in the first place. Efforts to build defenses, according to this view, could only prompt the other side to increase its offensive power, leading its rival to do likewise, thus fueling the arms race. President Reagan added a new level of complexity to these debates when, in 1983, he proposed his Strategic Defense Initiative (SDI), better known as Star Wars, whose goal was to protect the United States from missile attack—an ambition his critics called entirely unrealistic. And, to make matters more complex still, he excoriated the policy of mutual assured destruction on moral grounds and wedded SDI to a vision of nuclear abolition.

I asked Horner what his position was on defenses in the new era.

"I think the concept of the dominance of defense is absolutely critical," he answered. "And it cannot be for the United States only. This may be a difficult thing to swallow, but even if we set aside the whole nuclear issue, we need defenses. The world has become more unstable from a conventional fighting standpoint. It is easy to conceive that in five years a third country's missiles will be capable of reaching the United States. So whether or not we are in a cold war, we have an urgent need for ballistic missile defense. Right now, it is the one form of attack we can't stop. We can stop cruise missiles to some extent, but not ballistic missiles."

"Would defenses play a role in your conception of abolition?" I asked the general.

"Yes. We should propose that if you sign up for no nuclear weapons, you get a piece of the action with defense from ballistic missiles. Guaranteed."

"This was Reagan's idea," I noted. (Reagan had suggested that SDI technology might someday be shared with the Soviet Union.)

"That's right. The trouble was we weren't ready for it yet. Now the technology is emerging. The cost would be immense. We could not bear it in this country, but we could if we used a space-based system. One thing Russia can do well is throw satellites into the air. And one thing we can do well is build very capable satellites. So there's the price of admission for Russia and the United States. We could go into this together."

"What about other countries?" I asked.

"We're going to drag along our NATO allies, and the Russians will bring along the people they have special relationships with. Then you're left with the nations that are outside the camps and have nuclear weapons—Israel, Pakistan, India, and China. Consider Israel. One reason Israel has nuclear weapons is to preclude its annihilation. If you examine all the threats she may face, the greatest is a ballistic missile with a nuclear weapon. There's no conventional army that's going to come marching into Tel Aviv. If Israel couldn't stop it, the United States would. We've already signed up for that. They say, 'We can't depend on you,' but they've been doing pretty well with the Pentagon. If they keep nuclear weapons after others have gotten rid of them, though, they'd be outside the legitimacy club."

I observed that when Reagan had proposed sharing defensive anti-nuclear technology with the Russians, he'd been mocked.

"I know, but that was a valid vision and that's what we need—a vision of the future," Horner answered. "But don't ask the Pentagon to change the Pentagon. I think it has to come from outside. The Pentagon won't recognize truth. The executive branch has to provide leadership. If I had to fault the Clinton administration, amazingly enough it's because they've been the most stringent cold warriors of all.

"I don't think they have vision. Reagan had vision. You know, I'll never forget the Reykjavik summit, where he and Gorbachev talked about going to zero nuclear weapons. I mean, all the bureaucrats just about died of a heart attack. I thought: That makes sense to me. I don't know how you get two guys who can pull it off, but if you can, you've got my vote. And gee, everybody said: Well, Reagan really didn't mean that, or that he was asleep at the switch. They started to impugn the president for having the only legitimate idea that I've heard in twenty years.

"It's amazing how many people cannot envision a world free of nuclear weapons. It just scares the hell out of them. I find those people the most small-minded. You need the hardheaded businessman, the pragmatist, but you also need the visionary, the philosopher, the poet, to describe where we want to go."

"What have the reactions been to the position you've taken?" I asked.

"I guess the most negative reaction comes from the military people who are in the business of maintaining deterrence by being ready to launch war. Of course, they're very close to the subject, so they're very myopic. When I say things like, 'We don't need nuclear weapons,' I've just attacked their manhood." He laughed. "Interestingly enough," he continued, "I had a discussion with Dr. Edward Teller [the 'father,' together with Stanislaw Ulam, of the hydrogen bomb], who agreed that we could go to zero nuclear weapons—with the provision that we maintain our progress in nuclear technology. And of course what he was concerned with was providing safeguards against breakout. In fact, I was surprised. We were having lunch and I just laid into him on this, because I figured he would be very pro–nuclear weapons. And he was not. He was *pro-thinking*.

"In general, military people are reluctant to engage in this, because many of them—and I'm talking about the senior officers, the guys I deal with—came up through the ranks, commanding nuclear submarines, missile boats, or missile fields. They have to swallow hard because, of necessity, they've clung very close to these doctrines. I mean, they *have* to believe. So I guess the most amazing reaction I had was from the head of the Russian space program, General Ivanov. He's quite burly, imposing—obviously, a very intelligent guy. In 1994, we were out at Falcon Air Station, outside Colorado Springs. He was very proud of their space program, as he should be, because there are some things they do better than we do—space launches, for example. Yet you could also see how amazed he was that we had young high school graduates flying these million-dollar satellites. They respected the fact that our sergeants and airmen were doing jobs they expected commissioned officers to do.

"At one point it was kind of quiet and the time was right, so I decided to introduce the idea that we need to get rid of nuclear weapons. It shocked him. I said, 'You know, we're probably going to build ballistic missile defenses'—knowing full well that Russian insecurity is based on the fact that they believe we can do it and they can't. And I said, 'You know the same thing that shoots down the ballistic missile can also shoot down your satellites.' That got his attention. He took the position that they would never agree to the United States building ballistic missile defenses.

" 'Well, how are we going to get to zero nuclear weapons, then?' I asked. 'Because *you're* the guy with the problems. I don't have a problem. My problem is supposed to be Russia, but Russia's not interested in fighting and I'm not going to fight Russia.' He tended to agree with that. 'But,' I went on, 'you've got a problem with North Korea, China, India, Pakistan, Iraq, Iran, Syria—because they're all missile shots away from you. They all have incipient nuclear weapons programs, or maybe even possess nuclear weapons. What are you going to do about that?' That got him thinking. Then I said that we could share ballistic missile defenses and I made my appeal to him. I said, 'Your launch capability is so much better than ours. So why don't we develop the interceptors and the detectors in space to shoot down ballistic missiles for wide-area coverage, and why don't you launch them, because that's something your country can afford to do. Then we'd be equal partners in these shared defenses.'

" 'And as a first step,' I suggested, 'why don't you negotiate to put some of your people in Cheyenne Mountain, because we ought to be sharing this information, because you need it. And if we decide we're going to preemptively attack you, we'll just either shoot your guy, or wait till he goes to the bathroom.' He liked that.

"So then he asked, 'What's your problem getting the ballistic missile defense?' And I said, 'Right now, our problem is Congress. They are undecided whether to allocate the funds.' Then he stopped eating the meal we were having, and sat there in absolute silence for a good five minutes. Five minutes in absolute silence like that is an eternity.

His guys wouldn't speak—they wouldn't even move. They were just frozen. I drank a cup of coffee, and just sort of sat next to him. Finally, he said, 'O.K.'

"The next morning, when I took him to the airplane, he pulled me aside and said, 'I hope you have good luck with your Congress.'

"We didn't get to deterrence and containment overnight. Now we need a whole new way of thinking, a new intellectual construct and a change of awareness. I call this the war to replace the Cold War. And it is a war—a war against the proliferation and existence of weapons of mass destruction. I think reasonable people will find that the issue is not *whether* to get rid of nuclear weapons but how and when. But the debate cannot be only an intellectual one at Harvard University. We've got to get to the point where a guy driving a tractor in Iowa planting spring corn says, 'We really need ballistic missile defense, and we really need to get rid of our nuclear weapons.'

"The end is the elimination of nuclear arms and other weapons of mass destruction. When it's time to move out, walk away."

ROBERT MCNAMARA

Robert McNamara is by any standard one of the quintessential men of the Cold War. It was he who, as secretary of defense, first formally put the question, "How much is enough?" And it was he who, in answering that question, instituted the doctrine of deterrence in the form of mutual assured destruction as the declared policy of the United States. He was also one of the architects of the policies of the Kennedy and Johnson administrations in the Vietnam War. Lately, he has become a man of afterthoughts and regrets. In his book *In Retrospect*, he analyzed and condemned the policies in Vietnam that he had once championed. Some who opposed the war took him to task for not revealing his change of heart earlier, and some who favored the war upbraided him for revealing that change of heart at all—or for having it. Others, however, were grateful for an uncompelled act of accountability for which, in the annals of statesmanship, it is difficult to find much precedent. At the book's end, he placed an appendix that dealt with the nuclear

question. Here, too, there was reconsideration. Alluding to "a revolutionary change in thinking about the role of nuclear forces," he advocated "a return, by all five nuclear powers, insofar as practicable, to a
nonnuclear world."

When I spoke with McNamara in his office in Washington, he had
just agreed to be a member of the Canberra Commission. "Is it possible
and desirable to eliminate nuclear weapons from the world entirely?"
I asked.

"There are two questions," McNamara replied. "The answer to
both is yes. First, would it be desirable if it were possible to eliminate
nuclear weapons entirely, and, second, would it be possible? Would it
be desirable if it were possible means: Could we be assured that if they
were eliminated by the declared nuclear powers no terrorist group or
rogue state or other nation would break out and violate the agreement
and surreptitiously develop a nuclear weapon or weapons after we'd
all disarmed? If that's what we mean by 'if it were possible,' then
we should talk about that. But assuming for the moment that we could
be assured that breakout could be dealt with, then I think it's not
only desirable but essential that we eliminate nuclear weapons. They
have no military utility other than to deter one's opponent from using
nuclear weapons. And if our opponent doesn't have nuclear weapons,
we don't need them. I'm quoting almost exactly from a National
Academy of Sciences report published three or four years ago and
signed by, among others, the former chairman of the Joint Chiefs of
Staff, General David Jones. Now that report, oddly enough, having
made such a clear-cut and, I think, correct statement, goes on to say
that we can't—we shouldn't—go below fifteen hundred or two thousand warheads. The reason they say it's not possible to get rid of nuclear
weapons altogether is that we must protect against rogue-state or terrorist breakout. What I think they have in mind, to put it in simple
terms, is that if Russia and the United States sign an agreement to get
rid of those weapons, and we destroyed ours, thinking that they had
destroyed theirs, they might have retained their capability, and have
plans ready to quickly rebuild their nuclear forces. To prevent that,
since we might not learn of it until it was too late, we needed the fifteen hundred or two thousand weapons."

"What would your answer be?"

"Going to zero has been considered so undesirable that no thoughtful study has been made of it. I defy you to find a thoughtful study of whether it's possible to get rid of nuclear weapons completely while remaining assured of protection against a terrorist or rogue-state breakout.

"Now why is it *desirable* to eliminate the weapons? Even if someone agrees that there is no military utility in them, they may say: 'McNamara, you denigrate nuclear deterrence. You don't seem to understand that there is still some deterrent value.' Some may agree with me that the deterrent value has eroded, because now it's so clear that any nuclear response to a conventional attack by a nuclear-equipped opponent would be a disaster, and therefore it's not credible as a deterrent to say we would respond with nuclear weapons. 'But McNamara,' they go on, 'there still is a deterrent there.' McGeorge Bundy characterized it with a very interesting and apt term. He called it 'existential deterrence.' And I'm prepared to accept that there is some existential deterrence, though I would consider it quite limited.

"Why am I not eager to preserve that? Two or three reasons. The first is that it's very, very risky. Even a low probability of catastrophe is a high risk, and I don't think we should continue to accept it. If you don't believe it's a risk, then read the reports of the Cuban Missile Crisis Retrospective Meetings and the recently published Kennedy tapes. I believe that was the best-managed Cold War crisis of any, but we came within a hairbreadth of nuclear war without realizing it. There were mistakes made by Khrushchev and his associates, and by Kennedy and his associates, including me. We made miscalculations, misjudgments, in what I call the best-managed crisis. It's no credit to us that we missed nuclear war—at least, we had to be lucky as well as wise. So I want to say that's a risk I don't believe the human race should accept."

"For some fifty years, there has been a school of thought which teaches that you wouldn't want to get to zero even if you could, on grounds that a world without nuclear weapons is inherently unstable, owing to the danger of breakout."

"Yes, I know that," he put in.

"But you rebut it?"

"I want to put aside, for a moment, the breakout question. I want to describe why, *if* I can protect against breakout, eliminating nuclear weapons is highly desirable. It's highly desirable, first, because using nuclear weapons against a nuclear-equipped opponent of any size at all is suicide, and, second, because using them against a non-nuclear-equipped opponent is, I think, immoral. And I do not believe any political leader of this nation would or should use nuclear weapons in that situation. Even if he would, it wouldn't be more than one or two or five. So this doesn't have any relationship to the numbers that we presently have.

"Now, is it possible? I was just talking to a friend about exactly this point. He said, 'The goal of zero is desirable, but is it possible? What about terrorists and rogue states and breakout?'

"I said, 'Suppose we have an agreement under which there aren't going to be any nuclear weapons or no one is going to have any more than we retain, whatever that number is, then how many would we have to retain in order to protect against breakout? One? Five? One hundred? Certainly not more than one hundred.' All right, then: Why don't we agree—we're going to make a study about how to get to zero. But while we're making the study, we're going to go from thirty-five hundred down to a hundred. So I'll accept that there is a problem. I think there's an answer that can get us to zero, and clearly the fact that there's a problem doesn't in any way justify the current program of nuclear weapons."

At the time we spoke, McNamara had already participated in preparing the Stimson report. To its statement that the elimination of nuclear weapons "does presume that, over time, states will become less reliant on military force, and will not rely on nuclear weapons at all to settle their differences and secure their interests," he and his colleague Will Marshall, president of the Progressive Policy Institute, appended a footnote that reads in part "[we] do not agree that the achievement of elimination [of nuclear weapons] requires the resolution of regional conflicts and wide-ranging renunciation of the use of force." The point thus tangentially asserted was a fundamental one. Many agree that nuclear abolition—or general and complete disarmament, for that matter—would be both possible and delightful if, first, all political quarrels in the world were resolved. What need would there be for arms of any sort if no one had anything to fight about? McNamara and Marshall, however, were insisting on urgent, present action to achieve abolition, even in a quarrelsome world.

"The report basically says you've got to have collective security before you can eliminate nuclear weapons," he explained, "and I don't believe it. The requirement reminds me of Clinton's Nuclear Posture Review. In a sense the report says, 'McNamara, you don't seem to understand the Russians. True, they're acting peaceful today, but they may move back to become aggressively imperialist.' Therefore, we must 'hedge' against them by maintaining nuclear weapons. And I say, I agree, they may become aggressive. Do you want to face aggressive imperialists with large numbers of nuclear weapons or with small numbers or none? I want to face them with none."

"What do you think of administration policy?" I asked.

"Well, you know, the problem is a very simple one to me. The first words out of Clinton's mouth after he took office were about homosexuals in the armed forces. If I'd been deciding, I would have accepted homosexuals, but I sure as hell wouldn't have made a public statement, and in particular I wouldn't if I hadn't been drafted and gone to Vietnam. You put those two things together and he has no capability to take initiative in these matters. And there has been no leadership in the Defense Department. Those guys are my friends. I know them and I respect them. But that Nuclear Posture Review was a disgrace, an absolute disgrace."

McNamara was worried that what he referred to as "the lessons of the Cold War" might be lost. It was not just that a new generation was growing up without the experience of full-fledged terror; even the Cold War generations, he feared, might have missed the most important lessons of those decades. "There are many," he remarked, "who still don't understand the degree of destruction that would occur if nations used these weapons. Also, many people don't understand the risk that, quite unintentionally, we can maneuver ourselves into a position where these things would be used. They don't understand the fog of war. It's not just nuclear risk. It's other kinds of risk. You make mistakes in war. That's the lesson of the Cuban missile crisis. Unless you've been in it and have been responsible at the upper level, you don't recognize how often you make mistakes and how serious they can be and how utterly destructive if they involve nuclear weapons.

"The Canberra Commission initially put major emphasis on practical steps to monitor an agreement to eliminate nuclear weapons. My advice was, in the first instance, to address the risk in *not* eliminating nuclear weapons, and then to compare that risk with whatever risk there is of violation of an agreement to eliminate. Put very simply, the risk in not eliminating is totally unacceptable, because it is to me a risk of the *destruction of nations*. It became very clear to me as a result of the Cuban missile crisis that the indefinite combination of human fallibility (which we can never get rid of) and nuclear weapons carries the very high probability of the destruction of nations.

"The people who best understand that risk are those who at some point have had to actually think about their personal responsibility to recommend using them. I actually had to think about it: would I be prepared to recommend to the president the use of these things?"

"What did you answer?"

"I said, 'No.' "

"You did?"

"That's right. I've been called a liar in public because I now say that in '62 and '63 and in '64, when Johnson came in, I said to Kennedy and, later, Johnson, 'Don't follow NATO policy.' " (During the Cold War, NATO policy called for the United States to answer a Soviet conventional attack on Europe with nuclear weapons.) " 'Go out tomorrow, say you will follow NATO policy, and I will go out tomorrow and say I'll follow NATO policy—but don't ever do it,' I said.

"Well, I didn't lie. I worked hard for eighteen months to really think through exactly what all of this meant; and what it meant was, if we followed NATO policy, we would destroy the nation. I said to the president, 'I don't care what happens, if the Soviet Warsaw Pact is, in fact, overrunning West Germany, don't launch nuclear weapons.' "

McNamara's surprising disclosure of his private advice to two presidents reminded me of another question I had often asked myself during the Cold War years. At the heart of deterrence theory, it had seemed to me, lay a basic contradiction: According to the theory, the way to prevent the foe from launching a first strike was to threaten to launch an annihilating second strike; but if a first strike were actually launched, ensuring that the United States momentarily would become a waste-land, the retaliatory strike would have lost its purpose. It would be an act of pointless revenge. The problem worried strategists because they feared that the evident senselessness of the threatened retaliation robbed it of "credibility," thus weakening its deterrent effect. My ques-tion had been different. I wondered whether, if the first strike had ever arrived, the president would actually have ordered the pointless retalia-tion. The answer, it seemed to me, was of some historical interest. If the president had planned to launch that second strike, he would have committed himself to unparalleled slaughter for no apparent reason. Yet if the president had planned to hold back, then deterrence had been a gigantic bluff. I put the question to McNamara. "What about the case in which the other side used them first? What would you have recommended to the president?"

"Well, that's a good question, for which there's no easy answer. But that question is what led me to give, in 1962, what is known as the Ann Arbor speech, in which I said to the Soviets: 'Let's, for God's sake, not destroy each other. Let's recognize the great risk we face, and if we ever have to use these things, let's start out with a few and respond with a few.' I called it 'controlled escalation.' Although that might have been feasible when they had a few and we had a lot, it sure wasn't feasible a few years later. But if there had been a first strike against us, I'm quite confident about what would have happened: we would have unleashed a very, very substantial force."

I noted that by Ronald Reagan's second term, the president had concluded that a nuclear war "cannot be won and must never be fought."

"Well," McNamara replied, "he had two simplistic views. One was the right view. The other simplistic view—it was the wrong one—was that we can have an effective defense against ballistic missiles."

McNamara also dismissed the idea of sharing antinuclear defenses with the Russians. He called it "absurd," adding, "We'd have never shared anything like that." If Reagan had succeeded, as he had suggested at his preparatory summit meeting with Gorbachev in Reykjavik, McNamara added, "his own cabinet would have impeached him."

He mentioned the remark by Reagan's deputy secretary of defense, T. K. Jones, that "if we have enough shovels," our society could survive a nuclear war. "That guy had never been in the position in which he had to say, 'Well, Mr. President, under these circumstances, I urge you to launch. And I'm prepared because, you know, we've got enough shovels.' "

McNamara and Horner, I reflected, were both in favor of abolishing nuclear weapons but seemed to belong to different schools of abolitionism. McNamara, steeped in the doctrine of deterrence, not surprisingly seemed to rule out defenses as an aid to disarmament, whereas Horner, who had never had much affection for deterrence, looked forward, as Reagan had, to a defense-dominated world without nuclear weapons. In fact, the question of the role of defenses appeared to divide abolitionists almost as much as it had once divided cold warriors.

I asked McNamara what he thought should be done now.

"If I were president, I'd have a national security advisor and policy-planning staff in State and Defense focus on these issues. I would assemble the best people in the world. I'd want an informal discussion of the issues among the leaders of the largest countries—the great powers, plus India and a few others. As leaders of the great powers, we ought to be thinking about the next century. The Chinese would say, 'The problem isn't us—it's you damn Americans, who joined with the others to make us feel inferior, and now you want to talk about this. You're trying to hold us in.' And so on. It would take time. But I would start now."

McNamara told me that his earliest memory was of the day the First World War ended. "The city was exploding with joy," he recalled. "The date was November 11, 1918, Armistice Day. I was two years old. The city was San Francisco, celebrating the end of World War I, but also the belief—a belief held by Woodrow Wilson—that we had fought a war to end all wars and we had won it.

"And yet in the wars since then, we lost 160 million people, depending on how you count those dead from conflict. It was the bloodiest century in all human history. Now that we're at the end of that century and at the beginning of a new millennium, shouldn't we think about how to confront this terrible human problem?"

JOSEPH ROTBLAT

Joseph Rotblat is an exemplary man of the nuclear age. In 1939, he initiated research on atomic weapons in Liverpool, England. In 1944, he came to the United States to work for the Manhattan Project. In December of that year—seven months before the weapon was first tested at Alamogordo and eight months before it was dropped on Hiroshima—he resigned his position. Rotblat had agreed to work on the bomb only because he feared that Hitler would win the war. He resigned when he learned that the German atomic bomb program had failed. When the peril that had justified his work on the bomb ended, he ended his work on the bomb. He was the only scientist working on the Manhattan Project to do so. His act provides lonely testimony to the capacity of human reason and will to resist the powerful momentum of nuclear armament.

Today, the justification that Western nations gave themselves for possessing nuclear weapons—the Soviet threat—has ended and the question the entire West has to ask itself is the one Rotblat asked in 1944: When your reason for having nuclear weapons vanishes, do you end your work on them, or do you search for some new reason to go on?

In the poem "Anthem for St. Cecilia's Day," W. H. Auden characterized modern man as the "impetuous child with the tremendous brain." Rotblat, and Rotblat alone among the nuclear scientists in the months just before the advent of the atomic age, gave proof that it was possible for people to act with restraint and take moral responsibility for the products of that tremendous brain. After the war, Rotblat went to work to rein in and eventually eliminate the weapon he had helped to create. He became, among other things, a cofounder of the Pugwash Conference on Science and World Affairs, an international organization of scientists that has worked since its inception in 1954 to reverse the nuclear arms race, and it was for this work that he won the Nobel Peace Prize.

I asked him to describe his reasons for agreeing to work on the bomb.

"My rationale was that the only way to stop Hitler from using a bomb against us would be if we also had it and threatened to retaliate. In other words, it was the concept of nuclear deterrence. I may have been the first person to develop this concept." Rotblat laughed at the thought. These days he derides the idea that during the Cold War, nuclear deterrence prevented wars. "How many more wars are needed to refute this argument?" he asked in his Nobel acceptance speech. He also rejects the claim that deterrence stabilized the relationship between the two superpowers. "Neither side," he said to me, "was ever sure that it could destroy the other side after suffering a first strike. That is why each side kept trying to make its own arsenal more powerful and the other side's more vulnerable until they built the unbelievable number of some 100,000 nuclear weapons."

"What do you make now of the reasoning that led you to work on the bomb?"

"I often ask myself how I would behave if the same situation recurred. And, yes, I feel that I might make the same decision, although in several respects I was mistaken. First, I didn't know that the Germans had given up work on the bomb a long time before I quit. Second, I didn't realize that so-called nuclear deterrence doesn't work with people who are irrational, as Hitler was. I now think that if he had had the bomb he would have used it. And, third, I was naive in believing that once we scientists had produced a weapon, the military and civilian leaders would listen to us regarding how it should be used."

"And your decision to leave the Manhattan Project?"

"Well, this part is very simple. I left the project when I learned that the Germans had abandoned their atomic bomb project." Rotblat explained that the head of the British team, James Chadwick, for whom he had worked in England, had informed him that the Germans were no longer trying to make an atomic bomb. Chadwick, however, became worried about the effect of Rotblat's decision on the morale of the other scientists at the Manhattan Project. In addition, American security put together a dossier casting doubt on Rotblat's loyalty—reports, as it happened, that he easily was able to disprove, actually winning an apology. (He had been at meetings at Los Alamos at many of the times when the dossier claimed he was having suspicious meetings elsewhere.) Nevertheless, a gag rule was imposed on him: he was forbidden both from revealing to his colleagues the reason for his decision to leave and from otherwise staying in touch with them. Thus, within the secret precincts of the Manhattan Project, was the sole dissenter from the continuing work thrust into even deeper secrecy. (Since the still-uncompleted bomb, of course, remained a secret from the world at large, there could be no question of speaking publicly.)

I asked why he thought the other atomic scientists had not acted as he had done once Hitler lost the war.

"I believe that war has a terrible effect on our behavior, on our moral standards," he answered. "One person who comes immediately to mind is Robert Oppenheimer. If you looked at his outlook on life, his philosophy, you wouldn't believe that such a man would advocate the use of the bomb on Hiroshima—on civilians—and yet he did. He could have stopped, he could have said no, but he did not, and later on I found that his moral decay—in a way, his moral disintegration—had begun even before that, in 1943. You know that the first reactor came into being in December 1942 in Chicago. This was the first time it became possible to produce large amounts of strontium 90, the radioactive fission product. He wanted to spray it on German soil, so as to poison the food and kill people. And there's a letter that he wrote in 1943 to [Enrico] Fermi, who was in charge of the reactor, saying that we should not begin the project unless we could produce enough [strontium 90] to kill half a million men. This was utterly barbaric. It tells me that the war had affected him. It's one reason that I'm so much against war—not only because of the physical privation and suffering but also because of the mental breakdown."

We turned to the present and abolition. There are three areas in which Rotblat, who has written extensively on abolition (and edited a book, A Nuclear-Weapon-Free World, on the subject), has brought his attention to bear with particular insistence and force. The first is his advocacy of a nuclear no-first-use treaty—no-first-use being the policy that nuclear weapons should be dedicated solely to the mission of deterring other nuclear weapons. They should have no role, he believes, in deterring conventional war, much less in actually repelling conventional attacks. No-first-use has had many champions, including, during the Cold War, Robert McNamara. If the pathways of escalation from conventional war to nuclear war were blocked, Rotblat has suggested, nuclear war would become less likely, but he advocates no-first-use for another reason: its role in making nuclear abolition possible.

"The most important step at the present time—and this can be taken virtually overnight—is for the nuclear powers to declare that the only purpose of possessing nuclear weapons is to deter a nuclear attack," he said to me. "If the nuclear powers can agree on this, and follow it up with a global treaty of no-first-use, this in my opinion would be the breakthrough we need. It prepares the way to go to zero, for if each nuclear power possesses nuclear weapons only to deter other powers' nuclear weapons, and all were to agree to eliminate them, then no one would have any reason any longer to retain them. And it is something that can be done without an extraordinary verification system. I would put it at the top of my list of things to do."

Unfortunately, he observed, the nuclear powers cling, overtly or tacitly, to other justifications for keeping nuclear weapons. As the Nuclear Posture Review and the new Presidential Decision Directive made clear, the United States deploys nuclear weapons to deter a potential threat from some future hostile Russia and to deter chemical or biological attacks by rogue states. Rotblat joins General Horner in arguing that a nuclear-weapon-less United States, which would remain "the most powerful nation in the world," has less to worry about and more to gain from abolition than any other country.

Still, Rotblat calls for the most stringent verification systems technically possible for any future abolition agreement. Of particular importance, he told me, would be the verification of commercially produced plutonium, whose global stocks are already far greater than the amount of plutonium that might be removed from decommissioned nuclear weapons. He has concluded that verification within a range of 99 percent accuracy might be possible. Still, considering the amount of plutonium in the world, even 1 percent is "too much, because even 1 percent would be enough to make many bombs."

This admission brought him to the second area in which he has taken a particular interest. "We should establish a system of societal verification," he said. "In societal verification, citizens—including, especially, scientists—acquire a legal obligation to report on any efforts to build weapons of mass destruction." Any global abolition treaty should itself create such an obligation. "A clause of the treaty would mandate all signatory nations to pass national laws that make it the right and the duty of every citizen to notify an international authority of any effort to circumvent the treaty. This would apply especially to scientists. To make nuclear weapons you need two things. One is special equipment and the other is a certain brainpower. If violations are occurring, scientists will realize that something is going on. With this societal system of verification in place in addition to all the technical means, the chances of any nation's building up a nuclear arsenal in a completely clandestine way, without its being detected, are extremely small."

In connection with his work on verification, Rotblat has subjected the various possible forms of breakout to analysis. The most likely violator, he has observed, would be a former nuclear power. Such a power, however, would be highly unlikely to circumvent an abolition agreement merely to confront a conventional threat by a smaller power. That leaves "the possibility of a political situation that deteriorates so badly between two great military powers that they feel compelled to resort to military measures, even leading to the use of nuclear weapons." However, such a crisis probably "would be seen coming for a long time." Even if "both sides start to rebuild their nuclear armories," the outlook, however ominous, would be "better than at the present time," in which nuclear powers already possess large arsenals on full alert. Another possibility would be a small power that "clandestinely" built up "a nuclear armory for aggressive purposes." Such a country would undoubtedly face "the combined conventional military might of the whole world. . . . No rational leader is likely to take that risk for gains that are bound to be short-lived." There is, of course, the danger that an "irrational leader" or "fundamentalist regime bent on launching a holy war" might build nuclear weapons. The special difficulty in such cases is that a military reprisal might "not be a deterrent." But this is precisely the rogue-state threat that is "unmanageable even today." Rotblat concludes that while the dangers of breakout are real, taken together they are far smaller than the dangers we run daily in our nuclear-armed world.

Rotblat's conviction that scientists should take responsibility for the consequences of scientific inventions leads him to a third area of concentration. He believes that although nuclear abolition need not await general and complete disarmament, it nevertheless should be seen as a way station to a world without war. "Even now," he said, "many people still feel that we can fight a nuclear war and get away with it. They don't realize that for the first time in history man has acquired the means of destroying his own species in a single action. But even the elimination of nuclear weapons will not bring full security. Nuclear weapons cannot be disinvented. Therefore it is true that in a military confrontation nations will be tempted to rebuild them. Also, while nuclear weapons are the first means man has developed for destroying his own species, they will not be the last. Scientists can invent other means for the full destruction of the species. It is already recognized that further research is likely to bring these means into being. In such circumstances, any war can threaten us, because any war can escalate without limit. These are my reasons for believing that the long-term objective must be not just nuclear disarmament but a world without war.

"Of course, people say that this is utopian, much harder than the abolition of nuclear weapons. I argue that if you look at the actual trend in history in recent years, you find that we are halfway there—or perhaps more than half. In my own lifetime I have lived through two world wars and in both of these France and Germany were the principal antagonists, mortal enemies, and yet in the course of a few decades the idea of France and Germany going to war became inconceivable. In Latin America, only a few years ago, most governments were dictatorial military regimes. Now, except in one or two countries, they are democratic and no longer talk about fighting one another. The main enemy now is poverty, which we don't need a war to fight."

ALAN CRANSTON

"What we seek is the reign of law, based upon the consent of the governed and sustained by the organized opinion of mankind," President Woodrow Wilson stated on July 4, 1918, expressing, as he said, "in a single sentence" American objectives in the First World War, which, he famously hoped and believed, would be the "war to end war." The Wilsonian project of ending war by establishing an international organization based on the rule of law, of course, became a prominent—some would say a dominant—strain in American foreign policy in the first half of the twentieth century. (The depth of Wilson's influence is suggested by the fact that Richard Nixon, though regarded by many as a master of realpolitik, considered himself a Wilsonian.) Wilson's single sentence is approvingly quoted in Alan Cranston's book of 1945, *The Killing of Peace*, a narrative history of the campaign that led in 1919 to the Senate's repudiation of Wilson's League of Nations. Cranston hoped the story would serve as a cautionary tale against any impulse to reject the United Nations, which, in a second flowering of Wilsonian ideals, was being founded in that year.

Between the United Nations' conception, in 1944, and its foundation, in 1945, came the advent of the atomic bomb. That development caused Cranston, among many others, to conclude that an international organization much stronger than the United Nations was needed. If Horner was a military man inspired by Ronald Reagan's vision of a defense-dominated world without nuclear weapons, and McNamara was a civilian cold warrior in rebellion against the burdens of a deterrence doctrine he had helped craft, and Rotblat was a scientist in rebellion against the physical product of his own mind, then Cranston was a Wilsonian liberal internationalist who, at the beginning of the nuclear age, sought to bring traditional Wilsonian answers to bear on nuclear dilemmas. The sudden arrival of nuclear danger redoubled his commitment to the necessity of a task to which he was already devoted: the foundation of an international order that would replace war itself.

Cranston joined the United World Federalists and, in 1949,

became its president; but when, with the onset of the Korean War, the Cold War began in earnest, political support for world federalism dropped off precipitously. Although there is no doubt that the Cold War was the principal reason for the decline of Wilsonian hopes, the bomb also played a role. Its influence, however, was equivocal. On the one hand, its existence obviously added urgency to the cause of international peace; on the other hand, it came to seem, in the minds of many, itself to guarantee international peace, through the mutual balance of terror.

However that may be, Wilsonianism, although surviving in oratory, was eclipsed in practice, and before long the doctrine of deterrence came to mark the limits of mainstream opinion: there was no place in it for international political systems to end war. Cranston, who went on to serve as a Democratic senator from California from 1969 until 1993, and as Democratic whip for fourteen of those years, accepted the limits and worked in Congress for passage of the SALT II and the START treaties—agreements based on the underlying framework of deterrence.

What had happened, I wondered, to the great current of Wilsonian liberal internationalism, which had flowed so powerfully in the United States in the first half of the century? Had it simply petered out? Certainly, the end of the Cold War brought no surge of Wilsonianism, as the ends of the First and Second World Wars had done. No plan for a new international organization or the abolition of war was widely entertained. (President George Bush's invocation of Wilsonian principles to justify the Gulf War proved to be more an epitaph for the creed than an announcement of its revival.) Curiously, it was perhaps the nuclear possessionists whose goals were closest to Wilson's. Like Wilson, they offered a comprehensive solution to the problem of major war in the world. But whereas Wilson's solution was an international organization and the rule of law, their answer was the bomb and the rule of nuclear terror. Listening to the nuclear possessionists of 1997, one is often reminded of the world federalists of 1947. Both sought peace—nuclear and conventional—and both hoped that it would last forever. In contrast, most of the current abolitionists, notwithstanding the undoubtedly radical character of their principal aim, emerge as gradualists. For instance, none—not even Rotblat, who wishes to abolish all war—claims that nuclear abolition will do the job. All are prepared to postpone that task to a later date.

Cranston, I found, was now decidedly of this gradualist school. He did not, after leaving the Senate, return to his earlier world federalist passion. What he did do was begin to work, in his capacity as chair of the State of the World Forum, to quietly but intensely rally important public figures to the cause of ridding the world of nuclear weapons. He was an initiator and a moving force behind the statement by the international generals in favor of abolition, a press conference held by Generals Butler and Goodpaster, and the statement in favor of nuclear abolition that was signed in February of 1998 by civilian statesmen, including many former and present heads of state.

The job of Senate whip is one of lining up support for party positions. Now, in retirement, Cranston has become a kind of whip for a position that he himself has arrived at—the elimination of nuclear weapons. Through his many initiatives, he has quietly done more, in all likelihood, than any other American to marshal public opinion behind the abolitionist cause.

At eighty-three, Cranston is rail-thin and has somehow entirely failed to acquire the flourish and bluster that so often characterize successful politicians.

I asked him how he made the transition from president of the United World Federalists to elected official in the Cold War era.

"When I entered politics I was concerned that the United World Federalist association would be thrown against me and perhaps make life difficult on the grounds that I was trying to give up American sovereignty to build a world superstate. I was protected in two odd ways. First, when I was active in the World Federalists at the grassroots level in California, a local progressive-minded Republican named Bob Kirkwood joined the Federalists. As it happened, he became my opponent when I first ran for office. Second, when I was national president of the United World Federalists, one of its members was Ronald Reagan. So those two things wiped out the issue."

I asked to what extent he thought Wilson's vision was applicable to the post–Cold War era.

"The way to do things now is step by step," he answered. "And the first step is to deal with the nuclear danger. As we develop international institutions to do that, we will build some elements of world law—I like that phrase, 'world law,' better than 'world government,' whose use was a mistake, I think, in the forties."

During the Cold War, he said, the gradualist approach had proved itself. "The nuclear arms agreements between the United States and the Soviet Union did cap and reverse the arms race. Now we need much deeper reductions in nuclear stockpiles between the United States and Russia. When we get down near to where the United Kingdom, France, and China are, we need to draw them in, and move together to very low numbers. At this stage, we should draw in the threshold states—India, Pakistan, and Israel. You'd build confidence during that process, which brings abolition within reach. I don't think we should try to determine now what it takes to achieve final abolition. Nevertheless, it's an ultimate goal that should be proclaimed to ease the concerns of nations that don't like the idea that we're going to have the bomb forever and they are not—a state of affairs that can lead to proliferation. The goal is needed to set a moral tone—as a rallying point."

Another crucial step in this gradual progress to the goal of elimination, Cranston thought, was taking nuclear arsenals off alert. "De-alerting, which has already begun with first steps taken by Bush and Gorbachev and the modest de-targeting agreement by Clinton and Yeltsin," he pointed out, "can ease tension immediately by reducing the danger of accidental launches. If you move away from that brink of catastrophe and have it verifiable that, for example, you have separated warheads from missiles and taken them apart to some extent, and all of that can be witnessed, then if anybody reverses the process and starts putting things back together it will become known, and there will be time to deal with the situation."

"Do you think abolition requires a powerful world organization to make it work, as many of its opponents have said?"

"I don't think that it will take an elaborate collective security system. What's needed, many agree, is a strict inspection and surveillance procedure, a firm global inventory and control of fissile material, and a firmly agreed upon procedure for dealing with a rogue seeking to develop nuclear weapons or actually acquiring a few. We would surely find out before it has very many bombs in its hands. The threat would be large, but we wouldn't need a detailed body of world law or collective security system to deal with it. A procedure whereby the United Nations or a concert of great nations moved in, as they did in the Gulf War, would suffice."

Cranston was suggesting that the abolition of nuclear weapons would be possible even without world government, or anything close to it. The development of international law, to which he was still strongly dedicated, would come about gradually and incrementally, and full nuclear disarmament would be a part of the process. "More and more transactions—in business, in the area of the environment, in communications—are taking place without respect for national boundaries," he observed. "At present, no democratic process is involved in these developments, and sooner or later people are going to feel there has to be a more democratic voice in these global events as they unfold, in order to limit them."

I asked Cranston what relation this thinking had to his earlier belief in world federalism.

"There is one thread, certainly, that runs throughout: the need to accept abridgments of national sovereignty. Actually, this is already occurring as borders become less significant, and as nations increasingly face global problems with which they cannot cope alone. The kind of intrusive inspections already agreed to in several arms treaties represents, in fact, such an abridgment.

"National sovereignty is not the only sovereignty. Many of our founding fathers were very clear on this point. They spoke of the individual person's being sovereign. Jefferson, drafting the Declaration of Independence in 1776, wrote that 'governments derive their powers from the consent of the people governed.' Madison, drafting the Bill of Rights in 1789, declared, 'All power is originally vested in, and consequently derived from, the people.' A lone individual lacks the power to do all the things that he wants to see done. So the individual has to grant some of his sovereignty to the school district, the county, the state, the nation. But in a democracy, the grant is conditional, and people have the right to retract their sovereignty from those to whom they have granted it. The problem today is that we have no worldwide place to lodge those portions of individual sovereignty that are needed to solve the problems that, like the nuclear question, overpopulation, and many environmental problems, can only be solved at the global level. But the first step is to remind people that they—and not the nation—are truly sovereign, and that they have the right to vest their sovereignty, or a part of it, where they wish."

I observed that public interest in nuclear disarmament seemed low at the moment and asked Cranston how, politically speaking, abolition might come about.

"The likelihood of a nationally influential grassroots movement against nuclear weapons doesn't seem very high right now," he agreed. "There are other issues on people's minds, especially economic ones. It's not on the agenda of major governments, either. But there are people of considerable influence who intend to provide some leadership and feel that a response is possible from the people who have the power to make decisions. That's true not only in the United States but elsewhere in the world. Two governments—one in Australia, and one in Japan—have taken the lead. South Africa, with the great moral leadership of Nelson Mandela and the fact that they have actually abandoned a nuclear program, is another. And there are key people in Russia and Europe who are starting to speak out, as some are here.

"I'm thrilled that there is now a moment of opportunity. It may not last very long, and I want to help seize it. One virtue of being out of the Senate is that I am free to set my own agenda and can focus on this effort more than I could in the Senate, much as I wanted to. The period from 1914 to 1991 has probably been the bloodiest, most catastrophic in all human history. But we're approaching a millennium, which is something new and different for everybody now on earth. And the feeling is we've just got to make the twenty-first century better. What does it take? Among other things, it takes getting rid of weapons of mass destruction, and reducing or ending war, as we've done in North America and Western Europe—creating an enduring peace."

MERAV DATAN

Merav Datan, who was born in the United States in 1962 and emigrated eight months later with her parents to Israel, where she grew up, is now a dual American-Israeli national. In 1994, she graduated from Columbia University School of Law and last year became director of research for the Lawyers' Committee on Nuclear Policy. She spends much of her time working on the Model Nuclear Weapons Convention, a citizen's draft of a global treaty abolishing nuclear weapons.

After studying physics at the Weizmann Institute in Rehovot, she went to work with the Ethiopian consulate in Jerusalem, where her work proved highly important in making possible the exodus, by secret airlift, of more than fifteen thousand Ethiopian Jews to Israel. The experience impressed on her the importance that the work of a single person can have. However, she was not drawn to politics. "Politics seemed to me so much a matter of one side blaming another," she said to me when I met her at the committee's New York office. "I was more drawn to the law, and especially international law. If you view the use of force and militarization as a common enemy, you have a foundation for adversaries to work together."

As director of research for the model convention, she has drawn on the advice of several dozen arms control experts and international lawyers in coordinating the drafting of the treaty. Although the model uses legal and technical language of the kind that would appear in an actual treaty, the purpose of the enterprise is not to lobby for abolition in exactly the form specified in the draft; it is to bring to the surface the innumerable issues that such a treaty would raise, to provoke discussion about these in all their complexity, and to bring abolition out of the mist of wishes and into the clearer light of an actual plan. Accordingly, instead of offering definitive provisions for every point, the model sometimes supplies alternatives. For example, there are two possible definitions of what a nuclear weapon is (a surprisingly thorny question, as it turns out). One is from the Treaty of Tlatelolco, which established Latin America as a nuclear-weapon-free zone, and the other is based on the physical characteristics of the weapons. Datan hopes for and expects criticism. "We consider it a discussion draft," she said. "When the model is criticized, it succeeds." The model is the only effort of its kind that I know of in the world today.

Datan was startled by the demand for the first draft of the treaty when it was made available in April 1996. More than a thousand copies have been requested, many by U.N. delegations or other government offices around the world. Datan was amused, however, to note that among the delegations from acknowledged and unacknowledged nuclear powers, the only two that did not request a copy were her two homelands, Israel and the United States. (Regarding this, one is tempted to comment that a prophet is not honored in her own countries.) Recently, the model was submitted by the government of Costa Rica to the secretary general of the United Nations, Kofi Annan, as a discussion document.

I asked what she had found to be the most troublesome obstacles to abolition.

"The obvious one is the lack of political will," she replied. "And one reason for drafting the convention is to draw attention to this lack of will. Clearly, there are large technical issues in question, too, including the question of verification. It's difficult, for instance, to develop a system that permits inspection while safeguarding design secrets. Then there is the issue of control over nuclear materials. We incline to a 'dual key' system, in which national authorities and an international agency must cooperate to gain access to nuclear materials. Another difficult issue is nuclear power. Our treaty permits it but offers an alternative in which it is ended."

I asked for her opinion on the dangers of breakout from an abolition treaty.

"It seems to me that we are heading toward a situation in which breakout is more and more possible right now. The only difference is that we don't call it 'breakout'; we call it 'nuclear terrorism.' Part of the purpose of our work is to help reverse that trend. One important aspect of this is leading people to pay more attention to the weapons applications of nuclear physics and technology. It's often said that you can't control nuclear weapons because the genie is out of the bottle—the knowledge can't be removed from the world. We try to address that point head on. The response of scientists should be to develop another kind of knowledge: knowledge of the dangers that go with scientific inventions.

"We also note that the threat of proliferation is not due just to splitting the atom; it is the result of a lot of effort, a lot of expenditure, and the devotion of a lot of talent to military purposes. Proliferation is a consequence not just of knowledge but of policy decisions and spending on research and development."

I asked whether she was convinced that zero could be achieved.

"I'm perhaps a little less optimistic than some of the people I work with," she said. "Some of them firmly believe we can abolish nuclear weapons. I'm not sure—perhaps because I grew up in a very militaristic society. But the point for me is to think about zero, rather than ask at every step of the way whether or not it is possible. We should instead put to ourselves the question, 'If it is possible, then how would we get there?' For instance, one important question is how all the elements of the plan can fit together. This will involve compromise. If we consider the elements in isolation, we won't discover how they might fit."

3 THE HORIZONTAL PATH

During the Cold War, the number of nuclear weapons in the American and Soviet arsenals first grew exponentially and then, after reaching a high-water mark of some 100,000 warheads in the mid-1980s, began to drop. The success of nuclear arms control negotiations was measured, above all, in numbers of weapons. Nuclear disarmament of this kind may be called numerical, or vertical, disarmament. Abolition, obviously, occurs when the number falls to zero. However, abolition so conceived in a world of nuclear deterrence gave rise to a doctrinal crisis, for if deterrence theoretically placed a ceiling above which more nuclear weapons were useless, it also placed a floor beneath which it would be dangerous to reduce them. If safety depended on possessing nuclear forces, then reducing them too far—not to speak of abolishing them—was bound to seem perilous. In fact, as long as deterrence remains military dogma, abolition is impossible.

In the doctrinal crisis lies one of the reasons for the immunity that nuclear arsenals have shown to otherwise powerful tides of political change. It also helps explain why there are, among dovish arms controllers, so many proposals for "minimum deterrence" or "deep cuts," in which numerical reductions are allowed to proceed very far but then—at the last minute, so to speak—are pulled up short, leaving perhaps a thousand, or a few hundred, or maybe even as few as a couple of dozen nuclear weapons to serve in the deterrent role. For to go to zero would be to dissolve deterrence and thus dissolve security. It was this point of view that General Brent Scowcroft, former national security adviser to President George Bush, was expressing when he said, "At some level . . . future reductions could become severely destabilizing, [because] at very low levels, for example, nuclear weapons are much more easily targeted." Scowcroft embraces without evasion the doctrine that nuclear weapons are the world's best protection against nuclear weapons. "The evidence," he says, "that nuclear weapons did deter all nuclear nations from using them is impressive." Thus he rejects—as a believer in classical deterrence must—the "false identity" between "reductions" and "the all-important continual goal of [global] stability." It is this fear of excessive reductions that also sets the stage for the most alarmist statements regarding breakout, in which a nation shorn of its retaliatory nuclear force is portrayed as helpless in the face of just a few nuclear weapons. In the land of the disarmed, according to deterrence theorists, the possessor of one nuclear bomb is king.

If deterrence cannot countenance abolition, then some other strategic or political framework for disarmament seems to be needed. But what is that new framework to be? The current debate can be seen as a many-sided search for an answer to this question. Wilsonian collective security—or even world federalism—is one possible candidate. But as the former world federalist Alan Cranston acknowledged to me, that venerable, noble, quintessentially American idea is in eclipse at present.

It is into the space between deterrence and full-fledged Wilsonianism that a younger generation of analysts has stepped to offer a new approach to nuclear disarmament that we might call the horizontal path. Although they do not constitute a self-conscious school, their thinking, taken as a whole, contains many of the elements of a new conceptual framework. If vertical disarmament involves lowering the number of weapons in nuclear arsenals, horizontal disarmament involves progressively standing down, dispersing, disassembling, or partially dismantling arsenals. Establishing ceilings on nuclear arsenals, abolishing certain classes of weapons, and drawing down the number of weapons are steps along the vertical path. "De-alerting" nuclear weapons, "de-mating" warheads from delivery vehicles, storing warheads at a distance from delivery vehicles, removing parts from warheads or delivery vehicles (or adding parts that spoil their performance), or adulterating weapons-grade fissile materials are steps along the horizontal path. Vertical disarmament makes a catastrophe, should it ever occur, smaller. Horizontal disarmament makes a catastrophe of any size less likely to occur. The verticalist looks at the size of the arsenals. The horizontalist looks at their operation.

Vertical disarmament has reached its destination when the last nuclear weapon has been destroyed. The final destination of horizontal disarmament is harder to define. Absolute zero along the horizontal path would, technically speaking, consist of the disassembly of every last component of every last nuclear warhead and delivery vehicle, leaving in existence only the bare knowledge of how to rebuild nuclear weapons. This knowledge is, in the last analysis, the bedrock of the nuclear age, which neither disarmament nor any other human act can remove. The perdurability of this underlying knowledge is the irreducible basis for the danger of cheating or breakout in a nuclear-weapon-free world. As the possessionists see it, the country that uses this knowledge to violate an abolition agreement stands to gain an insuperable advantage. The violator, they seem to suggest, would put itself in the position of the United States in August 1945, while those obedient to the treaty would be in the position of Japan at that time. The unique historical experience of being the sole country to possess nuclear weapons, and of using those weapons to end a great world war, may well underlie the singularly American preoccupation with the idea of breakout.

To such pessimism, however, the horizontal disarmer offers an answer: Because that knowledge must remain in the world, it is possessed just as much by those who obey the agreement as by those who violate it. In obeying the agreement, they do not render themselves helpless before their enemies. Both cheater and victim remain in the nuclear age. Those who have been faithful to the treaty retain the capacity, if all else fails, to reconstitute their own nuclear arsenals. The violator's advantage would be at best temporary. The violator, therefore, would not be in the position of the United States in 1945. In 1945, no other nation possessed the knowledge of how to make the bomb. Today, scores do. They have the capacity, as every national leader contemplating violation would know, to build nuclear arms themselves within a definite period, thereby sharply reducing and quickly nullifying the advantages of sole possession.

In actuality, it would not be feasible to disassemble all the devices that could be used as parts of nuclear weapons or delivery vehicles. Many of them are deeply embedded in civilian life or in arsenals of conventional weaponry. If abolition were defined in a treaty in terms of precise levels of disassembly, a great many levels, ranging from de-alerting and de-mating to prohibitions on virtually all nuclear technology, including nuclear power plants, would be imaginable. Yet, while each step along the horizontal path would further attenuate the danger of a nuclear holocaust, there would never come a point at which, through technical measures alone, nuclear danger finally disappeared. Like the possessionist, the horizontal abolitionist knows that nuclear danger has descended upon the world forever and draws conclusions from that fact.

Vertical and horizontal disarmament are not mutually exclusive. They are, to a certain degree, two angles of vision on the same process. Every weapon that has been "reduced" has also been "disassembled" to one degree or another. (For example, all arms control agreements so far have pertained solely to delivery vehicles. No warheads have yet been destroyed; they have only been recycled or stored. This does not make these agreements fraudulent. It only means that the "reductions" they secure are of a more horizontal nature than common parlance might suggest.) Likewise, when a nuclear weapon has been (horizontally) dismantled to a certain point, it would not be wrong to say that it has been (vertically) "eliminated." Nevertheless, the vertical and the horizontal approaches to nuclear disarmament are substantively different. It's quite possible, for example, to imagine disarmament agreements that leave a large, horizontally disarmed arsenal (many warheads, all kept under inspection in locations distant from any delivery vehicles), just as it is possible to imagine ones that leave a small, fully constituted arsenal (few warheads, all on full alert).

BRUCE BLAIR

In the early 1970s, when Bruce Blair, now a senior fellow at the Brookings Institution, was serving as an air force launch control officer for Minuteman nuclear missiles in Montana, he noticed a discrepancy between the declared nuclear policies of the United States and the drills he was being called on to carry out as a military man. Policy of course specified that for the purpose of deterring a Soviet nuclear attack a retaliatory force capable of surviving a first strike and then devastating the Soviet Union must be held in readiness. Blair, however, found that he was almost never called on to carry out a drill in which he fired off his missiles after sustaining a full-scale Soviet attack. Instead, he was ordered to practice drills in which no Soviet attack had yet occurred. It appeared that either the United States was launching first, preemptively, or else on warning of an incoming attack. This discrepancy between policy and practice prompted him to embark on a path of investigation and discovery that has continued to occupy him to this day, turning him, in the words of the *Washington Post*, into the country's "leading expert" on nuclear command and control.

It was important for the character and duration of Blair's investigation that his interest in the nuclear question originated in a missile command post rather than in, say, a graduate seminar. In a field ruled by theorists, he is a rare empiricist. In a world of scholastic—or even, as some have called it, "theological"—deduction, he is one of the few who intrude Baconian induction.

To begin with, instead of asking what the requirements of deterrence were, Blair asked what it was that the United States was actually doing. On-the-spot experience led him to two issues that became lasting and fruitful concerns. The first was nuclear "safety," by which he meant not only safeguards against accidents but the integrity of the nuclear force's command and control structure from top to bottom in both the United States and the Soviet Union. The second was the management and operation of nuclear arsenals.

In the company of a handful of scholars and writers (including Desmond Ball, William Arkin, and John Steinbruner), he began to piece together a previously unavailable picture of the U.S. nuclear arsenal and its deployment. In a backhanded tribute to his work, the Pentagon demanded and won exclusive custody of a top-secret study that he wrote for the Congressional Office of Technology Assessment. His study became, as a *Wall Street Journal* headline put it, "The Ultimate Secret: A Pentagon Report Its Author Can't See."

Nuclear practice, he discovered, had departed in fundamental ways from the doctrines that supposedly guided it. In his first book, *Strategic Command and Control*, which appeared in 1985, he demonstrated that while the United States was in theory prepared to wage "protracted nuclear war" involving "rideout" of an initial Soviet attack followed by repeated, carefully designed, limited retaliatory strikes interspersed with pauses to allow for diplomatic activity, in operational fact no such capacities existed. Owing to the extreme vulnerability of command and control, it was doubtful that the United States could deliver even the single prompt, massive retaliatory attack that was the sine qua non of deterrence—much less the series of strikes found in the scenarios of "flexible response."

This truly shocking finding, supported with voluminous detail, threw into question not only the nation's declared policy of flexible response but also the entire policy of deterrence. Blair's conclusions cut clean across the ideological divisions of the day. On the one hand, they more than confirmed the fears of conservatives, who were concerned with the vulnerability of American forces to the Soviet nuclear buildup of the time. (However, he located the danger not, as they did, in the vulnerability of the land-based Minuteman force to an annihilating first strike but in the inadequacy of command and control over the entire nuclear system.) On the other hand, his finding provided some support to dovish opinion, which was greatly exercised at the time over the many declarations of Reagan administration officials suggesting that they hoped to fight and win a nuclear war. (For instance, Secretary of Defense Caspar Weinberger had said, "You show me a secretary of defense who is planning not to prevail [in a nuclear war], and I'll show you a secretary of defense who ought to be impeached.") If Blair was right, none of that was, in practice, remotely conceivable.

In a second book, *The Logic of Accidental Nuclear War*, based in part on conversations Blair had in the Soviet Union and its successor, the Russian Federation, he showed that Moscow's command and control system was, if anything, even more vulnerable than Washington's. He then concluded that "retaliation after ride-out was an abstract idea in the theory of stability but not a viable option in the real world." Hence, to those who say that in the Cold War "deterrence worked," readers of Blair must answer that, technically speaking, it never quite existed.

The vulnerability of command and control networks, though rarely mentioned in public debate on nuclear strategy, was well known to high-level military officers, who quietly sought to take remedial steps. They adopted plans to strike back in the short interval between the moment warning of an attack was received and the moment the first missiles landed. Launch-on-warning, Blair writes, was a sort of halfway house between preemption (a form of first strike) and rideout. Its adoption drastically compressed decision-making time for nuclear retaliation. The estimated time from the liftoff of Russia's intercontinental ballistic missiles to their detonation on U.S. soil is about half an hour, while for submarine-launched ballistic missiles it is as little as ten to twelve minutes. Detection of such an attack could come half a minute after liftoff. After some five to ten minutes, a missile attack conference of the president and other high-level officials would be called. If the attack originated from a submarine, the conference might come to an untimely end a minute or two later. If it originated from land, twenty or so minutes would remain before detonation, of which as little as three minutes might be available for presidential decision making. (The remaining minutes would be needed for the orders for retaliation to be received, processed, and successfully executed.)

Obviously, these deadlines place extraordinary pressure on the entire decision-making procedure and on the decision makers. Successful launch-on-warning, requiring as it does the smooth meshing of innumerable parts, technical and human, is itself a formidably difficult and demanding operation, and it is very much open to question whether either side has actually achieved the capability, especially in view of the short flight times of submarine-based missiles. Nevertheless, it is this fragile—possibly nonexistent—capacity that, formally speaking, saves deterrence from collapse. In reality, of course, many factors, including the irreducible unknowability of events once a nuclear war is under way, prevent—or "deter," if you like—sane leaders from launching nuclear first strikes.

In sum, the increasing accuracy of missiles and the growing explosive power of nuclear weapons have menaced nuclear command and control with "decapitation," in the language of the trade; the threat of decapitation has forced both sides to adopt launch-on-warning policies; and launch-on-warning has perilously shortened the time available for evaluating warnings of attack and deciding what to do in response. When both sides in a confrontation adopt this stance, the "logic" of accidental nuclear war comes into play—increasing, in a crisis, "the chance for military operations to overrun the intentions of the political leadership and cause the unpremeditated use of nuclear weapons."

Surprisingly, these "technical" perils have actually worsened since the end of the Cold War, owing to the steadily increasing accuracy of missiles and other military miracles of the information age. Blair did not suggest that any of this was likely in itself to bring on war between Russia and the United States. But he noted the frightening independence of technical developments from political ones, and he drew a lesson that transcended the Cold War. If Russia and the United States, two superpowers, were unable to protect their nuclear forces sufficiently to support a policy of mutual assured destruction, how could smaller, poorer nations that manage to obtain nuclear arsenals (say, Israel and some future nuclear-armed Arab antagonist) accomplish that feat? "An important lesson of the cold war," he writes, "is that when archenemies acquire the ability to deliver nuclear weapons, each will fear command and control decapitation."

If the principal weakness of deterrence was the vulnerability of command and control and the consequent hair trigger on which the two superpowers placed their arsenals—postures that have survived the Cold War itself—then the most pressing need in nuclear arms negotiations, Blair believes, is to relax these postures. It is this need that is answered by his proposal for global zero alert. He begins by drawing a distinction between the needs of deterrence and the needs of nuclear safety. In a word, deterrence requires that the use of nuclear weapons be made prompt while safety requires that their use be made difficult. To give just one example, the needs of deterrence in a world of vulnerable arsenals may require delegation down the line of command of the authority to launch nuclear weapons, so that retaliation can occur even if the president and other high officials in the chain of command have been killed or cut off from the nuclear forces, owing to the destruction of command and control. The needs of safety, on the other hand, are served by centralization and a sharp restriction of launch authority. During the Cold War, Blair observes, the needs of deterrence were understandably uppermost in planners' minds and safety was sacrificed. But now "the problem of nuclear security needs to be reframed with safety at the center." "Safety," in Blair's thinking, is a concept that can be expanded almost without limit, extending in a smooth progression all the way from mere technical devices designed to prevent the accidental or unauthorized launch of nuclear weapons through a full-scale restructuring and reduction of the nuclear arsenals that would lead, finally, to their elimination.

As conceived at present, arms control tends to overlook the issue of safety. The traditional approach to arms control, Blair observes, involves "diminishing numbers of weapons but no slowing of their reaction time." On the other hand, a purely horizontal approach to nuclear disarmament might leave in place large, disassembled arsenals. But in fact, as Blair acknowledges, there is no need to choose between the two paths; the logical course lies in the direction of ever smaller, ever safer arsenals.

Recently, I asked Blair to describe the discrepancy that, as a young missile officer, he observed between policy and practice.

"What really stimulated my interest," he said, "was the great debate that occurred in 1974, when the secretary of defense, James Schlesinger, announced a new nuclear policy of limited nuclear options. The media discussion portrayed it as a supposed shift from one kind of deterrence to another—from an old policy of 'counter-value' to a new one of 'counter-force.' " The policy of "counter-value" envisaged an immediate, all-out retaliation on the society of the other side in the name of mutual assured destruction. The policy of "counter-force" envisaged a preliminary attack, which might be limited, or might be pre-emptive, on the nuclear forces of the other side. Only after this card had been played would the option of destroying the society as a whole be considered. "Academic writings portrayed it in the same way, and the description struck me as being completely off the wall," Blair continued.

"In the first place, we had all along mainly been covering military targets, including nuclear infrastructure. In the second place, we were trained to go through a drill for launch that took no more than three minutes. I knew from my stint at the Strategic Air Command that this basically meant we were in a counter-force posture, with considerable emphasis on preemption. Also, we were practicing to be able to get our forces out of the ground on warning, very, very quickly—to send them en masse very largely at nuclear targets well before any incoming nuclear weapons would arrive. The policy of mutual assured destruction was based on retaliation after attack. But no one in our underground capsule was really thinking much about that. We were mainly prepared either to fire first or to quickly fire second, on warning."

"Did you know what targets your missiles were aimed at?"

"We knew the country and the category of target."

"What were you supposed to do in the event that your missile field was subject to nuclear attack?"

"Well, if we had launched only part of the force, we would have battened down the hatches and waited for further orders—to launch the rest or terminate the war. If some of our missiles hadn't been launched because they were under maintenance or some such, we were supposed to wait for them to 'go green,' as we used to say. We were supposed to wait until we had launched all the missiles in our squadron, which numbered fifty."

"And then?"

"We were supposed to climb up a ladder and remove a large plate over a tube, which was full of sand. Enough sand to fill half our capsule would pour out, and then we were supposed to crawl through the tube, and break our way through the final six feet. The trouble was, we discovered that there was a heavy coat of asphalt topside. Then our instructions were to make our way through the ground zero of a huge nuclear war to a National Guard Unit in Helena, which was about a hundred miles away. It was not a prospect that anyone cared to think about, really."

After leaving the air force, Blair went to Yale, where he put a background in applied mathematics to use studying command and control.

"It became abundantly clear to me," he said, "that our forces were on a hair trigger. Our military planners realized that they probably couldn't get political authorization for a preemptive strike on the basis of mere intelligence, and that they would need something more definite, which would be evidence of a missile attack en route. Paradoxically, this sharpened the hair trigger. If you think about it, the time for decision is likely to be smaller for launch-on-warning than it is for preemption. I then investigated the time lines for decision and learned that as in the United States as little as three minutes might be available for decision-making.

"The whole system was geared to launch-on-warning," he told me. "Could a president override that? Could he stop that? It's an open question. I think it would have been very difficult. Furthermore, there were provisions made to delegate authority down the chain of command into the military sphere in the event of a breakdown in communications, as almost certainly would have occurred."

"How did you turn to the question of Soviet command and control?" I asked.

"Soviet strategic rocket force officers and general staff officers got copies of my book and were astonished at the detail on command and control and astonished at the conclusions I had drawn. They began to seek me out to talk about these topics. Gorbachev's science adviser set me up with some real experts. Then, of course, glasnost came along and people ready to talk about this stuff came crawling out of the woodwork. It turns out that they had drifted into the same posture of launch-on-warning that we had, and for the same reasons, except that they were about ten years behind us. They explained to me that, sure enough, their president had a three-minute constraint on his decision making. Launch-on-warning is today the dominant option in Russian strategy. So now I had the other half of the equation fleshed out. The

Russians were telling me, 'This is really crazy—we're both in this posture.' "

His findings, I commented, seemed to suggest that nuclear arsenals had an internal momentum highly resistant to interference from without.

"One of the frightening things about the end of the Cold War," he replied, "is that these dangerous configurations of forces seem to be divorced from the political process and immune to political manipulation. What's more, this immunity has been explained and codified. A view has developed holding that whatever the current political context may be, there is always some hypothetical danger to be found in the future that can reverse the situation. It's also a little disconcerting to think that there has developed such a sharp separation between the purposes of nuclear forces and the immediate threat they were supposedly designed to counter that you can now hook up these same forces to vague possibilities that lie ahead. This gives rise to what you could call a sort of 'virtual deterrence'—deterrence of some threat that the future may hold."

"How would the universal de-alerting of nuclear forces, which you call global zero alert, help?"

"For one thing, it would bring deployments better into line with policy. It would also help relink nuclear forces with politics. It would be something positive to do in the military sphere that would correspond to the harmony that has developed between Russia and the United States in the political sphere. At a stroke it would remove the dangers of quasi-intentional or intentional nuclear war that stem from the launch-on-warning postures of the two sides. The fears of each side that the other might launch an annihilating bolt from the blue would be almost entirely removed. A second benefit of de-alerting forces is the purchase it gives on the problem of the disintegration of the Russian military in the wake of the disintegration of the Soviet Union. This is the aspect of de-alerting that resonates most within the government. De-alerting offers relief from the danger of unauthorized or accidental or inadvertent use, and this is something that the American military as well as the public at large is quite concerned about."

Opponents of de-alerting have argued that it would create an inherently unstable situation in which one side might race back to full alert and launch its arsenals before the other side could catch up. Blair responds, however, that stability could be assured by keeping in place invulnerable de-alerted forces, submarines being the obvious candidates.

An important benefit of de-alerting forces would be "immediately to bring other nuclear-armed countries into the dialogue," he said. For whereas numerical reductions are unlikely to draw in the lesser nuclear powers until U.S. and Russian arsenals are reduced from their present thousands to hundreds of weapons, proposals for zero alert require their immediate participation. (Russia and the United States might not fully de-alert their forces, for example, unless China, France, and Britain did likewise.) "Finally," Blair went on, "de-alerting can happen almost instantly. We don't want to move toward zero in twenty-five years, with the last missile on hair-trigger alert—and, if present strategic thinking prevails, that's what we're looking at. There is, in fact, a significant precedent for de-alerting. In 1991, Bush decided to de-alert all bombers, 450 Minuteman II missiles, and the missiles in ten Poseidon sub-marines. Gorbachev followed suit by deactivating five hundred land-based rockets and six submarines. The moves took only a few days. If you or I had proposed these steps, we would have been laughed out of town. But Bush did it and Gorbachev did it."

"What, concretely, was done?"

"The crews in the launch fields had their launch keys taken away from them."

"Like keys you put in a door?"

"Yes, keys that you put in, and have to turn, as in the ignition of a car. Take away the key and you can't drive the car. They also did some-thing else. They went into the missile silo and put a pin into the motor of the rocket—into its ignition. An analogy might be taking the spark plugs out of a car, or inserting some plastic in the gap of the plug so there cannot be ignition. In order to reverse that step, maintenance crews have to go back out to all the silos and pull the pins. Actually, it takes a long time, so a delay is built into the process. However, these steps were not verified."

"What else could you do?"

"There are all sorts of variations on the theme. A next big step would be to separate warheads from delivery systems and perhaps put them into storage under international monitoring. Steps beyond that would be to dismantle components of bombs and delivery systems. Ultimately you would be left with blueprints."

Blair has, in fact, drawn on his store of knowledge of nuclear operations to work out concrete proposals for de-alerting each of the legs of the nuclear strategic "triad" of airborn, sea-based, and land-based forces. Although the arrangements are technical and necessarily complex, Blair is confident that the job is doable. "The question," he says, "is how to configure forces so that they are survivable and reconstitutable but not readily available—certainly not for quick launch. The idea is to extend the time to reconstitute—from days to weeks to months to years. I think it is very practical, very feasible, if only the military and the agencies of government would put their minds to it."

A zero-alert plan, if it went deep enough, Blair has written, "is tantamount to nuclear disarmament." If it could be accomplished, something that truly deserves the name of safety would be attained in the nuclear age.

FRANK VON HIPPEL

Frank Von Hippel, a physicist and Professor of Public and International Affairs at Princeton University, has worked closely with Blair on issues of nuclear disarmament in general and de-alerting in particular. He is the chairman of the research arm of the Federation of American Scientists and, from September 1993 through December 1994, served as assistant director for national security in the White House Office of Science and Technology Policy—his one stint as an insider. There, he found that "the interagency process spends most of its time reducing good ideas to mush," as he wrote in the newsletter of the Federation, and before long had decided that he could be more useful as well as better informed working on the outside. He, Blair, and Dr. Harold Feiveson, a senior research policy analyst at Princeton's Center for Energy and

Environmental Studies, are editing a book that will recommend concrete steps toward nuclear disarmament, including de-alerting and deep
cuts in the arsenals.

As my conversation with Blair had already made clear, the word *de-
alerting* could refer to many different concrete steps. Some of these
steps are known, but others remain to be invented. Because de-alerting
is the first of the possible steps along the horizontal path of disarmament, and stands a chance of happening quite soon, I decided to pursue
the subject with Von Hippel.

"What criteria must proposals for de-alerting satisfy?" I asked.

"There are certain objections that a proposal must overcome," he
said. "First, the steps must be verifiable. Second, they must be consistent with the survivability of the forces. Third, they shouldn't be too
complex. Finally, of course, they should really reduce the readiness of
the forces."

"You, Blair, and Feiveson published an article in *Scientific American*
advocating de-alerting. What specific steps did you have in mind?"

"We're talking about de-alerting all the forces, but without, at first,
calling for the verification of the steps for submarines at sea or mobile
missiles away from garrisons. Verification of de-alerting for these forces,
which depend for their survivability on their ability to hide, is the most
difficult part of the task, and we wanted to avoid delay. Our answer to
the requirement of survivability is to keep some hundreds of warheads
at sea—not on alert, but capable of being re-alerted on receipt of signal.

"For silo-based missiles we adopt an idea first proposed by the Russians. Under START II, they were required to dismantle all of their multiple warhead missiles by the year 2003. The Russians responded that
they did not have the facilities to implement this so quickly. Therefore,
at Helsinki Clinton said, we'll give you five years, but in the latter four of
these you must deactivate the missiles by removing the warheads. Deactivating is the same as what we mean by de-alerting. The United States
suggested that the way to do this was to take the warheads out of the
missiles. But the Russians answered that they didn't have enough secure
places—places with the necessary tight environmental controls—to
store the warheads, whose temperature and humidity must be very carefully monitored and maintained.

"They suggested that instead they would immobilize the missiles in place. They proposed two methods. One was to immobilize the missile with a forty-ton lid on the missile silo. You'd have to bring up a huge crane to open it, and that would be observable. There are some questions about whether it would be possible to sneak in some hydraulic device to open the lid of the silo; but I think some version of the plan would work. Richard Garwin, the senior nuclear weapons adviser, had a similar idea. He suggested piling up a large hill of gravel over the silo—in other words, just bury the damn thing. It's well worth exploring.

"The second method was to remove the battery that operates the guidance system. But in fact you cannot fully evaluate any of these ideas with pure thought; you have to visit the facilities and talk with those responsible for them and see what the requirements are for maintenance, emergencies, and so forth.

"Could inspection of battery removal be arranged?" I asked.

"Yes. Under the START I treaty, each side is allowed ten random inspections each year, on very short notice, of multiple warheads on missiles, to see if only the specified number is there. The inspectors say, 'I want to go to such and such a base and go into silo three in five hours.' This is happening now routinely.

"Another idea we've had for de-alerting is to remove the nose cone—the 'shroud'—without which the missile can't fly. However, the Russians pointed out that the nose cone has a little bubble of air in it that is necessary for keeping the warhead air-conditioned. We responded by suggesting that you might replace the existing cones with flat-topped ones. This, too, would prevent the missile from flying, but it would preserve its air-conditioning."

I observed that the idea of de-alerting seemed to come down to interposing one or more easily verified obstacle in the way of using the weapon. I noted that it was striking, in our high-technology age, that some of these steps, such as disabling a big lid on the silo or using a pile of gravel, appeared to be of Stone Age simplicity—on the order of rolling a big rock in front of a cave.

Von Hippel commented that he had in fact proposed exactly this: "I suggested placing a twenty-ton boulder in front of the garage doors for the missiles. However, this is not a well-developed idea."

He then returned to the difficulties of de-alerting submarine weaponry. Nothing as crude as a big boulder had been discovered to do the job. He described a scheme in which the guidance systems of the missiles would be removed in port in the presence of inspectors. Those inspectors then would place electronic seals, capable of conveying a coded message, on the doors of the chambers where the missing guidance systems had resided and would periodically require that the code be sent and verified by remote communications in order to confirm that the doors had not been opened and guidance systems placed within.

Some of the techniques for disabling and degrading advanced nuclear technology might be surprisingly simple but others, evidently, were going to tax the ingenuity of even the best scientists.

ROGER MOLANDER

In matters of nuclear policy, there is normally a sharp divide between the worlds of those who frame policy within the government and those who criticize it from without. Roger Molander is one of the surprisingly few who have moved between the two worlds. Under Presidents Nixon, Ford, and Carter, he served as nuclear warfare and arms control adviser on the National Security Staff. In 1982, as the nuclear freeze movement was getting under way, he founded Ground Zero, an organization devoted to informing the public about the basic facts of the nuclear age. In support of Ground Zero, he traveled throughout the country, speaking to citizen groups, visiting newspaper editorial boards, and appearing on radio and television. In 1983, he became president of the Roosevelt Center, a nonprofit organization devoted to invigorating the public realm by encouraging citizen participation in both domestic and national security issues. At present, he works at the Washington think tank RAND on the issue of nuclear proliferation and the new subject of strategic information war (attacks on critical information systems and infrastructure *by* other information systems).

In 1993, Molander and two of his colleagues at RAND, Marc Dean Millot and Peter A. Wilson, conducted a study for the air force called

"The Day After." It consisted of four war-gaming exercises in each of which it was posited that nuclear weapons had been used in one of four regions: the former Soviet Union, the Middle East, South Asia, or the Korean peninsula. In each of the war games, some two hundred participants from the military, executive agencies, Capitol Hill, news organizations, and fellow think tanks were invited to decide what course of action they would recommend to the president. The novelty of the study lay in its examination of the post–Cold War nuclear policies of the United States in the light of crises that might arise elsewhere than in the theaters of the former Cold War.

Since 1991, fear that a rogue state, perhaps armed with nuclear weapons, might embark on a path of aggression has, to a certain extent, taken the place in official circles of fear of the late Soviet Union. Saddam Hussein's annexation of Kuwait, the American-dominated military campaign that drove him out, and the subsequent news that he had been well on his way to developing nuclear as well as chemical and biological weapons gave substance and urgency to the new concern. The danger was underscored by fears that controls over nuclear weapons and technology had been seriously weakened in the wake of the collapse of the Soviet Union and news that North Korea was probably diverting nuclear materials to the production of nuclear weapons. During the Cold War, nuclear proliferation had been a secondary concern; now it was becoming primary.

As the 1997 Presidential Decision Directive made clear, official policy has, if only in vague terms, assigned to nuclear weapons the task of dealing with nuclear-armed rogue states. In January 1992, for instance, Secretary of Defense Dick Cheney stated, "We must be prepared to face adversaries on their own terms, possibly involving the use of weapons of mass destruction and ballistic or cruise missiles." In 1994, President Clinton himself had of course stated that the United States should retain strategic nuclear forces adequate to deal with "any future hostile leadership with access to strategic nuclear forces."

However, none of the public statements has dealt with the question of what, concretely, the United States should do if a rogue state not only acquires nuclear weapons and threatenes to use them but actually does use one or more of them. Would it make sense for the

United States to retaliate by using nuclear arms against the rogue state? If not, does it make sense to rely on the threat of their use? Should the United States rely instead on conventional arms? Should it do anything at all? The RAND war games were designed, in part, to force answers to these questions into the open.

In one of the RAND scenarios, Iran menaced other oil-producing states of the Gulf with destruction. As the scenario opens, Iran, thanks to military help from China and Pakistan, has already fought a war with Iraq and won. American intelligence has reported that Iran possesses a handful of nuclear weapons and a few intermediate-range ballistic missiles. The United States has sent a heavy division to Saudi Arabia and other forces to Kuwait and Bahrain.

On "day one" of the game, Iran demands that Kuwait and Saudi Arabia cut oil production. A few days later, Iran attacks American and other ships in the Gulf and then detonates a hundred-kiloton nuclear weapon on its own territory, as a "demonstration" of its nuclear capacity and resolve. U.S. intelligence soon reveals that Iran possesses thirty-five to forty intermediate-range missiles. (Iran is in fact widely believed to have a program to build nuclear weapons, and its efforts to acquire ballistic missile technology are a matter of lively current concern in the United States as well as controversy among the United States, China, and Russia.)

The game players were invited to advise the president on a response to these events. Hanging over the gaming were some lessons of the Gulf War. Darkening that heady triumph of American arms had been two ominous shadows. The first of course was the surprisingly advanced state of Saddam Hussein's nuclear weapons program. (In the RAND game plan, this discovery was reflected in the assumption that Iran had nuclear weapons.) The second was the failure of America's overwhelming airpower to destroy Iraq's Scud missiles. (This fact was reflected in the assumption that Iran had mobile intermediate-range ballistic missiles.) Conjoined, the two capacities added up to a fact of high significance: in RAND's game plan Iran possessed that crucial desideratum of nuclear power, an effectively invulnerable nuclear force. Once that supposition was made, the RAND game players discovered, favorable military options for the United States dwindled away, and desperate choices and preposterous outcomes forced themselves on the attention of the players. Many noted that the Gulf War might have proceeded along very different lines—or not occurred at all—if Hussein had already acquired nuclear weapons. They doubted, for example, that "the U.S. would have committed itself to a buildup dependent on a few airfields and ports"; that "King Fahd [of Saudi Arabia] would have allowed U.S. troops into Saudi Arabia"; that "the United States would have demanded Iraq's immediate and unconditional withdrawal from Kuwait"; or that "the coalition would have tried to destroy the Iraqi high command."

In the exercise at hand, when some suggested a buildup of American conventional forces, others were quick to point out that these would be mere "nuclear hostages" likely to be "lost in a nuclear attack" by Iran. On the other hand, a U.S. nuclear attack, in addition to crossing a moral and political threshold that had remained inviolate since the bombing of Nagasaki, might fail to destroy all of Iran's missiles. In that case, the annihilation of cities of key allies, such as Israel and Saudi Arabia, might ensue. (There would of course also be the possibility of retaliation, then or later, against American cities, perhaps with smuggled weapons. During the Cold War it was often asked whether, at the moment of truth, the United States would be willing to lose New York to save Hamburg. In a regional crisis of the future, would it be willing to lose New York to save Riyadh?)

Two broad groups formed among the game players. One favored a policy of "containment," patterned on Cold War policy toward the Soviet Union. The other, fearing that an Iran deranged enough to have already detonated a nuclear weapon would be uncontainable, favored a policy of "eliminating the Iranian regime" through nuclear attack. Moreover, those supporting nuclear attack feared that even if Iran restrained its use of nuclear arms Congress and the American public would be unwilling to support a protracted conventional war. On the other hand, it was anything but clear that the American public would support American initiation in the Middle East of the first two-sided nuclear war in history.

A scenario in which North Korea acquired—and used—nuclear weapons in an invasion of South Korea disclosed similarly fruitless and horrifying alternatives for American policymakers. Participants were again "roughly divided" between those advocating nuclear retaliation and those favoring conventional retaliation. The former believed that conventional airpower was inadequate and urged a "decisive use of tactical [nuclear] power at a key point to stem the invasion, [and] give the North Korean force . . . the same 'shock treatment' the South was just subject to." Opponents argued that nuclear retaliation "would assure a North Korean nuclear retaliation against U.S. forces, South Korea, and Japan and escalate completely out of control."

It was one thing, apparently, to threaten nuclear retaliation against "any future hostile leadership with access to strategic nuclear forces" but quite another to frame specific operational plans for making good the threat. The practice of nuclear war against rogue states, it appeared, was in its own way as full of absurdity as plans to fight a nuclear war with the Soviet Union had been. Indeed, for a number of the military participants one conclusion stood out in both exercises: "nuclear weapons offered little military or political value to the United States in regional conflicts, even against adversaries using nuclear weapons." They "maintained that conventional weapons now could (or would soon be able to) destroy virtually all types of targets . . . as effectively as nuclear weapons and with lower collateral damage to noncombatants." (An exception, it was later pointed out, might be facilities placed deep underground.) But if nuclear arsenals were of limited or no use in regional crises in a world of proliferating nuclear weapons, then might not a world without nuclear weapons be entirely desirable, even from a narrowly military point of view? Several air force officers, including Generals Horner and Butler, were moving toward this position, and the RAND exercises of 1993 were one of the first signs of this radical shift within the U.S. military.

The intention of the game planners had not been so much to advise officials on how to fight regional nuclear wars as to prompt reflection on policies that would make such wars unlikely. Both the report and a subsequent report called "The Nuclear Asymptote," by Molander and Wilson, set forth several portraits of what the broad nuclear future of the world might be. In a recent conversation, Molander described to me the need that he and his fellow authors had felt for such reflection. His starting point, he said, was his conviction that the end of the Cold War had brought the nuclear question to a "critical juncture" and that decisions made in the next decade might be "decisive for the overall shape of the nuclear future." The conjunction of the end of the Cold War and of nuclear proliferation may lead, he feels, to a second "nuclear awakening, a nuclear transformation."

"There has a been a vacuum of thought in government about these new issues," he said. "Washington is the place you might look to for answers to questions like this, because Washington is where all the power is, but in fact the bureaucracies work on a very short timescale. Washington got comfortable with nuclear strategic arms control, which became obsolescent in its later stages when the Cold War ended. The questions had been whether three thousand or four thousand warheads apiece were sufficient for deterrence. Now the appropriate question is whether the number might drop by an order of magnitude. I used to make a living arguing the difference between twenty-two hundred and twenty-one hundred nuclear delivery vehicles. Now a new paradigm is needed, and the people in the bureaucracies are not ready to deal with that possibility. It's an interesting question where the impulse for a change in paradigm can come from in the United States. I don't expect much from politicians generally, who tend to flee from difficult issues, especially when politically viable solutions are not available. The presidency is certainly a strong candidate for addressing such issues, and perhaps Clinton will step up to it." Yet in truth, he notes, the days when Washington and its former adversaries in Moscow alone could make the crucial decisions may be numbered. It's in the nature of proliferation that "the number of actors is steadily increasing."

"The Nuclear Asymptote" identified four asymptotes, by which the authors mean "end states" of policies that might be inaugurated now. The first was "High-Entropy Deterrence," which means that the end state is reached as the result of drift. Approaching this asymptote, proliferation proceeds apace, nuclear weapons remain the currency of power, and deterrence becomes a universal doctrine. In such a world, however, deterrence, now required to preserve a balance among perhaps a dozen or more powers, might break down once or twice, and nuclear weapons might be used, requiring the international community to figure out how to react "to the third or fourth use of nuclear weapons." What if nuclear use led to victory? Would a successful violation of the fifty-three-year taboo make their use as acceptable as their possession had been during the Cold War? Or would it cause a sudden reversal of opinion regarding both use and possession?

The second asymptote involved a sort of managed proliferation, in which the de facto nuclear powers India, Pakistan, and Israel would formally be admitted to the nuclear club. The third was simply the present two-tiered system projected into the future. As now, the world would be divided into nations that possess nuclear weapons and nations that have agreed to forgo them. However, the Non-Proliferation Treaty, which ratifies this state of affairs on a strictly temporary basis, of course obligates the nuclear powers to work in good faith to eliminate their arsenals. Therefore, if the third end state is to be lasting it would require radical revision of the treaty to remove this obligation—no light matter in view of the fact that this global agreement has been joined by 185 countries.

The fourth and final asymptote in the RAND study was consistent with a much longer continuation of the Non-Proliferation Treaty. It would be "virtual abolition," which means getting rid of all but perhaps a few hundred nuclear weapons, whose role would be to guard against breakout. The fact that RAND, home of the renowned writer on nuclear strategy Herman Kahn, has published a study mentioning nuclear abolition as a feasible goal in any shape or form is in itself something of a milestone of the nuclear age.

Interest in the possibility of some form of abolition grew stronger among many in the air force, Molander told me, as they reflected on the prospect of fighting (or ducking) regional nuclear wars in a world of advanced proliferation. "Yet the steps between the START levels of thirty-five hundred warheads and zero had not been developed intellectually *at all*. It was one thing to talk about reducing to a few hundred or zero, but what was the rest of the picture? The asymptotes and the war games were ways of beginning to ask these questions."

As a component of virtual abolition, the report advocated what it called *virtual arsenals*. Somewhat confusingly, perhaps, the word *virtual* in the phrase *virtual arsenals* meant something different from what it meant in the phrase *virtual abolition*. In the phrase *virtual abolition*, it had the common meaning of "almost." But in the phrase *virtual arsenals*, it had the more recondite, scientific meaning of "substitute"—a usage that has become popular in the vocabulary of the information age, in such phrases as *virtual reality*. A virtual arsenal, the authors wrote, was an arsenal in a de-alerted or partially dismantled state that would require some days or weeks to be brought back to full military readiness.

Some years before, Molander, as president of the Roosevelt Center, had done preliminary studies of the possibility of virtual arsenals, but the RAND study was (as far as I know) the first prominent mention of the idea in the voluminous literature of official and semiofficial Washington. In the RAND study, virtual arsenals are an adjunct to at-the-ready arsenals, not a replacement for them. Molander hoped, he told me, to introduce the idea that partially dismantled arsenals still possess deterrent value—that for example, a thousand weapons capable of being brought to readiness in a month might be a stronger and more important component of deterrence than a hundred alert weapons, which might be ready immediately or in a few hours.

In the conclusion of their report, Molander and Wilson observed that the people of Nagasaki were getting ready to mark the fiftieth anniversary of the atomic bombing of their city with a proclamation expressing their hope that just as Hiroshima always would be the first city to have been destroyed by a nuclear weapon, Nagasaki would prove to be the last. "Fifty years hence," the RAND report adds, "the citizens of Nagasaki will mark the one hundredth anniversary of the bombing." Expressing the hope that those years, too, will have passed without the use of nuclear weapons, Molander and Wilson ask, "And if for a hundred years, why not forever?"

MICHAEL MAZARR

In my quest to define the steps along the horizontal path, I next spoke with Michael Mazarr, the director of the New Millennium Project at the Center for Strategic and International Studies in Washington, D.C.

In the autumn 1995 issue of the scholarly quarterly *Survival*, he published an article called "Virtual Nuclear Arsenals"; he then proceeded to edit a book called *Nuclear Weapons in a Transformed World: The Challenge of Virtual Nuclear Arsenals*.

Mazarr offers what might be called a realist's approach to radical nuclear disarmament. He went in search of "detailed outlines of potential nuclear end-states that are verifiable, stable, and respect U.S. extended deterrence requirements." To satisfy these criteria, he too suggests virtual arsenals, which, he hopes, would permit the world to "ban the existence of all assembled, ready-for-use nuclear weapons and thus to push them to the background of world politics without abandoning all their alleged benefits or leaving the major powers vulnerable to nuclear blackmail." The RAND report, which Mazarr quotes, presented virtual arsenals as an adjunct to small, residual, fully assembled arsenals. Mazarr offers virtual arsenals as possible full substitutes, in a nuclear-weapon-free world, for assembled arsenals. He cites the example of Sweden, which inaugurated a nuclear program in the 1940s that continued throughout the 1960s, after which it was discontinued but not dismantled. In that country there remains a reactor, shut down but intact, and a small group of physicists who study nuclear weapons and have the benefit of a "two-decade-long weapons program." The pertinent question about Sweden's nuclear capacity, he notes, is "not whether [Sweden] could build" nuclear weapons but "*how quickly.*"

Virtual arsenals, Mazarr claims, answer the objection to an abolition agreement that it might leave nations that sign on without recourse in the event of breakout. With virtual arsenals in the wings, he writes, "no renegade state could obtain enormous leverage by constructing a handful of nuclear weapons; the nuclear powers would simply reassemble a few dozen of their own." The horizontal path, then, would begin with Blair's global zero alert, proceed with further measures of disassembly and dismantlement, and end with a precisely quantified, internationally agreed upon, fully inspected array of "technical resources" that, while not constituting a nuclear arsenal, would enable the country possessing them to respond to breakout by returning to nuclear armament within a certain calculable period of time.

Mazarr is willing to go very far to preserve the deterrent effect of virtual arsenals. He even proposes building into any nuclear disarmament treaty a "withdrawal clause," whereby a nation that believes itself mortally threatened—by, say, biological weapons—could announce its intention of reassembling a specified number of nuclear weapons. Blair has pointed out that in a world of large arsenals nuclear safety and nuclear deterrence are competitive goals. The same would be true, evidently, in a world of virtual arsenals. In the matter of the withdrawal clause, Mazarr gives deterrence the edge over safety.

In a conversation with Mazarr in his office at the Center for Strategic and International Studies, I asked what the response had been to his article and book project.

"I'd noticed that in the field of arms control, there remained a great division between those who believed in ultimate abolition and those who believed in going a long way yet still thought that ultimate abolition was crazy," he said. "It seemed to me that it would be useful to find concepts that might bring these two groups together—to bridge the difference between the advocates of, say, very deep cuts and the advocates of full disarmament, however defined. Reading Bruce Blair and others, I began to realize that if you moved to a really extreme form of de-alerting, functionally it became the equivalent of disarmament. It seemed worthwhile to try to lay down an analytical foundation for what some years down the road would inevitably emerge as a substantial debate.

"The reaction has been receptive. The more people thought about it, the more they realized that there was some substance there. One place where reaction has been especially good is Japan. The project became quite well known there, and several Japanese journalists have asked me about it. You can understand why. It could permit them to enter the ranks of the deterrent powers without actually developing nuclear weapons.

"Japan has, in fact, caused a certain alarm around the world by acquiring large stocks of plutonium, which it claims are strictly for civilian use but which also would be useful for building nuclear weapons. A lot of people have noted that Japan's plutonium acquisitions have made them a sort of virtual nuclear power already. The Koreans will certainly tell you that. I don't think the Japanese have a sinister motive.

But they are attracted by the idea that if we can establish the international principle that the virtual arsenal is the goal the nuclear powers ought to aim for, then Japan can reassure itself that it would never be tempted to build up beyond that point."

Even fully alerted arsenals, Mazarr observed, have a "virtual aspect." "There is, in fact, no nuclear arsenal in the world whose weapons are all ready to use immediately," he noted. To be ready for immediate launch, some of the weapons have to be placed on a higher state of alert than they are at present. American arsenals are now at DEFCON 5. The highest level of alert is DEFCON 1. "In the early phases of a shift to virtual arsenals, you retain certain specific components in assembled form. But you can imagine that in tens or hundreds of years every last component will be thoroughly disassembled, yet even then there will be a capacity to rebuild nuclear weapons. I was just reading a story in the paper about a young scientist in New York who's building a replica of the Soviet Sputnik satellite. It took the entire apparatus of the Soviet Union to do this in the fifties, but now he can do it himself."

It occurred to me that virtual arsenals might be described as at DEFCON of a much higher number than any available today—say, DEFCON 37, or DEFCON 252. Some people, I noted, have suggested that if virtual arsenals are adopted as an international goal, many nations now at zero might build up to that level. Virtual arsenals might touch off a virtual arms race.

"I don't find that persuasive," he said. "A few countries, such as Brazil, might do a few quiet things. I don't think that in a world that has backed away from nuclear arms to the extent of adopting virtual arsenals as the limit, you are going to have a lot of medium powers rushing in to expand their capabilities."

His idea for virtual arsenals includes an escape clause—a sanctioned return to nuclear armament under certain as yet undefined circumstances. The definition of those circumstances, it seemed to me, would be of fundamental importance in any disarmament treaty based on his plan; for that definition would mark the dividing line between nuclear armament whose prohibition would be the whole point of the treaty and nuclear armament that was needed to enforce the treaty—between, that is, a violation and the remedy for that violation. Any blurring of that line could be fatal to the treaty's success. Furthermore, if the treaty were completely reversible, then nuclear arms would retain considerable legitimacy. Recalling that some people have held that the use or possession of nuclear weapons ought to be considered a crime against humanity, I asked Mazarr how he would frame his escape clause.

"It's a difficult question," he answered. "Almost all treaties have some sort of escape clause. Because in the abolition treaty a potential for reconstitution of a deterrent against breakout is permitted, there has to be a very clear provision for nuclear rearmament."

"But what would trigger that right?" I asked. "Might it be notification by an international agency that a nation had violated the abolition treaty and was building nuclear arms?"

"I can't imagine that any sovereign country would surrender its right to rearm to an international bureaucracy," he replied. "My own view is that this sort of legalism is really impossible, yet I feel confident that the arrangement would work for other reasons. You could provide in the treaty that a nation can withdraw only if it is threatened with cheating. One difficulty, though, would be the situation in which a country was being overrun in a conventional war, not a nuclear war. I'd say that if you're invading a country that possesses a virtual nuclear arsenal, you've got to know that when push comes to shove they're going to draw their nuclear sword and use it against you. Therefore, you'd know that if someone was conquering someone else, it could become a nuclear war; therefore, the conquest could not occur. At that point, the country using nuclear threats to avoid being overrun would be in violation, but they wouldn't care. I'm not worried about that, though. The genius of the arrangement is that it will not be in anyone's interest to violate this treaty once it has been established, apart from a very narrow category of exceptions you can imagine."

"Why is that?"

"One question that is rarely asked about a country that built an arsenal in violation of a disarmament treaty is what it would do with the arsenal. To presume that a breakout has some advantage is to presume that the violator would use the weapons very quickly. Otherwise, it would be a wasted asset. Its leadership knows that if they try to use their nuclear arms for coercion, the other side will eventually hit back—if not immediately, then in a couple of weeks. So deterrence would still hold. But in fact, it seems to me that events would proceed quite differently. Let's imagine that China and Russia are on the verge of war. I doubt that either would be trying to conquer the other. Their objectives would probably be more limited—seizing or securing a disputed border area, for instance, or an oil field. The threatened country, as I see it, would go to the international community and say, 'Well, we're under attack here. They say they only want a border area, but we don't know how far they will go. If you don't do something about this, we're going to have to start reassembling our nuclear arsenal in a week.' But if the threatened country were to go this far, it would probably be a bargaining chip to win international support rather than a real plan to launch a nuclear strike."

I noted that there is a peculiar precedent for just such a situation. When white South Africa built its nuclear arsenal, it framed no plan to use the weapons against its potential attackers. Its only plan in the event of attack by other African countries had been to pressure the United States into intervening by revealing its nuclear capability and threatening to use the weapons. As one South African official has said, "South Africa never had any idea of waging a nuclear war." The limit of its plans in an emergency had been to "quietly reveal its nuclear capability to leading Western governments, principally the United States," as Mitchell Reiss described South African nuclear strategy in his book *Bridled Ambition*.

"The case of proliferation I know better," Mazarr continued, "is North Korea. It has done the same thing, if not quite as explicitly. The stakes in our day are rarely conquest. Systems like the Soviet Union don't always exist. And so in today's world, who are we deterring? North Korea? Fine. Maybe Iraq. Despite our foolish expansion of NATO, we're not really deterring Russia from anything. But this, of course, is another subject. In 3000 B.C., I imagine that everyone was deterring everyone else at all times. But we have moved away from that."

GEORGE PERKOVICH

George Perkovich, director of the Secure World Program of the W. Alton Jones Foundation and a member of the Council on Foreign Relations, has discovered support for the horizontal path in an unexpected quarter—the Third World. In an article in the summer 1993 *Foreign Policy* called "A Nuclear Third Way in South Asia," he pointed out that the "threshold" nuclear states India and Pakistan do not need to work toward de-alerted or virtual nuclear arsenals—a condition to which he gives the name "non-weaponized deterrence"—for they are already there. India detonated a "peaceful" nuclear explosion in 1974 and possesses a large civil nuclear establishment that employs more than twenty thousand technical and scientific people. It has developed and tested a short-range missile, the Prithvi, and a medium-range missile, the Agni. Pakistan has developed all the components of nuclear weapons, including enough weapons-grade fissile material to make six to ten bombs. It has also developed a short-range missile, the Hatf, and may have received components for medium-range missiles from China.

Yet, in Perkovich's words, "despite all their expense and effort ... India and Pakistan have not yet deployed nuclear arsenals or even declared themselves to be nuclear weapon states." The calculated ambiguity of this stance is reflected in the statements of both countries' leaders. "I am telling you in straightforward terms, an Indian planner should assume that Pakistan has a certain nuclear-weapon capability," General Krishnaswami Sundarji, a former chief of staff of the Indian army and a hawk in the Indian context, has said, "and similarly any prudent Pakistani military planner ought to assume that India has got a certain nuclear-weapon capability." Pakistan's foreign minister, Gohar Ayub Khan, commented last year, "On our part, we have enunciated a clear and consistent policy on this issue. We have stated that Pakistan has acquired nuclear capability but has made a conscious political decision not to make nuclear weapons." He added, "Our commitment to nuclear non-proliferation is absolute but we cannot accept a discriminatory and inequitable regime." He also reminded the world that Pakistan has "been persistent in our quest for the elusive dream of a nuclear-weapon-free South Asia."

"Neither Pakistan nor India," Perkovich writes, "is believed to have coherent, detailed doctrines to guide the use of nuclear weapons. Nor does either country have an extensive community of analysts and decision-makers versed in Western-style strategy." The "arsenals" of the two countries exist in a kind of doctrinal limbo, exerting, at most, a virtual variation on McGeorge Bundy's "existential deterrence," which he described as an aura of menace that inheres in nuclear arsenals and radiates from them, whether or not their possessors make specific, defined threats or adopt elaborate targeting plans. The two South Asian nations, evidently, have found that they can radiate this menace without building the actual hardware.

Perkovich sees in these amorphous arrangements a state of affairs that, if inspected and ratified in treaty form, might not only prevent a nuclear buildup in South Asia but offer a destination for the disarmament efforts of the full-fledged nuclear powers. Its key elements would be disclosure and verification of nuclear preparations, a cap on the missile race that threatens to break out between the two countries, and the creation of obstacles to further armament by "injecting time buffers into the entire process." Perkovich also takes note of the many agreements for reductions, de-alerting, and inspection that had already been arrived at by Washington and Moscow and wonders whether, in time, further steps of a similar nature might "wither nuclear weapons establishments." If so, he asks, might the South Asian arsenals prove to have been "harbingers of a time when all that remains are blueprints and disassembled components?"

I asked Perkovich about recent developments in nuclear strategy in South Asia.

"Developments in strategy have not been that important," he said. "Things work differently in South Asia from the way they work in the West. At present, the prime ministers have fairly good control over nuclear policy. The adoption of formal strategy might undermine this control. Indian leaders want to avoid the erosion of political control that they saw occur in the United States and the Soviet Union during the Cold War. In general, those who provide more elaborate analysis are hawks who want deployments."

"Has India been moving toward deployments?"

"Here, too, the situation is murky. There was a report recently that India had 'deployed' Prithvi missiles toward the border of Pakistan. When they developed the system, they did not think through where it was going to be based, or what its command and control would be, so when they ran out of storage space, they placed them in the north of India, about 150 kilometers from the border. The prime minister said he didn't know, which is evidently true. We can recall American decisions that were made in the same routine way. For the army it was a routine movement. The Prithvi is a short-range, liquid-fuel missile that takes twenty-four hours for fueling, and it's not clear that there are fuel trucks anywhere nearby. Furthermore, the Indians say they have no intention of putting nuclear warheads on the missiles, and it's not even clear that they have the capacity to do this. So if weaponization is going on, it's very much in slow motion. Both governments have been pretty self-restrained. It's not like the Cold War, in which each side would boastfully declare a new capability. In South Asia, they move forward but say, 'We don't mean this; we're not doing anything here.'

"In India, the most important event was the extension of the Non-Proliferation Treaty, which India still refuses to agree to. Many Indians were shocked that the United States rolled over the opposition to the treaty's indefinite extension without being forced into more concessions on disarmament by the nonweapon states. No one bought India's argument that nonweapon states should block the treaty if more disarmament concessions were not forthcoming from the United States, and this created a crisis for India's nuclear establishment, which is quite powerful politically. This group seized on the Comprehensive Test-Ban Treaty, whose renewal was coming up soon, and to which India was committed. They began preparations for an Indian nuclear test before the treaty was signed. There was a great furor over testing, and a strong international response against it. Prime Minister Rao struck a de facto deal with the proponents of testing, in which he in effect said to them, 'You're not going to get the test you want, but I won't sign away your opportunity to do it in the future.'

"I had a chance to talk to former prime minister [Inder Kumar] Gujral. He had no visceral interest in having nuclear weapons. He didn't see them as invaluable or useful. On the other hand, he loathed the non-proliferation regime. He saw it as a kind of nuclear imperialism and believed that India's dignity required resisting it."

I mentioned the South African case and asked whether he thought it might not offer a likelier model for the role of nuclear threats in a nuclear-weapon-free world than the usual American one of covertly building, and then using, a nuclear arsenal as an instrument of aggression. That is, was blackmail a likelier prospect than breakout?

Perkovich, like Mazarr, thought of the North Korean case. "When North Korea said it was going to withdraw from the Non-Proliferation Treaty, the international community immediately began to make threats and offer bribes, including offering them the light-water nuclear reactors that have since been agreed upon. It seems likely that something similar might happen in crises in a nuclear-weapon-free world. I doubt that countries in a currency crisis could say, 'Give us twenty billion dollars, or we'll build nuclear weapons.' But countries with serious security problems could use the threat of nuclear rearmament to demand help. The reality is that in every war India has had, the first thing it did was to ask for help from the international community. The fact of the matter is that neither India nor Pakistan has enough supplies to wage war for more than three weeks. Their strategy—especially Pakistan's—is to bring in the international community.

"To believe that a force of ten or a hundred weapons obtained through cheating would be as crippling to the world as those who fear breakout suggest, we have to imagine that events are occurring in a complete vacuum. Such a nuclear threat could not have any objective of a political kind; for that would require time for negotiation, and negotiating time would allow other states to reconstitute their nuclear forces. Whoever was doing this could not be trying to change politics or acquire territory, because those things also require time. In other words, a nuclear breakout force would conceivably be advantageous only for as long as it took the United States or some other power to regenerate its forces, and this need not be a defeatingly long time. In this case, the 'breakout' force amounts to a terrorist tool, and we're back to the current situation where nuclear arsenals provide no effective role to deter or defeat terrorism."

SETTLERS

Those who bring about radical changes in an established order of things can be divided into pioneers, settlers, and the new establishment. Pioneers, in the nature of things, are visionaries: They imagine a new order that does not exist anywhere and place their faith in it. Some, like Martin Luther, are great renegades who fracture existing orthodoxies. Others, like Alexander Solzhenitsyn, are outsiders—voices crying in the wilderness—who somehow make themselves heard in the settlements. The settlers, a more numerous class (and so less likely to be known to us by name), are pragmatic, enterprising souls who follow in the wake of the pioneers, clearing a field and building a house where before only a trail had been blazed. In the wake of both follows the new establishment, creating an orthodoxy out of what not long before was only a dream. Without the pioneer, nothing begins; without the settler, the pioneer is forgotten; without the new establishment, the settler's clearing returns to the wild.

Of course, not every dreamer witnesses the fulfillment of his dream, but one example of a transformation that did occur was the abolition movement that brought on the prohibition of slavery. The reversal of opinion was total. Today it is more shocking by far to favor slavery than it was to propose its abolition in the early nineteenth century.

Sometimes, the first signs that a transformation is under way are oblique. At a distance from every "center" there are always "the extremes." Although those in the center and those far from it are usually antagonistic, they are often tacitly interdependent. If a respected person suddenly takes a strong position at an extreme, several things may happen. The defenders of established opinion circle their wagons against the defector. Immediately, a ready-made language of condescension, dismissal, and rejection is brought into play. (A good example in the matter at hand was Richard Perle's gibe, already quoted, that abolitionist generals had more stars in their eyes than on their shoulders.) Yet even as the machinery of expulsion is operating, another, opposite process may be taking place. The centrists find themselves, possibly without even noticing it, beginning to take their bearings from new points. And then the center moves.

Something like this dual process seems to be occurring in the new, post–Cold War debate on nuclear arms. The people I had talked to so far were, in ways large and small, pioneers in the abolition cause. Several recent studies may be considered evidence of the arrival of the earliest settlers. While still rejecting the full program of the pioneers, they have quietly picked up camp and moved a considerable distance in this new direction, even if there is no sign that the American government is ready to follow.

"Transforming Deterrence," a new report brought out by the National Defense University, provides a good example. In its introduction, Hans Binnendijk and James Goodby write, "The appeals of the 'abolitionists' have driven a knotty policy issue to the surface—to wit, should we seek to delegitimize nuclear weapons and reduce their salience in national defense to as close to zero as possible?" Something of the anodyne, bureaucratic tone of this introduction can be grasped in a passage that reads "Russia and the United States have declared themselves partners, but nuclear weapons remain a key element in their relationship." (It's a sentence whose flat, unelaborated conjunction of the oddly assorted elements of "partners" and "relationship" on the one hand with the threat of mass slaughter by nuclear weapons—elsewhere in the report called a "prudential factor"—on the other is perfectly in keeping with the emotionally flat tenor of current official nuclear policy and the Nuclear Posture Review on which it is based.) Yet, while rejecting abolition, the authors of the introduction recommend two steps that are very far-reaching: "study" of "reducing total nuclear weapons inventories in the United States and Russia to the low hundreds" and "deactivation of ICBMs and SLBMs."

The same impression of a bee's nest stirred into commotion, though not to flight to a new hive, is conveyed in "The Future of U.S. Nuclear Weapons Policy," a 1997 report published by the Committee on International Security and Arms Control (CISAC) of the National Academy of Sciences. It stops short of embracing abolition but travels surprisingly far in that direction, along both the horizontal and the vertical paths. Its introduction, by academy president Bruce Alberts, is a settler's manifesto. The members of the group, he writes, "have many decades of experience in nuclear policy, many in senior government positions, dating back to the Manhattan Project." Among them were Major General William Burns, former director of the U.S. Arms Control and Disarmament Agency; Wolfgang Panofsky, professor and director emeritus at the Linear Accelerator Center at Stanford University; and John Steinbruner, a senior fellow and former director of the Foreign Policy Studies Program at the Brookings Institution. Alberts reveals the settler-like ambitions of the report when, disavowing any pioneering intentions, he quotes approvingly a comment by his predecessor Frank Press that "rather than developing new ideas, the study's greatest value lies in the remarkable degree of consensus that the group was able to achieve on a wide array of important security issues." (President Alberts may in truth have been too modest about his organization's report. It visibly bulges with a diversity of views and does in fact contain fresh thinking in several areas, including its analysis of the logical puzzles and operational pressures that strained deterrence to the breaking point even during the Cold War and its subtle weighing of the role of verification in disarmament agreements.)

Since the report's purpose was to speak for a consensus, I decided against interviewing any one of its authors and instead conducted an "interview" with CISAC as a whole by framing questions to answers that can be found in the text.

"What is the committee's position on abolition?" I asked.

"The committee uses the word *prohibit* rather than *eliminate* or *abolish*," CISAC replied, "because the world can never truly be free from the potential reappearance of nuclear weapons and their effects on international politics."

"I'm not sure I understand you. Slavery was 'abolished,' but no one 'disinvented' it. Still, let's call it prohibition for now. Has the time come to prohibit nuclear weapons?"

"It is not clear today how or when this could be achieved; what is clear is that comprehensive nuclear disarmament should be undertaken only in circumstances such that, on balance, it would enhance the security of the United States."

"Doesn't it go without saying that an American policy should be in

American interests? What, more specifically, are the advantages and disadvantages of prohibition?"

"[Prohibition] would have three main benefits. It would virtually eliminate the possibility of use. . . . It would reduce the likelihood that additional states will acquire nuclear weapons. . . . [And it] would deal decisively with the uncertain moral and legal status of nuclear weapons."

"All this sounds very positive. Should we put prohibition on the agenda, then?"

"Nuclear disarmament poses risks as well as benefits. . . . The prohibition on nuclear weapons might break down via cheating or overt withdrawal from the disarmament regime. . . . Comprehensive nuclear disarmament could remove the moderating effect that nuclear weapons appear to have had on the behavior of states. . . . To reduce these risks, a disarmament regime would have to be built within a larger international security system that would be capable not only of deterring or punishing the acquisition or use of nuclear weapons but also of responding to major aggression."

Demanding a collective security system as a precondition for eliminating nuclear weapons has traditionally been the means by which abolition is pushed off indefinitely. "That sounds like a tall order," I commented.

"The committee has concluded that the potential benefits of a global prohibition of nuclear weapons are so attractive relative to the attendant risks that increased attention is now warranted to studying and fostering the conditions that would have to be met to make prohibition desirable and feasible."

In the meantime, the committee endorsed a series of measures that have emerged as something like the settled agenda of a considerable body of expert opinion: the measures go beyond the Nuclear Posture Review without, as yet, embracing abolition. One of these—a vertical step—would be the reduction of each former superpower's nuclear arsenal to one thousand warheads. (It's hard not to suspect that this number has been chosen simply because it is a good round figure.) This would be followed by reductions to "a few hundred" nuclear weapons on each side. A second measure—a horizontal step—would be de-alerting. The committee is ready to go surprisingly far along the horizontal path. "In the case of ballistic missiles," it holds, "it is possible to remove warheads, shrouds, guidance systems, or other key components"—with all of these steps to be subject to monitoring by other countries. A third measure is a radical change in nuclear targeting from the current quite rigid plans for retaliation against Russia to "a much more flexible planning system of 'adaptive targeting.' " A fourth is an inspected, comprehensive mutual accounting of warheads and a cutoff in the production of fissile materials.

All these suggested steps would be underwritten by an important policy shift also found in other proposals: a Rotblat-like declaration of no-first-use, which would leave nuclear weapons serving only what the committee calls the "core function" of deterrence—namely, deterring attack by other nuclear weapons. The committee's steadfast devotion to the central proposition of mutual assured destruction is evident in a statement that reads, "The reduced number of weapons would be sufficient to fulfill the core function, however, through its potential to destroy essential elements of the society or economy of any possible attacker." Thus, the committee, while not ready to abandon deterrence in the new era, would strip it of the "extended" role assigned to it during the Cold War. No longer would nuclear weapons be used to deter conventional attack or attack by chemical or biological weapons. The committee was also strongly interested in combining the horizontal and vertical paths to "prohibition."

"Do you think that with virtual arsenals in place deterrence could remain in operation 'below zero'?" I asked.

The committee's answer was positive. "Indeed, even the existence of the idea of nuclear weapons—more specifically the ability of many states to make them—is enough to create an existential deterrent effect against large-scale conflicts of all kinds. . . . It could provide a *part* of the assurance required. . . . In a sense, a prohibition on the possession of nuclear weapons is a logical extension of the de-alerting measures [we have] recommended, extending from hours or days to months or years the time required to reconstitute an ability to use nuclear weapons. A durable prohibition would expand as far as possible the firebreak between a decision to ready weapons for use and the ability to launch a nuclear attack, thereby allowing as much time as possible to resolve the underlying concerns, and decreasing the risk of nuclear catastrophe to an irreducible minimum."

"What problems do you see in this arrangement?"

"First, allowing states to maintain the capability to build nuclear weapons on short notice would make it easier for a state to cheat while at the same time making it more difficult to detect cheating. . . . Second, having states poised to resume manufacture and deployment of nuclear weapons could create dangerous instabilities in which states might rush to rearm during a crisis."

"What are your conclusions?" I asked.

"Achieving the conditions necessary to make a durable global prohibition on the possession of nuclear weapons both desirable and feasible will not be easy. Complete nuclear disarmament will require continued evolution of the international system toward collective action, transparency, and the rule of law; a comprehensive system of verification, which itself will require an unprecedented degree of cooperation and transparency; and safeguards to protect against the possibility of cheating or rapid breakout. As difficult as this may seem today, the process of reducing national nuclear arsenals to a few hundred warheads would lay much of the necessary groundwork."

The report can be seen as an effort to carry nuclear disarmament as far as it conceivably can go within the framework—pared down but intact in its essentials—of deterrence. The destruction by retaliation of "the society" of the nuclear opponent (who, strangely, is now our friend and partner) is still provided for and remains the bedrock of national security. Seen from this angle, the committee's proposal is still a form of deterrence, but a skeletal deterrence, not the "robust" kind favored by unreconstructed possessionists.

STANSFIELD TURNER AND
MORTON HALPERIN

Two individual settlers of recent vintage are Admiral Stansfield Turner, who served as director of central intelligence under President Jimmy

Carter, and Morton Halperin, who served on the National Security Council under Presidents Nixon and Clinton and is a senior fellow at the Council on Foreign Relations.

Turner, too, takes deterrence as his point of departure, demonstrating once again, if that were necessary, the powerful grip of this doctrine on the American mind. Setting forth along the well-worn pathways of the apparently endless maze of deterrence theory, he has reasoned his way to two new variations on the old question "How much is enough?" First, he has come up with the idea that an attacking force large enough to drive the opponent's economy to "the point of nonrecovery" is enough. Second, he makes new use of the term *self-deterrence*, a phrase that has been given many meanings over the years. In his hands it simply means the fear of launching a nuclear attack that is produced by the fear of retaliation. It leads Turner to a striking assertion: "There is no foreign policy objective today that is so threatened that we would employ nuclear weapons and accept the risk of receiving just one nuclear detonation in retaliation." His final variation is a targeting doctrine that he calls "controlled response," in which any retaliation to nuclear attack would be carefully designed to support political as well as military objectives.

With these proposed revisions of deterrence, Turner pares the doctrine down even further than does CISAC. His proposal, which goes several steps farther than theirs, accompanies a sharp vertical drop with bolder moves along the horizontal path. The steps he envisages are the familiar stations along that path: de-alerting, de-mating, storage of warheads at a distance from launch vehicles, removal of guidance sets from missiles, and even, at some point in the more distant future, the dismantling of the warheads themselves. The forces thus horizontally disarmed he calls a "strategic escrow." The significance of the word *escrow*, of course, is that what has been put in escrow can, in an emergency, be taken out again.

Turner's method of proceeding would not be for the United States to negotiate conventional arms control agreements but for it to make a series of unilateral moves, in the expectation of reciprocation by Russia and, eventually, by the other nuclear powers. He points to the limited, sequential, unilateral de-alerting of forces by Bush and Gorbachev in

1991 as a precedent. The end point of this "program of strategic escrow" would be that each nuclear power would possess some two hundred warheads stored separately from two hundred launch vehicles, with the whole arrangement monitored by international observers, guarded by limited defenses, and undergirded by a universal no-first-use treaty backed up by international sanctions.

Turner does not call his end point "zero." In fact, he distinguishes it from zero, which he considers "not feasible in the foreseeable future." Like CISAC, he believes that going to zero would require, among other things, "a mechanism to deal with violators, which would exceed any authority the world has yet granted to international organizations."

But his definition of this rejected zero is a stringent one. It would be, he writes, "equivalent to disinventing nuclear weapons, and would eliminate any concern that someone might employ one."

Morton Halperin's plan closely resembles Turner's. Halperin, too, would adopt full "transparency" for his demobilized arsenals and full, intrusive international verification of their status. He, too, would "separate . . . existing nuclear warheads from delivery systems on a step-by-step basis." But then, having taken this important step along the horizontal path, he would take one more: he would separate the nuclear cores from the nuclear warheads, and procedures would be adopted to prevent the cores from "quickly" being re-mated with the warheads. (Turner, too, mentions the possibility of taking this step but puts it off indefinitely. Halperin puts it on the immediate agenda and includes it in his end point.)

The greatest difference between Halperin's plan and Turner's, however, is not substantive but semantic—no small matter in the field of nuclear policy in which no use of the weapons in question has occurred for more than half a century. While Turner distinguishes his goal from zero, Halperin calls his zero. His aim, he begins by saying, is to "redefine" zero in a manner that will make it achievable, in part by drawing a distinction between nuclear weapons and mere nuclear materials. "As long as nuclear weapons exist, there will be a danger of inadvertent, unauthorized, or accidental use," he writes. "Thus, nuclear weapons must be eliminated." By removing the cores from the warheads, he de-weaponizes (to adapt George Perkovich's phrase) the arsenal. In the growing catalog of end points for nuclear disarmament, here was a new entry: two hundred nuclear cores, each separated from the rest of the warhead and its delivery vehicle.

FRED CHARLES IKLÉ

Fred Charles Iklé, who served as director of the U.S. Arms Control and Disarmament Agency under President Ford and as under secretary of defense for policy in the Reagan administration, is one of the nation's most elegant and least classifiable thinkers on the subject of nuclear strategy. His writings are not voluminous but they are lapidary, and pack a lot of thought into a small space. What is more unusual, they are rigorously free of the jargon that renders so much writing on strategic subjects opaque to the lay reader. Like the champions of minimum deterrence, Iklé calls for reductions of nuclear arsenals to lower levels but wants to stop there. But this is the end of his resemblance to the theorists of deterrence—a doctrine against which he has trenchantly polemicized for at least two decades. Like General Horner, he is an advocate of antinuclear defenses, and he was an advocate, in the mid-1980s, of the Strategic Defense Initiative. In an article in 1986 in *Foreign Affairs*, he ridiculed the policy of mutual assured destruction as a "flat-earth" theory—as intellectually untenable, morally questionable, and impracticable. "Like oil and water," he wrote in a notable passage, "the two ingredients" of the doctrine "will always separate: the accord on a stable equilibrium of mutual restraint is psychologically incompatible with the constant threat of reciprocal annihilation. The first ingredient of this mixture represents the best in international relations: a continued willingness to cooperate in restraining one's own military power, coupled with a serene reliance on the opponent's prudence and his common sense. The second ingredient . . . represents the worst in international relations: an endless effort to maintain forces that are constantly ready to annihilate the opponent, coupled with an unremitting determination to deny him escape from this grip of terror." The resulting strategic order therefore "is unstable at its very core." Worse, "upon an alliance of democracies, such a policy imposes a passive,

almost cynical resignation toward the possibility of an atrocity un-
surpassed in human history," he wrote, language not often found in
articles by government officials on nuclear strategy. He continued, "It
offers a prospect of anxiety without relief, an intellectual legacy crippling the outlook of each new generation, a theme of desolate sadness."

What then to do? Iklé, supporting some, if not all, of the antinuclear defense plan of the president he served, proposed a simultaneous buildup of antinuclear defenses accompanied by a sharp cut in
offensive forces, leading, finally, to a world in which defenses had the
edge. At that point, mutual assured destruction would be dissolved.
Iklé did not, however, embrace Reagan's vision of nuclear abolition. To
judge by the article, reductions to very low levels of strategic forces
were enough for him.

When the Cold War ended, Iklé weighed in with new reflections in
Foreign Affairs. The world, he now wrote, had become dangerously
accustomed to "nonuse" of nuclear weapons. During the Cold War,
many factors had combined to produce nonuse, including the discovery
by one president after another that, whatever the theorists of "limited"
nuclear war might say, the weapons were useless in actual wars such as
the ones in Korea and Vietnam, and the realization of the absurdity of
ever translating NATO's policy for first use of nuclear weapons into
practice. In addition, of course, the emphasis on mutual assured
destruction was in total contradiction to NATO's first-use policy.

Today, the record of nonuse has led policymakers to "take for
granted that a [local nuclear] calamity would remain confined to the
margins of the world order." The leaders of the great powers, Iklé writes,
suppose that "as the pygmies try to stir up chaos, the giants stay aloof
on their Olympian heights of thousands of nuclear weapons; at most
they launch a thunderbolt to restore order below." Iklé, who now is even
less impressed with the doctrine of deterrence than he was before, begs
to disagree. The end of the tradition of nonuse by one or more nuclear
explosions would unleash forces "that would transform the international system far more profoundly than did the collapse of the Soviet
Empire."

In his introduction to Michael Mazarr's book on virtual nuclear arsenals, Iklé stops well short of endorsing the idea, but he concludes with what he calls a "homework assignment" for nuclear strategists:

Please write a brief essay explaining why ready nuclear weapons prevent war, how only mutual assured destruction can keep the peace, and why preparations for instant retaliation and "first use" help maintain stability. But, instead of justifying these concepts by assuming a replay of the first half-century of the nuclear age, explain their validity—if any!—for a world in which the Soviet Union has broken up peacefully, in which NATO ambles eastward in search for the lost Warsaw Pact, and in which our best intelligence services cannot keep track anymore of the numbers and whereabouts of nuclear weapons in the world. Then reconsider your assessment of virtual arsenals.

I began my conversation with Iklé by asking if he favored the abolition of nuclear weapons.

"I do not," he answered. "The idea of abolishing nuclear weapons is for many people the first that comes to mind in trying to get out of the nuclear predicament. However, it wouldn't take very long for nations to build nuclear weapons again. Besides, the larger nuclear powers could easily conceal some of their weapons. Imagine trying to find all the nuclear weapons in Russia or China! And you would have to keep track of all the material to build weapons—the plutonium produced in reactors and enriched uranium. The Russian government today cannot even keep track of all its own materials; so how could American, or international, inspectors find all these things if future Russian governments tried to conceal them? Also, it seems totally implausible that Russia, China, or, for that matter, the United States would want to go down that path in the absence of some new horrible impact on the emotions of people in government."

Since Iklé sees the strong possibility of precisely the event—the use of one or more nuclear weapons—that could create this horrible impact, I wondered what he thought should be done *now*.

"You need—in the short term, I believe—a kind of concert of the major nuclear powers to maintain the tradition of nonuse as long as possible, not only among themselves, but to keep all the so-called rogue states from ever using nuclear weapons. These major powers would punish the use of nuclear weapons by rogue states, perhaps by letting one major party—the most effective one in each case—step forward and respond to prevent any repetition. If, for instance, North Korea were to use nuclear weapons against South Korea or Japan, the United States might handle the needed nuclear response, but Russia and China would tolerate the United States' doing so, much as they tolerated the Gulf War. This enforced nonuse policy, however, would have to apply not just to nuclear weapons but to any large-scale use of weapons of mass destruction."

Iklé also favors certain verifiable measures of de-alerting, not as stepping stones to abolition but for their own sake. He continued, "There are dangers in a taut alert posture, and some of the alert procedures in Russia, as Bruce Blair has written, are really spine chilling. If you review some of the past nuclear incidents you will discover that on some occasions we averted accidental nuclear war, you might say, 'by accident.' High-alert forces also have unhealthy consequences for political attitudes. We can see a vicious circle at work, in which having nuclear forces on high alert feeds the idea that you are in a serious military confrontation, and the feeling that you are in a confrontation feeds the alerting process."

Iklé has often commented on the moral cost of deterrence policy, and I decided to ask him whether the same objections might not apply to the reduced, less confrontational arsenals he was proposing. "One of the things that we hate about nuclear arsenals is that they implicate us in the consequences of their use, if only in retaliation," I remarked. "Even with 'small' numbers, we would have to have people making them, policies for their use, and so forth."

"That's a fair point," Iklé said. "The huge arsenals that we built up in the Cold War had a numbing effect on the minds of the people who did the planning—those few who did do it."

"But also on the average citizen," I suggested.

"Smaller forces," he responded, "would restore a sense of realism." They would overcome an attitude that, paradoxically, is both cavalier and apocalyptic—that regards nuclear war as the end of the world, as if a comet were about to hit, and leads people to say, 'What can I do about it?' During the Cold War people regarded nuclear war as almost transcendental. But it was not transcendental then and it is not now. It is a real possibility for *this* world."

"What if your plan were implemented?" I asked. "Would you then want to push on to abolition?"

"Other things will raise their ugly heads long before you get to zero," he said. "Science has not stood still. As we learned from the crisis with Iraq, there are other weapons of mass destruction that are easier to conceal and to make—especially biological ones. Let me illustrate this concealment problem with an example. The IRA has successfully used high explosives as weapons of terrorism to exert political pressure. Although Northern Ireland is under British military control and southern Ireland is controlled by a government that supports peacemaking efforts and opposes IRA terrorism, the British have not been able to 'abolish' these high explosives. Why do people assume one can 'abolish' all weapons of mass destruction by signing treaties?"

"Nuclear weapons are still considerably harder to make than high explosives," I commented.

"They are, thank God," he answered. "Maybe you can ban weapons-grade uranium, or do something about plutonium, although that's also hard. But biological weapons? Increasingly, biotechnology will be used for making pharmaceuticals, for healing, and the same techniques can be misused for making biological weapons."

I commented that in the face of this horrifying prospective concatenation of political disorder and many-sided scientific advance, the abolition of nuclear weapons seemed to me all the more desirable.

"Sometime in the far distant future, it might happen," he answered. "But other things would have to happen first. The world would have to come under the control of some global authority, and a rather intrusive and demanding one at that. Such a powerful authority could well turn into a tyrannical world government—a danger perhaps as horrifying as the dangers of nuclear weapons. Besides, neither governments nor people will seriously consider taking any really big steps until they are kicked in that direction by very intense emotions." Such emotions, of course, could be stirred up by the end of the era of nonuse of nuclear weapons that he had warned of in his *Foreign Affairs* article. For now, he said, "all that can be hoped for is a certain amount of preparation, so that the shock would not undo our democratic form of government and our political liberty."

EUROPEAN

VOICES

HELMUT SCHMIDT

During the Cold War, Western Europe was beset by two opposite anxieties in relation to nuclear arms. One was that the United States would not come to Europe's defense in a crisis. The other was that it would. In the first case, Europe might have been conquered. In the second, it might have been annihilated. The second anxiety became more acute in the mid-1960s, when the United States adopted the doctrine of "flexible response"—an option that supposedly made limited nuclear wars possible. Many Europeans feared that such wars would be limited to Europe, which might become a convenient atomic battleground for the two superpowers, whose territories would remain untouched. The two anxieties collided head-on in a political battle over U.S. deployment in the early 1980s of a new generation of medium-range Pershing missiles, whose presence was meant to counter Soviet medium-range SS-20 missiles. European governments hoped to bind the United States more closely to Europe by the deployment, while substantial, vocal sections of their publics, fearful that the United

States would indeed defend (and thereby destroy) Europe, vociferously opposed the deployments.

When the Cold War ended, Europe, released from both anxieties, was freed, like the rest of the world, to reexamine the nuclear question. Some analysts hoped that the British and French arsenals left over from the Cold War might somehow be incorporated into the defenses of the European Union. Others have concluded that nuclear weapons should be abolished. One of these is the former chancellor of West Germany, Helmut Schmidt, who originally called for the Pershing deployment.

"Maybe you are aware of the fact that I've signed my name to the statement by Alan Cranston and heads or former heads of state calling for the elimination of nuclear weapons," Schmidt told me when I met him in his office at the newspaper *Die Zeit*, in Hamburg. "That fact reveals to you my principal tendencies. Now, I want to qualify this. I am not at all optimistic that the goal can be achieved soon, but I think such an appeal does make sense now, because it may help reduce the number of existing weapons.

"The Non-Proliferation Treaty was an unequal treaty, which I think was morally and politically a bad thing. For twenty-five years, the superpowers failed to fulfill their obligations under the treaty. But since the early 1990s, they have started to reduce the number of weapons. They have to go much further today.

"A worldwide non-proliferation treaty would certainly require that the nuclear-weapon states disclose what they have and how they control it. Probably, this would not lead Israel or Pakistan to disclose its preparations. That would require pressure that can be exerted only by the nuclear powers, and their legitimacy for exerting such pressure could only derive from laying open their own balance sheets. It's going to be a long and drawn-out process. It might take fifty years for these weapons finally to be eliminated. I wouldn't rule out such a length of time."

I asked if he thought a world without nuclear weapons would be unstable because the weapons can't be disinvented and some nations might cheat.

"I would agree that the technology is very difficult to control," he replied. "There is always the danger and possibility of cheating. If I were an American, therefore, I would not rid myself of the last nuclear weapons until I was sure that everyone else was doing the same thing at the same time.

"You know, within the nuclear-weapon states—particularly in the United States and Russia—there is an enormous body of vested interests. And they are influential in many ways—not only through lobbying in Washington and Moscow but through influence on intellectuals, on people who write books and articles in newspapers or do features on television. It's very difficult as a reader or as a consumer of television to distinguish by one's own judgment what is led by these interests, and what is led by rational conclusion.

"Twenty-five years ago, I met Edward Teller. He was an irate man, full of argumentative capacity and power. But he had vested so much of his personal prestige in his position that he was unable to rethink anything." (Schmidt's assessment of Teller evidently had been quite different from General Horner's.) "There are thousands of people who are unable to rethink. In addition, there are the military and civilian bureaucracies. These influence the thinking of members of Congress, senators, members of the legislature in Washington and Moscow. Then, on the other hand, you have the extreme, psychotic enemies of nuclear things, whether weapons or reactors, and they also try to influence people. They also invested their prestige to a degree and cannot rethink. So it's going to be a very, very long process of struggling within the nuclear-weapon states.

"But I think it's a good time to set the goal. I remember very well the deep impact that the inauguration speech of John Kennedy had upon me when he told his fellow Americans that they shouldn't ask what America could do for them but what they could do for America. From time to time, you need a leader who says something like that and by his deeds and action convinces people that he really means what he says."

"Would it be useful today for a president of the United States to publicly embrace the goal of abolition, with all the qualifications that you've mentioned?" I asked.

"Internationally useful, yes," he answered. "Whether politically useful inside the United States, I wouldn't know. But you know, I'm not deeply engaged emotionally in the nuclear issue. Not at all. For instance, I was the one who instigated what later on got to be called NATO's double-track decision [to deploy the Pershing missiles]. I believe in the principle of balance in military situations. Balance doesn't rule out military conflict, but it diminishes the probability. Balance is better than when you feel superior by 300 percent."

Considering his comments on the balance of forces, I wondered what he would think of the idea that deterrence could persist even after the actual weaponry had been pulled apart. "If you eliminate the hardware," I asked, "is it possible that because of the technical knowledge that remains, deterrence might stay in force?"

"Yes, I agree," Schmidt answered. "The know-how cannot in principle be abolished. Even if you shoot all the people who have it, there are still the books and the scientific journals and what-have-you. And I would add that in a couple of decades you'll have to reckon with the fact that the knowledge of how to do it will have spread widely enough for terrorists to create nuclear weapons in their garages. Does the fact that I or my allies possess nuclear weapons deter that terrorist or, say, a little terrorist state? I have quite some experience with terrorists. No, it will not deter them. It's no use throwing a nuclear bomb on Benghazi, even leaving aside the moral question. But we also have to ask: Is it legitimate to do this? There's a civilian population there. I mean, one could raise severe moral questions about the bombings of Hiroshima and Nagasaki—severe moral questions. But I will be a little more worried if terrorists get on top of the government of a big state in the Middle East, with, say, forty or fifty million people, and then acquire nuclear weapons."

"Some have suggested that it would be useful if a concert of states were to embrace the goal of abolition publicly and begin to study what the shape of a nuclear-weapon-free world might be. Would you agree?"

"That depends on the composition of the group," he answered. "The Americans now think they are the only superpower in the world. This is a misunderstanding of their real situation. Russia will stay weak for at least another twenty-five years, maybe fifty, two generations. Nobody really knows. It's a country in turmoil. Yet they are still a superpower. After the death of Deng Xiaoping, there may be a number of question marks about the future development of China, domestically as well as internationally; but it's a superpower, which the Americans don't seem to understand. So far, they have regarded China only as a great future market. That is true, of course. Chinese exports to the world's markets will be as big as American exports, maybe even as big as the exports of the whole European Union. So it's not only militarily but economically that it is a superpower.

"So, coming back to your question about a group of statesmen: If an American president makes such a pronouncement, maybe together with President Chirac (who would not participate, by the way), and maybe with Chancellor Kohl, and maybe with Prime Minister Tony Blair—but then, in the last paragraph but one, invites the Chinese and the Russians to please participate, this would not work. The Americans have to deal with the leaders in Moscow and Beijing as people who are on an equal footing. As far as I can tell, the leaders in Moscow and Beijing would consider joining such an effort only if and when the United States ceased presenting itself as the world's sole leader while others were just trailing behind, saying yes, yes."

So far, Schmidt hadn't mentioned Europe. I asked him what role nuclear weapons should play in its policies.

"My feeling is that for a few decades, neither Britain nor, especially, France will give up its nuclear capability. On principle, they will do it not a second earlier than the other three main nuclear powers. As for the European Union, it is *in statu nascendi*. It has been *in statu nascendi* for decades, and it will take more decades. It is a unique undertaking—of a kind that has never happened before in history. Never. Not before the birth of Christ, nor after."

"What do you mean?"

"You have seen the creation of great empires, either by strategically gifted leaders or perhaps emperors or dictators—Alexander the Great, and before Alexander, Assyria, Babylon, and later, Egypt, the Roman empire, and so forth. We have seen two very short-lived attempts at creating empires in our time—by the Japanese and by Hitler. One hundred and fifty years earlier, Napoleon did it.

"In all these cases, people of differing historical and cultural backgrounds were forced into one empire. In Europe now, you have some thirty-six nation-states, and the present membership of the European Union is fifteen member states, with twelve or thirteen languages. Most of these nation-states go back about a thousand years. And this is also true of Poland, which is not a member state. If you asked a Britisher, he would probably say that his country has existed since the Battle of Hastings, in 1066. The French would certainly say, 'since Charlemagne.' And so the national traditions go back over centuries and centuries. Each nation carries its historical baggage on its shoulders.

"The attempt to create the European Union marks the first time in the history of mankind that nation-states that differ so much from each other nevertheless voluntarily—not under the pressure of a Napoleon or an Alexander the Great or a Hitler, but *voluntarily*—have decided to throw in their lot together. This is unique. On the other hand it explains why the process is so drawn out.

"It started in 1950, with the Schuman Plan. Most of the people who agreed to the Schuman Plan in Europe at that time did not really think of it as a United States of Europe, of which Winston Churchill had spoken in 1946, in a speech in Zurich. So from 1950 until today, which is almost half a century, this thing has suffered a number of setbacks, has overcome a number of crises, and is still going forward. I don't know how long it will take until we get to one common foreign and security policy. It could be another half-century—it could take that long.

"To come back to your question: for as long as I live and as long as you live, Britain and France will be nuclear powers, and the European Union will not. This, at least, is my guess."

"The buildups of arms, nuclear and other, of the past fifty years were justified as expenditures of the Cold War," I said. "But now the Cold War has ended. There is no angry, defeated power, like Germany after the First World War, that might want to upset the peace. Yet there has been no attempt to create a comprehensive settlement, as there was after the two world wars. Why do you think that is?"

"What should it settle?" Schmidt asked. "What could it have settled, if it had been attempted?"

"I'm thinking above all of disarmament, which continues very much on the track it was on during the Cold War," I said.

"No, no, I would not agree," Schmidt responded. "I think that in the second half of the 1980s, there was a very decisive turning point in the field of disarmament. This was the Intermediate Range Forces [INF] agreement. It was the first real measure of actual disarmament, even though it was limited to smaller nuclear weapons. It produced a qualitative change in the situation. Since that time, by agreement, there has been a decrease of nuclear weapons on both sides. You cannot deny this. You cannot say that this is the same situation as before."

"I'm suggesting, though," I replied, "that the treaties you mention, as important as they were, were all adopted during the Cold War, whose end has not brought much change."

"No," he said, "the INF treaty *was* the end of the Cold War. The Cold War did not end in 1990. It didn't end with the collapse of the Soviet Union. Vis-à-vis China, it could have ended after the visit of Nixon and Kissinger to Beijing. But the Americans got off track after that."

"What do you now think of the doctrine of deterrence?" I asked. "Can this doctrine guide policy in the politically new world we are living in? Or should we seek out some other doctrine?"

"Let me start with a footnote," he said. "You use the word *deterrence*, without an adjective. This seems to indicate that you understand the meaning of the word as either exclusively or in the main related to the nuclear field. But deterrence has been an element of foreign policy for thousands of years. Any fortification of a township in principle said to a potential enemy, 'No use attacking my city! We have a wall!'

"The Trojan War was three thousand years ago, and we had warriors on the wall who could shoot with their bows or throw their lances. So deterrence is not particularly a category in the nuclear field. Not at all. This has not changed since the arrival of nuclear weapons. Even without nuclear weapons, you will have wars in the future, plenty of them, if only because of the population explosion on this globe. And a little country will always seek refuge under the wings of a bigger one, and the bigger one will always try to subdue smaller ones. This is human. At the time of Jesus of Nazareth, we were two hundred million people on earth. Now we are close to six billion. And it doesn't seem to me that this proliferation is going to end or stop. Soon, we will be eight billion people. The abolition of nuclear weapons doesn't make human beings more peaceful. There will always be some who attack or cross borders by force. You will always have people who want to defend themselves against such attacks. This will remain so, even after the disappearance of nuclear weapons. And the question—the old question—will remain: How does one maintain peace?"

GERD SCHMÜCKLE

When Helmut Schmidt was chancellor of the Federal Republic of Germany, the German general Gerd Schmückle was deputy commander of NATO. (The commander is always an American.) The combination of the end of the Cold War and the triumph of American arms in the Gulf War impressed him deeply. It led him to favor, and to publicly suggest, the elimination of nuclear arms.

"I proposed that if it were true that the Americans had conventional precision weapons that worked as well as they seemed to in the Gulf, then it would be time for America to proceed to total nuclear disarmament," he told me. "I do not believe in partial nuclear disarmament—that is too difficult to control. And elimination would make no sense if we had no *replacement* for nuclear weapons. The replacement would be conventional precision weapons, of the kind we saw in the Gulf War. It was interesting, too, to see that briefly in Bosnia they worked excellently against the Serbs. They hit just the military targets and saved civilian lives."

"What reaction did you get when you made this proposal?" I asked.

"My American friends were upset. They said, 'Ah, you will take away all our nuclear weapons, but this is the source of our strength,' and so on. They are good people, but they were very sour with me. Later, at a small conference in Paris, Robert McNamara agreed with me. We laughed, because military men were for elimination, while the civilians were for holding on to nuclear weapons."

I mentioned that many civilian analysts took the position that the United States should hold on to several hundred nuclear weapons.

"I disagree. You must replace them. I don't believe any statesman today will dare to use these weapons. World opinion would be against him. You Americans bombed Hiroshima and Nagasaki, and still you are suffering from it. In the case of any new use you could not say, 'Well, it was necessary for this or that reason.' Even Edward Teller, a good friend of mine, said to me, 'We should first have demonstrated it to the Japanese over the ocean.' I think that self-deterrence is very, very powerful. It's very hard to think of a statesman who would be willing to take on himself the burden of using nuclear weapons."

I asked if he thought that the United States would have used nuclear weapons to defend Europe.

"I said to my chancellor, Helmut Schmidt, 'It's really doubtful whether the Americans would use nuclear weapons to defend us. Why should they commit suicide for the sake of Germany?' But at the same time I believed that as long as the Russians believed there was a 3 percent probability that the Americans would use them, it would be enough."

I noted that many of those I had spoken with thought the United States had failed to take sufficient advantage of the end of the Cold War.

"The great opportunity arose, I believe, after the Gulf War. But the opportunity could have been taken only with the leadership of the Americans. You Americans are very talented at coming up with marvelous phrases for such things, which can really convince the world: in this case, conveying the message that we want a nuclear-weapon-free world now. You must take the lead in developing a conception of how to live together without nuclear weapons. No one would pay attention to the Germans, or the French, or the British. You are the only nation that can do it. A president could do it, with the tremendous power of the country behind him. I would say that it is the greatest opportunity that America has ever had. In fact, I would go farther and say that objectively it's the greatest opportunity that the world has had. But now I'm afraid that the opportunity may be over."

"Why is that?" I asked.

"Six years have passed since the Cold War ended. China has been steadily developing and could become a serious problem. Russia is getting worried that it has lost too much territory. If I were a Russian, I would be hoping again to become a world power. Other, smaller countries have been developing their ambitions, and there has been a proliferation of civil wars, as in Somalia, Rwanda, and Bosnia. It's difficult to know what the great powers can do in such situations. But one thing is certain: nuclear bombs are of no use."

ROBERT O'NEILL AND LORD MICHAEL CARVER

Robert O'Neill is Chichele Professor of the History of War at All Souls College, Oxford University, and a former director of the International Institute of Strategic Studies in London. Lord Michael Carver is the former commander in chief Far East of the British army and the former chief of defense staff. I met both when the Canberra Commission, on which they were serving, held a meeting on Long Island.

I talked first with Robert O'Neill. "What do you regard as the most substantial arguments—the ones that have the most weight with you— against a nuclear-weapon-free world?" I asked.

"The one we're going to come up against most frequently is that nuclear weapons exercise a disciplinary function in the world. They make impossible a direct conflict between the United States and Russia. They make smaller powers think very hard about how far they will go in provoking a nuclear power, for fear that they get a nuke back. They reinforce the power status of nuclear-weapon states. This is tremendously important to Britain and France as well as China. As I teach at Oxford, I'm very much aware that the issue of status is what it's all about in Britain, and that we are going to have great difficulty in selling the message of the Canberra Commission there."

"What's your response to these arguments?" I asked.

"I would say that it's currently unprovable whether or not nuclear weapons kept the peace between NATO and the Warsaw Pact. We have a lot of work to do on the history of the period. We are missing many of the documents from the Russian side, in particular. And what we hear at the moment suggests to me that we made some serious mistakes in likening the Soviet Union under Stalin and Khrushchev to Nazi Germany under Hitler. They probably were totally different sorts of governments, with different sorts of aims. That's the way it looks in hindsight, in any case. I think we can say that. Certainly, the risks we ran in depending so heavily on nuclear weapons are of a kind we would not really want to accept for the long term. I think we have a very good prospect now of maintaining peace without nuclear weapons."

"What about a disciplinary role in the future?" I asked.

"Well, they *could* play a disciplinary role," he said. "But I would think that there are other much more important disciplinary factors. International economic cooperation, the democratizing process, the forces of electoral opinion are going to focus the minds of the former Communist countries—and perhaps even present Communist countries—much more sharply than military advisers have suggested."

"Could deterrence work at all in the period ahead?" I asked.

"In a very limited sense, perhaps—that is, nuclear weapons may deter other people from using their nuclear weapons on you. It becomes suicidal; therefore, you don't. But if the other guy doesn't want to do that anyway, maybe he would rather be free of the burden of nuclear weapons, too. So you could both give them up. I think it might be akin to the paradigm shift that occurred when Gorbachev decided in the mid-1980s to change Soviet foreign policy. All of a sudden, they found that military superiority wasn't a necessity. I'm hoping that, all of a sudden, some national leaders will simply say, 'Well, we just don't need nuclear weapons. What earthly purpose do they serve?' Once that happened in Washington and Moscow, it would obviously lead the way for others.

"The Americans sometimes bring up another argument in favor of nuclear weapons: that you need them to deter other weapons of mass destruction, biological or chemical. However, my view is that nuclear weapons are very poorly situated to play such a role. They destroy a massive area, killing the wrong kinds of people, and they do nothing to protect your own forces, because the chemical and bacteriological weapons will probably be released from sites dotted all over the adversary's country, as were Iraq's Scud missiles in the Gulf War. In addition, such a use of nuclear weapons would certainly draw a very negative reaction from international public opinion. So nuclear weapons are really not useful in dealing with that situation.

"A third argument the Americans raise is that they might be usable in regional conflicts against an aggressor. The Iraq case is relevant here. There was no way that you could sensibly have used a nuke to get Saddam Hussein out of Kuwait. He would have said, 'Well, go and do it.'

"There's a long history of looking at how to use nuclear weapons in regional crises. Truman considered the possibility in Korea, and Eisenhower also looked very hard at how to use nuclear weapons in Korea. Remember, Eisenhower was elected on a vague promise that he would do something to end the Korean War. 'I will go to Korea,' he said. He didn't say what he would do there. But one of the things he did when he went to Korea was to talk to his military advisers about the feasibility of using nuclear weapons. And he didn't come back with any good answers. The defeat of the French at Dien Bien Phu was another situation where they were considered and found unusable. In the Berlin crisis, nuclear weapons were looked at once more, and once more found inappropriate. The right targets just were not there.

"Then we can look at the Vietnam War, and the various wars in the Middle East. Again no one used nuclear weapons. In sum, there's a long history demonstrating that nuclear weapons just don't have a role in controlling conventional conflict, even when you are losing. The Russians in Afghanistan are another case in point.

"Another argument I'm sure you would hear in Washington is that nuclear weapons are very important to alliance leadership. They would also say that if the United States were to carry out nuclear disarmament, it would have to rearm conventionally."

"What do you think of that argument?" I asked.

"I think there's some truth in it," he answered. "But I think America probably has as much conventional force as it needs, with the possible exception of some ground forces. In the next fifty years, it may be extensively involved in peacekeeping operations, but I think its function as an alliance leader really has to be asserted more by political and economic means these days. We're in a different phase of international relations, in which political and economic factors have far greater currency than military ones. Germany and Japan are the best cases in point. Countries don't need to have very substantial military forces at all to be tremendous factors in the important global political decisions. The United States has to deal with them very delicately, and military force doesn't help with this in any way. I think the upturn in American productivity and competitive power is very evident and we're starting to see some dividends coming out of it. And good luck to the United States! To put a lot more money into a new phase of nuclear weapons development is just going to be money down a rat hole."

"What arguments against abolition do you hear most frequently in England?" I asked.

"That the structure of power in the world is based on force, and that the United Kingdom has been very well served by maintaining strong forces. It needed to build them up during the Second World War. It used them throughout the Cold War, and the effect has been, as [Foreign Secretary] Douglas Hurd puts it, 'punching above its own weight.' It's acquired more leverage than its economic power would justify, because it's been a very important NATO ally, because it has nuclear weapons, because it's ready to be an active partner of the United States in things like the Gulf War, Bosnia, and so on. There is a certain amount of truth in all this. But I would say that nuclear weapons have had almost nothing to do with it. Actually, I suspect the United States would secretly be quite relieved if Britain were to give up its nuclear weapons.

"Different American administrations have taken somewhat different positions on this, but the United States is interested in an orderly world, and the fewer independent nuclear decision-making centers you have, the better. So I don't believe that British nuclear weapons really contribute anything significant to the alliance. Actually, they create problems.

"Yet a country that went through the dreadful experience of the Second World War, of making the change from Chamberlain's appeasement to Churchill's defiance, is going to cling to its weaponry, and it's not going to give it up quickly."

"How do you judge the United States' receptivity to the idea of abolition?"

"It seems likely that the bureaucracy—of the State Department, the Pentagon, the National Security Council—is going to be very hostile. Very few people there would have anything other than an orthodox view of the utility of nuclear weapons, mostly because few of them have taken the time to sit down and really rethink the fundamentals of the question in the post–Cold War situation. The most important thing they should bear in mind is that the United States is now likely to be the principal target for nuclear weapons in the world. Previously, the Soviet Union was the likeliest target, and the initiator would have been NATO, which had a first-use policy. Now the situation is reversed because there could soon be possessors of nuclear weapons, whether governments or subgovernmental groups, that will prove just incapable of being deterred. They'll be like the guys who blew up the World Trade Center; they simply hated America so much that they were willing to die for their cause."

I asked O'Neill for his assessment of the horizontal approach to nuclear disarmament.

"My reaction is very favorable," he answered, "because—for one thing—this approach creates time barriers to a return to acute nuclear tension. Once we started such a process, it would help all of us rethink our attitudes toward nuclear weapons. It would lead people to see much more clearly how little use they are."

I asked in conclusion for his opinion of the view that in a nuclear-weapon-free world a cheater would be king.

His answer was crisp and brief. "Well, no king, because using a few nuclear weapons or threatening to use them would be of very limited value. Either the bluff could be called, or, if it turns out not to be a bluff, and someone does use them, they would open themselves to unimaginable retaliation by the whole international community, backed by intense public outrage around the world. For the nation that did use nuclear weapons, it would just be another way of committing suicide. We might have to go through an incident like this before the point was driven home, but I think it's better to accept that risk than to accept, as we do now, the continuing risk of the whole planet being blown sky-high."

Lord Michael Carver joined the conversation just as Dr. O'Neill was offering his opinion on the various horizontal steps that might most effectively lead to abolition. Lord Carver expressed a certain anxiety that in pursuing either the horizontal or the vertical path the goal of zero might be lost in, or replaced by, goals that fell short of zero. "As I see it," he said, "the most important thing at this moment is to persuade everyone, even those not inclined to accept it, that the target has got to be total elimination. If you start peddling solutions which are not perhaps quite total elimination but something that comes close to it, you lose the whole force of the argument. Until you've dramatically fixed zero as the target, you'll just get the sort of silly thing you get now. Of course, when you come to actual details and a verification system, you've got to face all these problems; and of course, you have to have steps along the way. But don't let's say that a target less than the absolute target would be acceptable."

"Some favor minimum deterrence," I noted.

"It's a totally ridiculous thing," he answered. "I used to ask questions in the House of Lords, and one young hereditary peer after another, speaking for the Ministry of Defense, used to say the same thing: 'We give you solemn insurance that all we're planning is minimum deterrence through last-resort weapons.' I asked, 'What do you actually *mean* by "minimum deterrence of last resort"?' Naturally, they couldn't answer.

"One of the only valid arguments for the British nuclear force, really, was that since NATO's policy depended on nuclear weapons, British nuclear policy showed solidarity with the alliance as a whole."

"How and when did you arrive at the conviction that zero nuclear weapons was the destination to aim at?" I asked.

"For a long time I thought that most of NATO's nuclear policy was nonsense, because, fundamentally, the moment you fired one missile off, you were going to get one back, and nobody was more vulnerable than Britain. It would have been not only absolute folly to do it; it would have been criminally irresponsible, even if the nuclear weapon was one of the smallest. I mean, when I was chief of defense staff, there was this absurd idea—I was laughing about it with Lord Carrington, the foreign secretary—that you would fire one off into the Pripet Marshes, or somewhere, and say, 'That's to show you that I would be prepared to use nuclear weapons.' Now what happens? He fires one back, and it lands in a bog in Scotland. He says, 'That's just to show *you*.'

"Yet my view, before the end of the Cold War, was that I was *not* in favor of total abolition. I was in favor of reduction—eventually, I hoped, to two small ballistic missile submarines, one in the hands of each of the superpowers. That would have been stable.

"But I thought at that time that there was a danger in getting rid of them altogether, because they had been a deterrent to the major nations, and especially the nuclear nations, getting into a war with each other. Whereas if you did away with them, you would have lost that advantage, yet the danger would remain that they would *come back*.

"Then last year, I had a message that a Senator Garreth Evans, external affairs minister of Australia, was going to call. I expected some old senator who wanted to talk about his war memoirs. But Evans explained to me that he wanted me to join the Canberra Commission. I answered that I wasn't sure I was in favor of total abolition, and that probably I wasn't his chap, but he was very persuasive. Then I got two bits of paper that seriously persuaded me. One was the Stimson report, signed of course by Robert McNamara and Andy Goodpaster, whom I happen to know very well. I was very impressed with their statement that they believed it was in the security interests of the United States that nuclear weapons should be done away with. Then I read a paper that had been written by Professor Michael MccGwire, arguing that while *of course* there were risks in reaching total zero, they were nothing comparable to the risks in going on forever and ever with nuclear arms.

"The basis of his argument is that all the risks the objectors talk about—that somebody might cheat, or you might have breakout—were not to be compared with all the risks of keeping nuclear arms—from the Americans loosing off nuclear weapons to an Oklahoma bombing incident with a nuclear weapon. Incidentally, the argument that the only weapon to which the United States is really vulnerable is a nuclear one applies equally to the United Kingdom.

"Now, having read the background papers of the Canberra Commission, I'm totally convinced that not only the nuclear powers but everybody would be physically safer—and their interests better protected—if we did away with nuclear weapons."

"The great job now, I believe, is to persuade the Americans that this is the way to go, that they should commit themselves to it. Then I don't think you really would have any trouble with the British, although no doubt the French would encourage the British to keep them. One of the arguments for the British and French nuclear systems has always been that we might be deserted by the Americans. Therefore, the French might say, 'Ah ha! Here you are, you see what's happened. Now, isn't it lucky that we've got our own?' But of course that argument, too, would collapse, provided that Russia was committed to elimination.

"I think that if the battle of public opinion could be won in the United States, the next battle would be for the public in Russia. Then I don't think that the British and the French could say that we don't accept elimination as a vital goal. They would say they'll get involved when the other arsenals get down to our level. I think that the Chinese position would be the same."

"Is it the end of the Cold War that has made abolition possible?" I asked.

"What made it possible," he answered, "was the *total* change of atmosphere brought about by the Gorbachev-Reagan meeting at Reykjavik. And don't forget: it isn't only a changed atmosphere. You no longer have a large, very modern, very efficient Soviet army in East Germany, only a few miles away."

I remarked that in the post–Cold War world, the most important question seemed to be a general one: Could nations in general be safe if they did not possess nuclear arsenals?

"The crux of the matter in that case is Israel," he observed. "There is only one reason for almost any other country to have nuclear weapons—to deter another country that has nuclear weapons. But who now would attack Britain or France? Israel is in a different situation. It's subject to conventional attack. It's in the same situation as West Germany during the Cold War: it can't trade space for time, certainly not with the situation being what it is on the West Bank. Therefore, someone might say that there's a perfect justification for Israel to have nuclear weapons. After all, otherwise in a short period of time the Arab states might use conventional weapons to obliterate the country.

"But no, that is a false argument. Israel's possession of nuclear weapons immediately provokes the surrounding countries to want them. It would in any case be unacceptable in American minds for Israel to use a nuclear weapon against a nonnuclear state. So, in fact, I reckon that Israel is worse off. Her chances of reconciliation with her neighbors are made more difficult by her being a nuclear power. It hasn't done her any good at all.

"But persuading people that all of us—even Israel—would be better off if we could get rid of nuclear weapons is only the first part of the task. The second part is to make sure that they *have* been eliminated; and to get people to accept the first argument, you have to persuade them of the second."

ROLF EKEUS

Rolf Ekeus, now the Swedish ambassador to the United States, has an experience unique in the history of the nuclear age. As executive chairman of the United Nations' Special Commission, he was assigned the task, together with the International Atomic Energy Agency, of inspecting Iraq's compliance with its post–Gulf War agreement to dismantle all its weapons of mass destruction (chemical, biological, and nuclear, as well as missiles with a range above 150 kilometers). Ekeus became the first person to seek to inspect a reluctant nation's commitment to eliminate such weapons. The experience was all the more significant in view of the fact that Iraq's government is a brutal, secretive dictatorship. In 1997, when Ekeus resigned his position to become ambassador, he was unable to state categorically that he had discovered and overseen the destruction of all Iraq's long-range ballistic missiles— though he gave assurances that all production of missiles had stopped. He could not guarantee, either, that all facilities for the production of chemical or biological weapons had been eliminated. However, he did declare to the world that "Iraq has no nuclear weapons, and, with the existing monitoring regime, Iraq will not be able to acquire nuclear weapons." The importance of this assurance—the first of its kind ever given—in any consideration of a worldwide treaty abolishing nuclear weapons is obvious.

I asked Ekeus what some of the biggest surprises had been in his experience inspecting Iraq.

"Well, Iraq is a country with large financial resources, including readily available cash," he said, "so perhaps we shouldn't be surprised by what they accomplished. They also have an industrial base, and a reasonably solid social network—I mean food, health care, and so on. Nevertheless, I think we must say that Iraq is a developing country. The industrial base is primitive compared to the West, and there is a primitive development of law. It is striking how such a country could advance so far in *all* aspects of the technology of nuclear weapons and other weapons of mass destruction.

"There are many reasons. One was a centralized leadership, which eagerly wanted these weapons. They began by sending students all over the world—and especially to the industrially advanced Western countries—to study not just nuclear physics and related skills but also the techniques of biological and chemical science. So I would say that their effort was based not on a quick decision but on a grand strategy to acquire the underlying skills. Of course, so much knowledge is available in the open literature—especially in the nuclear field, surprisingly.

"My first discovery therefore was the capacity of a country with a modest industrial base and educational system to acquire, through centralized, highly directed efforts, the know-how for building such weapons. Second, it's striking that Iraq directed its efforts at acquiring all basic aspects of the production of nuclear weapons. It developed parallel programs to obtain the fissionable materials, the weapons' designs, and the material for the weapons. Third, it worked on delivery systems—it didn't forget that. They especially studied missile technology, establishing a vast procurement system."

"How much of this was known before the Gulf War?" I asked.

"That Iraq had nuclear ambitions and a nuclear program was, I think, known to all the intelligence services. But it was not high on anyone's agenda. There was—certainly, I can speak for myself—a sort of Western arrogance. We thought that this Saddam Hussein might be able to talk a good game but not really do very much."

"What measures in the future could give confidence that secret programs like Iraq's could be detected in time?"

"There was no place in the world—not even the United States— that put together a systematic, comprehensive picture of what was going on in Iraq. Maybe the United States was more concerned with Iran and therefore overlooked the significance of exports of weapons technology to Iraq. Policy was guided by people looking more at the current geopolitical situation than at proliferation. Nor was there coordination among governments to put together the whole picture. Since then, there has been improvement in cooperation among the supplier countries.

"The problem is large because of growing transfers of technology in the global economy. The transfer of technology is a good thing, but it can also be an agent of weapons proliferation. What we need to put at the top of the agenda is transparency. For example, a special export-import control requirement has been adopted for Iraq by the U.N. Security Council. It requires all member states to notify the Special Commission about exports to Iraq of any items that the commission has listed as dual-purpose—that is, items that can be used for legitimate purposes, such as pesticide and fertilizer production, but also can be used for the production of weapons. The beautiful thing is that this gives the Special Commission access to information about where the items end up, so it can then make sure they are being used only for nonprohibited purposes. This is an idea with a great future, I believe. Ironically, Iraq finds it not such a bad thing. It permits states to trade with Iraq, and even sell it fairly advanced equipment. Iraq must accept openness, transparency, and control. But in return it will get technology. That is the trade-off."

Ekeus went on to say that the principle underlying this trade-off could be enlarged to bring about a transformation in the whole field of arms control. "The key is the preventive character of this program," he explained. "Now, we make a report only if there is a violation, and then there is the right to inspect and intervene. It's after the fact. But under a transparency regime, operating according to the principle of the trade-off, you would detect adverse trends early. There would be a much richer menu of actions, not merely punishment after the fact. There could be a constructive dialogue, international agreement to block certain equipment, a procedure for grievances—all sorts of creative things. In general, countries that wanted advanced technology would be able to get it, but only by accepting controls.

"You would have to proceed carefully, because it would be very easy to destroy. Some countries might refuse all half-measures and hold out for complete disarmament. This is the argument India has used to reject the Comprehensive Test-Ban Treaty. It must be understood that this would be a major undertaking. It would mean the creation of an international database. One difficulty is commercial confidentiality, which must be protected. But I believe that the obstacles could be overcome."

I asked Ekeus what his position was, in light of all he had learned, on the abolition of nuclear weapons.

"I don't believe," he said, "that nuclear weapons provide any state with real security. The Gulf War was an enormous display of what can be done with the opposite of nuclear weapons—namely, high-tech, precision arms. The interest of military people now is chiefly in these. For the most advanced states, the fact that interest in nuclear weapons is declining is very important. They have become rather absurd, esoteric, big, clumsy clubs—it is difficult to outline a scenario for the use of nuclear weapons."

I sketched out the argument that an abolition agreement would be undermined by cheating or breakout.

"Yes, there is something to this argument. Yet if you suppose that Iraq had acquired one bomb, which was highly possible, and the United States had no bomb, I doubt that it would have made any difference. Would the United States blow up Iraq with a nuclear bomb? It's not credible. But the United States could easily take other measures. What's more invaluable is good intelligence, good surveillance. Or let's say Iraq blew up Tel Aviv, or an American carrier in the Gulf. What would be the appropriate response? To blow up Baghdad? Again, the United States would use its smart weapons.

"So I don't entirely deny that there is an argument in favor of keeping nuclear weapons, but what is the argument against? There is one very powerful argument: that if they exist they can be used, bringing enormous destruction, killing hundreds of thousands of people. And to what end? I mean these are such base, negative, primitive calculations that it is almost inconceivable modern man can entertain them if he has any pretensions to moral responsibility. I have spoken to many specialists in this field, including enthusiasts of nuclear weapons, and no one has ever been able to say there's a system that can preclude their use. They can say the odds are low, but they can never say that a system is foolproof. The only way to prevent their use is to get rid of all of them.

"Second, as long as some countries possess them, it is inevitable that you will have proliferation. Let us consider the case of Israel. I have great respect for Israel. I do not believe that its leaders would ever use these weapons in an irresponsible fashion. It's a highly civilized, responsible society, in spite of all its tensions. But by apparently having this weapon they create the urge for Iraq to have the weapon. It's sort of a disease that spreads from one country to another. So in the long term I think it is a necessity for all nuclear-weapon states to eliminate their nuclear weapons. Or consider South Asia. China's nuclear armaments ensure that the Indians will hold onto their nuclear weapons option. I have discussed the question with Indian strategists. I point out that in its relations with Pakistan, India would gain by eliminating nuclear weapons, because it would be left with its superior conventional forces. And Pakistan already says it is ready to give up its nuclear weapons option, providing India does the same. But then the Indians say, 'Yes, but we have to worry about China.' It's not a private matter, having a nuclear weapon. You poison the well.

"Today, it's feasible for almost any country at the technical level of Iraq, or probably lower, to obtain nuclear weapons. Consider Serbia. It is more advanced than Iraq. Its missile system definitely is better."

"Some say that nuclear weapons can't be abolished because they can't be disinvented," I observed.

"That is a very weak argument, in my opinion. We learned how to build zeppelins, but we don't say that because we can build zeppelins we are going to. I don't think nuclear weapons are very useful. They are outdated, outmoded."

"Then you reject the argument that abolition is impossible because the inspection question can't be dealt with."

"It can be dealt with," this dismantler of Iraq's arsenals of mass destruction said.

MAJ BRITT THEORIN

At a Canberra Commission meeting on Long Island, I spoke with Dr. Maj Britt Theorin, a former member of the Swedish Parliament who served for nine years as Sweden's ambassador for disarmament and is now a member of the European Parliament. I asked her to assess European opinion on the nuclear question.

By way of illustration, she described to me the reaction in Sweden and in the European Parliament to French nuclear testing in 1995. "I've been involved in nuclear disarmament for twenty years, and the strength of the reaction surprised me. For instance, in Sweden, sales of French wine dropped by 50 percent. We have a water festival in Stockholm, and some restaurant owners as well as ordinary people poured French champagne into the streets. The reaction in Sweden was especially strong, but it was strong throughout Europe. Polls showed that a majority of the French were against the testing. And France is probably the last bastion of support for nuclear weapons.

"You know, on the very day that Chirac decided to start testing, our [European] Parliament demanded that our president tell Chirac that we don't accept it. Chirac addressed the Parliament two weeks later, and I was there. I climbed over some small barriers on the side on which he would enter. In my hand I held a small poster showing an atom bomb with 'No!' written over it. A security guy tried to stand in the way so Chirac wouldn't see the paper. He was greeting people and smiling from ear to ear. After he had walked about a half-yard past me I said, in my best French, '*Monsieur le President*,' and he turned back to me. I was glad I was a woman. I held up my poster. You should have seen his face. He was so confused, he didn't know what to do. And suddenly—you know the French—he said, *'Merci.'* If he had said 'Mercy' I could have understood it. When he tried to give his speech, about two-thirds of the Parliament rose to its feet and chanted, 'No! No!' and wouldn't let him speak for five or six minutes."

"What do you think the reaction would be in France to an initiative to abolish nuclear weapons?"

"If you have a good idea, and introduce it at the wrong time and place, it may not amount to anything," she replied. "But when you have the right idea in the right place and at the right time, you can make things happen. And that, I think, is the case now with the idea of a nuclear-weapon-free world.

"The French traditionally have said that they would be willing to get rid of their nuclear weapons when everyone else did. In the Cold War, the statement didn't cost them much. Therefore, what the United States and Russia do is essential. If you propose a program in which the two great nuclear powers are committing themselves to a nuclear-weapon-free world, then it will be quite impossible for France, Britain, or even China to say, 'We won't do it.' They have always stated that if the two great powers commit themselves first, they will come on board."

HARALD MÜLLER

The concept of virtual arsenals makes some abolitionists unhappy. They don't like the idea that the answer to the violation of an abolition treaty might be nuclear rearmament by the potential victims. When I described the idea of horizontal disarmament to McNamara, I found him open-minded but largely unimpressed. I began by describing the steps along the horizontal path, starting with de-alerting and continuing through de-mating to some further state of disassembly.

"Well, that's all right," he answered. "But I don't think you solve the problem that way. I believe that we should, in effect, get rid of them—I mean literally, physically get rid of them, with no remnants, except those that are commercially available. You'd have those components remaining, together with the ideas in men's minds. The point I would make is that you can still have breakout from your horizontal position. And this is what you have to guard against.

"Otherwise, you will have this material spread out, separated by a hundred miles, with pieces tagged and monitored by international inspectors, and so forth, yet it will still be possible for a nation— particularly the Russians but others as well—to obtain or create components that are not monitored and put a group together to build nuclear warheads. Then they could come to us one day, and say, 'Ah ha! You and we agreed to keep this horizontal standard, and we've abided by it, but now we have a hundred warheads, and we're going to launch them unless you do A, B, and C.' That's what you've got to protect against. There are various ways of doing it. But this is a problem that has *not* been adequately thought through."

When I asked Rotblat—who has opposed nuclear weapons from a time when only "virtual arsenals" can be said to have existed—for his reaction to future virtual arsenals, he replied, "I'm not happy about using this argument. It works against us. Suppose that in a truly nuclear-weapon-free world there is a dispute between two nations— India and China, for example. Let's say that they then decide they want to build up new nuclear arsenals. I'm saying that it would take quite a while for them to build up. This time could be used to solve the problem in other ways."

"But suppose those methods were to fail?" I asked. "Isn't it worthwhile pointing out now that the threatened countries would then be able to build nuclear weapons themselves?"

"Logically, you're right," he said, "but I would rather put the emphasis on the thought that we are creating a system that would make this very unlikely."

Blair, like Rotblat and McNamara, was uneasy with the idea of relying on nuclear rearmament as a solution to breakout. "It's not at all clear to me," he said, "that a nuclear response or capacity for response is needed to deal with the knowledge that makes it possible to build nuclear weapons, which will always exist in the world. There are other approaches that might work and that should at least be pursued first. They are based on trying to escape the deterrence trap—on approaches

that don't even invoke a nuclear response. It seems to me that you want
to develop a concept that allows you to escape the very idea of having
to think about mutual deterrence.

"Perhaps we have stopped our thinking too soon. By steadily lowering our nuclear profile we can at some point all but remove mutual
nuclear deterrence as the operative concern and allow other concepts
of relations among countries to take its place. And that has to be
some sort of cooperative security. You imagine a relationship similar to
the British-American alliance, in which both countries have nuclear
weapons, but there is no relationship of deterrence between them.

"There are many ways you can imagine escaping this relationship,"
Blair added. "One is to deploy massive defenses. Another is to acquire
overwhelming offensive superiority. But these two approaches don't
work. Another way is to have nuclear forces that can't reach each
other—as is the case, for example, with China and France. They're not
exactly on friendly terms and they both deploy nuclear weapons; but
somehow—because of lack of range, lack of planning—there is not
really an operative relationship of nuclear deterrence. That's another
reason for de-alerting. Even with a lot of weapons, de-alerting can move
you, in a sense, out of range of one another. You are moved not in physical distance but in time.

"There is also nuclear disarmament. That could eliminate deterrence. Then there's zero legitimacy. Biological weapons have something
close to zero legitimacy. Under the biological weapons convention,
you're not allowed to develop, test, stockpile, or use them. It's zero. I
would be content if nuclear weapons were driven to that point."

Somewhere in the chaff of all the argumentation pitting abolitionism against possessionism, minimum deterrence against extended
deterrence, antinuclear defenses against antidefense agreements, virtual against real arsenals, and virtual arsenals against more radical
versions of zero, there lurked a basic question whose answer was surprisingly elusive. The question was: What is zero? That is to say, what is
abolition? Sometimes it seemed that there were as many definitions of
abolition as there were abolitionists. The simple and clear-sounding
idea of zero became blurrier when examined in detail. The forest of
zero threatened to get lost in the trees of virtual arsenals.

This concern was thrown into sharp relief in a conversation I had in Frankfurt with Harald Müller, director of the Peace Research Institute Frankfurt, an organization founded by the government of the state of Hesse that counsels the federal government on disarmament issues. The meeting began as an interview, developed into something of a debate, and ended on a note of agreement that, for me, helped elucidate the shape (or shapes) of zero.

Müller was well acquainted with the proposals for weaponless deterrence or virtual nuclear arsenals, and he opposed them. Traditional abolitionists agree with the possessionists on one point: they place no faith in the capacity of nations threatened with breakout in a nuclear-weapon-free world to protect themselves by rebuilding their nuclear arsenals.

"Basically, I should tell you that I feel extremely strongly that virtual arsenals basically defeat the objective and the idea of zero," he began. "The first reason is that they would universalize the idea of nuclear deterrence and thus legitimize it. Therefore, the policy would undo more than three decades of successful efforts in the vast number of nonnuclear states to delegitimize the idea of nuclear weapons."

Müller's worry stemmed from a deep-seated resistance to what he considered a "typically American idea": that "the diffusion of technology leads automatically to more and more countries acquiring weapons of mass destruction."

"If you look at the nuclear sector," he said, "you've got fifty-odd countries that technically are capable of building nuclear weapons. But they don't do it. That was a decision. In the field of chemical and biological weapons, the number of candidates is even larger. But they don't build those weapons either. My point is that proliferation doesn't occur because countries say to themselves, 'Hey, we've got the technology—let's make the bomb!' There are only a handful of countries that want these weapons.

"There is a sickness in the American mind which says that everybody really wants to have the bomb because we have it and we don't want to get rid of it. But there is no evidence for this. Consider a country like Belgium, for instance. It has plutonium. But this does not mean it has a 'virtual arsenal.' It's so silly. It's not a virtual arsenal, because there is no thinking about nuclear weapons in any Belgian mind. They used to think about them, but now it's gone. We have to beat back this sick culture that tells us that everybody wants the bomb."

Müller added that he was doing a study of eighteen countries, including Hungary, Spain, Germany, the Netherlands, Canada, Argentina, and Nigeria, that were presumed capable of building nuclear weapons but had not. "Many of these are countries that not only have renounced nuclear weapons but are working actively to stop proliferation. For example, Germany and Japan are countries that supported the indefinite extension of the Non-Proliferation Treaty. In other words, the story of renunciation is a much bigger story than the story of proliferation.

"What I find pernicious in the virtual arsenal idea," he went on, "is the description of any stage of zero as a stage of preparation. I'm sorry to say it, but this can only come from somebody who is already infected by nuclear-weapon thinking, and in a very dangerous way. In our part of the world—and in this I think I speak for many people in the non-nuclear states, including the nonaligned—we are not in a stage of preparation for making nuclear weapons. The Mexican nuclear energy program, for example, is not a stage of preparation, nor is the Swiss. On the one hand, we do not wish to encourage such countries, under an abolition agreement, to make such preparations. On the other hand, we cannot accept the idea that they would have no preparations while the former nuclear powers would have them. That is something that we would never, never accept. That would be discrimination, and it's absolutely impossible to get it accepted anywhere outside the states now in the privileged position of having nuclear weapons—if you want to call it a privilege.

"The second reason I oppose the idea of virtual arsenals is that military organizations will be tasked with the mission of returning to nuclear readiness. This creates a vested interest in the whole idea of nuclear deterrence, which would force states to move closer and closer to rearmament, until only the last turn of the screw was left. And if we get into such a screw-turning race, I predict, we will end in a very short time in a world in which several countries—presumably more than today—will have nuclear weapons. They will believe there is so much risk that another party is turning the screw that they had better do it. In addition, if we adopt virtual deterrence as our answer to cheating, we completely eliminate the need to think about alternatives. People can relax, and military men can rest on their fat behinds, their virtual nuclear behinds, and never think about the possibilities and necessities for conventional answers to nuclear challenges."

"Yet even today," I answered, "when nuclear weapons are not merely virtual but actual, military leaders scarcely neglect their conventional forces. In a world of virtual arsenals, it seems to me, they would worry even more about conventional forces, since they would know that the return from a zero world to nuclear armament would be a drastic, history-changing step. They would be likely to seek every possible alternative first. Also, I wouldn't say that virtual arsenals legitimize nuclear weapons; I would say that they *continue but decrease* a legitimacy that nuclear weapons already have in many minds. Finally, you say that Germany and Japan do not regard their latent capacities to build nuclear weapons as states of preparation for building nuclear weapons. I'm happy to hear this, and ready to give them credit. But in their case, isn't this because they have been sheltered under the nuclear umbrella of the United States? I'd be more interested in examples of countries that faced nuclear opponents without nuclear allies yet did not build nuclear weapons."

"You're right about Germany," he said, "but at the same time, you have to look at a process that has been under way in German opinion. If in the 1950s or 1960s you had asked a hundred members of the elite—military officers, political journalists, security analysts—whether, if the American nuclear umbrella were folded, Germany should go nuclear, probably eighty or ninety would have answered yes. But if you asked the same question today I would estimate the number of yeses at only about twenty-five."

"Speaking more generally," I answered, "I accept all of your criticisms of virtual arsenals if we are comparing them with some more thoroughgoing radical zero state, in which reliance on nuclear retaliation has been forgotten, as in Belgium, or replaced with something else. But the more important point of comparison for the time being, it seems to me, must be our present, nuclear-armed world. Let's not forget that today we live in a world of many nuclear weapons and that we'd like to get out of that world. In our world, as you well know, the inequality between the nuclear states and the nonnuclear states is total. If we insist that the only acceptable zero is one in which reliance on nuclear weapons has vanished entirely, then we may create a very high hurdle of political requirements, such as successful collective security arrangements, that must be met before we can reach abolition. Yet we know from history—from the League of Nations, from the United Nations—that global collective security is dauntingly hard to achieve.

"Every level approaching zero is also, whether we like it or not, a stage of potential return to nuclear armament. Therefore, to accept and acknowledge this in a treaty is only to accept what is inevitable. The virtual idea has the merit of grappling with what, after all, is the root fact of the nuclear age, namely, the knowledge of how to build nuclear weapons."

"I find two very different points in your remarks," Müller answered. "The first I think well worth considering and might associate myself with. The second I find extremely dangerous and pernicious and, as a citizen of a nonnuclear state, would clearly and openly dissociate myself from. The first point is the idea that we can treat the virtual arsenal, or the various stages on the way to virtuality, as a transition period—a necessary transition period—from today's world to the world I wish to see."

"Could you define zero in that world?"

"It would be a world in which the answer to cheating is clearly defined as a conventional response, and in which nuclear possession and use is outlawed for any purpose."

"Would you make the treaty legally irreversible, specifying that even if one country were to rebuild nuclear forces, it would be illegal for its intended victim to rebuild?"

"Not right away," he answered.

"The key question then would be not just what level of technical nuclear preparation or technical devolution you would ordain in the treaty," I said, "but rather the point at which, as a matter of government policy, you would stop relying on those preparations and be ready to agree to that restriction in a global treaty."

"That's a very important point—and it's where I would dissociate myself from what I take to be your position. The distinction between a fake zero—and I would call it fake—and the real zero is one that I really want to uphold."

The distinction that Müller had made seemed to me to go to the heart of the elusive definition of zero. "So your true zero is defined as renunciation," I noted. "It is not a level of technical preparation or devolution. Rather, true zero is the moment when governments, for one reason or another, no longer look at the preparations as operational material but rather as just some old garbage."

"That's correct."

In our conversation, I commented, zero seemed to have divided itself in two. On the one hand there was the idea of technical zero—a destination very difficult to define. On the other hand, there was what we might call political zero, or else zero of the will, definable as the point at which, even though a country's technical capacity for returning to nuclear arms remained, the government did not rely on it, even in the remotest contingency, for national defense.

I said that thanks to our conversation this dual concept of zero now seemed to me probably the most adequate. Müller, completing the moment of harmony (peace, if you like) that had concluded our amicable debate, said that for his part he no longer thought of virtual arsenals as something he "outright rejected" but as a "potentially useful stage in the whole disarmament process."

IV

RUSSIA

THE SOVIET UNION AND RUSSIA

All countries that have possessed nuclear weapons have held them in secrecy, but in no country was it deeper than in the Soviet Union. Within the labyrinth of Soviet power, the bomb occupied the innermost, least-illumined chamber. So deep was this concealment that Soviet arms control diplomats were at times reduced to seeking basic facts about their country's arsenal from their U.S. counterparts at the negotiating table. Soviet academic writings likewise were given to citing American sources. Only the concentration camp system, with which the nuclear program in fact overlapped at many points, was as thoroughly hidden. It was no accident that Stalin appointed the same man—Lavrenti Beria, the head of the Soviet secret police—to preside over both. Only recently, with the opening of some of the former Soviet Union's archives, have studies such as David Holloway's book *Stalin and the Bomb* and Bruce Blair's *The Logic of Accidental Nuclear War* begun to lift the veil.

As a physical object, the Soviet bomb was of course substantially the same as the American bomb; but as a cultural, political, and moral presence it became something quite different. In the 1930s, before the possibility of making nuclear weapons was recognized, Holloway reports, the Soviet Union's community of nuclear physicists shared the fate of the entire elite of the Soviet Union: it was ravaged by Stalin's purges. In the 1940s, however, as Stalin and Beria slowly began to awaken to the power of nuclear energy, the physicists came to enjoy a degree of protection from the regime's terror. The paradoxical consequence was that at this intersection of the two innermost circles of Stalin's inferno—at the point of overlap, that is, of Soviet concentration camp terror and Soviet nuclear terror—there was born among the nuclear scientists what Holloway calls "a small element of civil society in a state that strove for totalitarian control over the life of society." (Something of the almost unimaginable atmosphere prevailing in this community is suggested by the saying, current in the late 1940s, when the scientists were striving to provide Stalin with his first nuclear bomb, that the prizes they would receive if the bomb succeeded would be proportionate to the punishments they would get if it failed. Those to be shot in the case of failure would, in the case of success, be made Heroes of Socialist Labor—the state's highest honor—while those slated for prison if the bomb failed would, if it went off, receive mere Orders of Lenin—the second-ranking honor.) Because the nuclear scientists were able to supply the brute Stalin with the most brutal instrument of terror of his or any other age, they were permitted to live in a top-secret island of comparative safety. Here, at the very center of Stalin's web, under the direct supervision of Beria, there existed "the nearest approximation to a citizen that could be found in Soviet society as a whole." Holloway notes the further irony that "the atomic bomb, the most potent symbol of the hostility between the Soviet Union and the West, saved a community that constituted an important link between the West and the Soviet Union." (One of the crucial links in that chain was Rotblat's Pugwash movement, which maintained contacts between Western and Soviet scientists even during some of the coldest years of the Cold War.)

If we are tempted to suspect that the idealism and "citizenship" of these figures occupying lofty positions in the "nuclear gulag" were merely a privileged elite's rationalization of its service to a hateful system, we need only remind ourselves of the luminous, courageous career of the best of their number, Andrei Sakharov, father alike of the Soviet hydrogen bomb and the Soviet human rights movement. His early pamphlet "Reflection on Progress, Peaceful Coexistence, and Intellectual Freedom," published in 1968, amounted to a credo of this hidden, liberal-minded community of scientists. Sakharov hoped, he wrote, that the Soviet and Western political systems would "converge," permitting both nuclear disarmament and liberalization of the Soviet system. Only later was he forced into the position of thoroughgoing "dissident" against the regime. There is, indeed, a profound consistency between Sakharov's eventual opposition to the regime and his opposition to the nuclear arms race, inasmuch as the stock-in-trade of both was, in the last analysis, terror. A similar consistency appears in the very different career of Mikhail Gorbachev, who, while Sakharov was being trod underfoot by the Soviet state, was rising to its apex. He, too, was both a liberalizer and a nuclear disarmer. (It is thus fitting that Gorbachev's telephone call to Sakharov ending his internal "exile" in the city of Gorky was a milestone on the road to *glasnost*.)

Notwithstanding the inner consistency of totalitarian methods of rule and nuclear threats, nuclear weapons never played the role in Soviet consciousness that they played in American consciousness. In the Soviet Union, there was no flowering of a distinctive nuclear doctrine comparable to nuclear deterrence. There was, for better or worse, no Soviet Thomas Schelling, Henry Kissinger, or Herman Kahn—no butting of big Communist brains against the barriers of "the unthinkable." On the contrary, Soviet nuclear doctrine remained poorly developed and obscure. At first subordinated to Marxist dogma, it later became imitative of U.S. thinking. In the 1970s, Soviet leaders, who had indignantly rejected the paradoxical requirements of deterrence— that, for example, one must not seek to defend one's cities from nuclear attack—suddenly embraced this U.S. doctrine. The fruit of the resulting meeting of minds was the SALT I agreement of 1972, whose centerpiece was a sharp limit on antiballistic missile systems. It was not until Gorbachev set out on his path of transforming the Soviet system and ending the Cold War that the Soviet Union became an innovator in nuclear policy.

The reasons for Soviet "backwardness" in developing a nuclear policy are many. One was simply lack of freedom. The invention of the bomb seemed to call for a revolution in military thinking, but Soviet thinkers were as unfree to challenge orthodoxy in this field as in others. Stalin failed throughout the Second World War to appreciate the potential of the atomic bomb, even though his spies were giving him voluminous reports on the progress of the Manhattan Project. Holloway has shown that even the news of the successful American test of the first atomic bomb at Alamogordo, delivered to Stalin personally by Truman at the Potsdam meeting in July of 1945, failed to goad Stalin into providing adequate resources to the Soviet nuclear weapons program. Only the concussion of Hiroshima moved him to act. The initial failure of the Soviet leaders to adequately support their atomic scientists, Holloway concludes, "suggests that the atomic bomb had no reality for them in the summer of 1945, that they had no conception of the impact it was about to have on world politics." (This was the second time that Stalin had shown himself unable to appreciate clear signs of a forthcoming revolutionary military development—the first being his catastrophic failure to anticipate Hitler's attack on the Soviet Union in June of 1941.) It is a tribute—though perhaps a dubious one—to the leaders of democratic America and England that they had the imagination, when given the relevant information by competent scientists, to grasp enough of the immense import of the proposed device to set about spending billions of dollars to create it.

A second reason for Soviet backwardness in nuclear matters was geographic and strategic. Owing to the size of its conventional military forces and its proximity to Europe, the Soviet Union enjoyed, in the opinion of both sides, conventional superiority in what was assumed to be the main theater of confrontation of the Cold War. Soviet nuclear weapons could be relegated to a secondary role there. The United States, by contrast, compensated for its perceived conventional inferiority by threatening to use nuclear weapons to stop a conventional Soviet attack in Europe.

A third reason for the backwardness was the fact that from start to finish of the Cold War the Soviet Union lagged behind the United

States in the development of nuclear technology. In 1940, for example, Soviet scientists learned of the importance of uranium in the production of nuclear energy in an article in the *New York Times* sent to the nuclear physicist V. I. Vernadsky by his son, who was studying in the United States. "This was the first news about the discovery to reach me, and to reach Moscow in general," the father wrote back to the son. "I quickly set things in motion." Although Soviet nuclear physicists were outstanding and surely would have succeeded in building an atomic bomb by their own efforts sooner or later, the fact remains that the general design of the first Soviet bomb was an American one, delivered into their hands by the spy Klaus Fuchs. Thereafter, with the exception of the intercontinental ballistic missile, every major innovation in nuclear arms—the intercontinental-range bomber; the hydrogen bomb; the solid-fuel rocket; the nuclear-powered submarine, with its submarine-launched, nuclear-armed ballistic missiles; the multiple independently targetable reentry vehicle; and, finally, the techniques for strategic nuclear defense—was pioneered by the United States.

Atomic weapons loomed larger in the American than in the Soviet mind for another reason as well. In the Second World War, the United States developed them in time to use them—at Hiroshima and Nagasaki. The bomb thereby became associated with the American victory in the Pacific and, soon after, with its new position of dominance in the Cold War world. Nuclear weapons were—and are—an enormous undigested fact of U.S. history (as was made clear by the 1994–95 controversy over the Smithsonian Air and Space Museum's exhibit of the *Enola Gay*, the plane used to drop the Hiroshima bomb).

The Soviet Union, on the other hand, won its Second World War with conventional weapons. Whatever else was on the Soviet conscience, the actual use of nuclear weapons was not. Soviet propagandists saw in this fact a welcome opportunity to brand the United States a brutal aggressor and to style itself the leader of "the peace camp" (though no criticism from that camp of Soviet nuclear policies was tolerated). America's use of the bomb and its brief postwar nuclear monopoly also justified the Soviet program in the minds of those working in it. Andrei Sakharov never repented his role in delivering the

H-bomb into Stalin's hands. Long after he had become a renowned human rights activist, he continued to believe that his act had been necessary to create a balance of power between the two great states.

When the Soviet Union was overthrown, the newborn Russian Federation fell heir to its nuclear arsenal. The handover—the first case in history in which the nuclear button was passed by an ancien régime to its overthrowers—was accomplished through a double transfer. First, the Russian military command transferred its loyalty from the Soviet Union to the Commonwealth of Independent States. Second, the former U.S.S.R.'s non-Russian republics on whose soil nuclear weapons were stationed agreed to send them to Russia for dismantlement. Nuclear weapons, the front line of defense for the Soviet empire, had proved entirely powerless to prevent its dissolution. The sole desideratum, shared by virtually all parties, was to pass the bombs safely into the hands of the new government.

The Soviet imperial nuclear arsenal was dead. The Russian national arsenal was born. But what was its mission? Could nuclear arms protect the Russian Federation? Against whom? According to which tactics and strategy? Was Russia more likely or less likely than its Soviet predecessor to agree to the control, reduction, or abolition of nuclear weapons?

In Russia, I raised these and other questions with a number of active and retired military figures, political analysts, and present and former officials. It is scarcely surprising that in the wake of the triple collapse of the Communist regime, the multinational union over which it ruled, and the global Cold War system of which it formed one side, the nuclear policies of the new possessor state should be nebulous. Russia's most pressing security need was to deal with centrifugal forces within the Russian Federation, including, above all, the rebellion in Chechnya. Only slightly less pressing were the ethnic and national wars blazing within and between nearby republics of the former Soviet Union. It was evident to everyone with whom I spoke that nuclear weapons were of no use in any of these conflicts.

"With regard to the separatist tendencies within Russia," General Leonid Grigorievich Ivashov said to me, "it's clear that nuclear weapons play no part." Even conventional weapons, he noted, had proved of limited value. "When military forces go to war," he observed, "it means that politics has failed to solve the problem. In the world at large, the United Nations and regional international organizations are still trying to elaborate some means for dealing with the outbreak of local conflicts. In some respects, the Commonwealth of Independent States has gone farther than the world community in addressing these problems. We have accepted the idea that we need to work not so much on intervening in these conflicts once they have arisen but in preventing them beforehand. I'd like to say that the military took the lead in suggesting these ideas for prevention—including political pressure and economic pressure—in the last years of the former Soviet Union. We know better than anyone that once a conflict is started, thousands of people will die and cities will be destroyed. Then the politicians turn the issues they have failed to solve over to soldiers. The politicians lock themselves in their cabinet rooms and await developments without. Next, they declare the military guilty: 'They have killed people,' they say, 'they have destroyed cities'; whereas in fact they are themselves guilty. For these are above all political problems, for which it is very difficult to find military solutions. That's why many of us in the military urge political solutions to these problems."

Dr. Michail Gerasov, deputy director of the U.S.A.-Canada Institute in Moscow, even feared that Russia's continued heavy reliance on nuclear forces might produce a "deformation" of Russian military thinking, since "nuclear weapons have nothing to do with regional or local conflict of the kind we have had in Afghanistan and Chechnya." It was more important, he said, to have "effective, well-equipped, well-trained general purpose conventional forces, organized to deal with the actual threats that Russia is facing."

It was only at the level of global security, General Ivashov remarked, that nuclear weapons remained important in Russian policy. Yet it was in just this sphere, of course, that the end of the Cold War had brought the deepest changes. In the first few years of the post-Soviet era, hopes had run high in Moscow that the former hostility of the superpowers might turn into friendship in an equal degree. The creation of the Marshall Plan to help the nations of Europe, including America's enemies in the Second World War, seemed to offer a clear precedent for such a turnabout, as did the foundation of NATO, which eventually came to include Western Germany and Italy. In 1991, President Yeltsin went as far as to suggest Russian membership in NATO. It seems likely that had such an alliance been forged it would have superseded the system of mutual nuclear deterrence. There is no need, after all, to deter those with whom one is allied. When, for reasons having mainly to do with domestic politics, Presidents Bush and Clinton both steered clear of any such embrace of newly democratic Russia, a feeling of disappointment and lost opportunity became palpable, especially in and around official circles in Russia.

The political analyst Alexander Konovalov described this disappointment to me in vivid terms. "When democratization began in the Soviet Union and, later, in Russia," he said, "many of the international steps taken by our leaders, including our withdrawal from Eastern Europe, were presented, in part at least, as concessions in preparation for our entry into the family of democratic nations, which would help us solve all our problems. Of course, expectations were too high. The idea of cooperation was oversold by the West and, even more, over-bought by Russia. This spirit of openness, frankness, and trust has now been lost. I doubt it can be revived in my lifetime. It was a situation in which it was possible to do immense things. One writer even wrote in 1992 that Russia had lost the third world war but, unfortunately, nobody would come to occupy us, even if we were to pay."

With the decision to expand NATO to include Poland, Hungary, and the Czech Republic but not Russia, disappointment acquired an edge of resentment. "Usually," Konovalov said, "the winners of the last war lay the foundations for the next era's security arrangements. This may be done even during the war, as at Yalta. But the end of the Cold War came as a complete surprise to everyone. At first, the West could scarcely believe it was true. Then it started to believe: we are the winners. But instead of proposing a new security system, it seemed that the West simply decided to share out the spoils. Of course, no one is afraid of American or NATO aggression tomorrow, but people no longer think the United States is a friend of ours. They are beginning to think the United States needs a weak, humbled Russia, perhaps as a source of cheap labor and raw materials."

The NATO expansion also reinforced the rationale for nuclear weapons in Russian thinking. In Russia, that expansion began to play a role similar to that played in the United States by fears of a possible collapse of Russian democracy. "The real challenges of Russia's future are in the south and the Far East," Konovalov said. "But because of NATO expansion, the West forces Russia to think about the European theater. Unfortunately, NATO enlargement means nuclearization of the European security issue, and this is occurring, by the way, according to a logic that coincides exactly with the logic that your generals taught our generals in the 1960s and 1970s. They told us in those years that they were not rich enough (and, reading between the lines, not stupid enough) to pay for sixty thousand tanks to balance Soviet conventional forces, and therefore they had to resort to a cheap equalizer, namely, tactical nuclear weapons. Now, as state after state leaves Russia and joins NATO, you hear that same reasoning in Russia. I'm not sure it will become state policy, but it is prevalent in military circles."

Major General Vladimir Belous, retired, who often writes on nuclear matters, similarly remarked to me—and his was a typical comment—that "for now, nuclear weapons, including the tactical ones, will be one of the principal means for Russia's defense, because of its conventional inferiority and its economic weakness." In 1993, in fact, Russia had abandoned the Soviet Union's no-first-use policy for a first-use one similar to NATO's.

For decades, Soviet strategists, like Soviet technicians, had been adapting Western nuclear inventions and ideas; now, in one of the stranger of the many strange twists of post–Cold War politics, a Western concept, deterrence, would serve to tighten Russia's grip on its nuclear arsenal. "Now nuclear deterrence has become a positive notion in Russia," Sergei Rogoff, the director of the U.S.A.-Canada Institute and an arms control expert, commented. "It's claimed that nuclear deterrence will prevent any kind of aggression against Russia. In this respect, Russia, while adopting some of the stupider notions of the Soviet regime, is also adopting some of the stupider American notions of the Cold War period, producing what in my opinion is an amalgamation that is rather ugly."

These specific new reasons for prizing nuclear weapons coincided with a vague and more general reason. Russia, as General Ivashov reminded me, wished to remain a great power. A great power, he reckoned, could be identified by six characteristics: a large territory, a large population, powerful conventional forces, a strong economy, membership in the U.N. Security Council, and possession of a strategic nuclear arsenal. Moscow's geographical sway (including its Eastern European satellites) has in recent years diminished by more than 25 percent; its conventional forces are in disarray; its economy in a state of semi-collapse. That leaves a large population, membership in the Security Council, and strategic weapons. "Russia wants to remain in the club of great powers. Therefore, it is not eager to give its nuclear forces away," he said. Nevertheless, Ivashov favored a negotiated elimination of nuclear weapons.

The new appeal of nuclear weapons is to some extent mitigated by other factors. For Russia as for the United States, the leftover nuclear "confrontation," however distressing on paper, remains an almost entirely formalistic affair, unsupported by even minor political conflicts. It is an outline of a prospective conflict that, for the time being, happily lacks any actual content. In Russia, as in the West, the former Cold War foe, though now a declared friend, serves as a sort of straw man for military planning. The traditional laws of the balance of power, which dictate that one must respond to a rival's capacities, not his intentions, seem to require that Russia respond to NATO's advance, yet few Russians, whether in official circles or on the streets, foresee actual military threats from the West. (Fear of trouble from Russia's east is far keener.) Still, within the framework of this formal thinking, Russian arsenals have come to play a more prominent role in military strategy than Soviet arsenals did. On the other hand, Russian observers, when invited to look beyond present circumstances, are far readier than most Americans to embrace radical solutions, including the idea of abolishing nuclear weapons.

MIKHAIL GORBACHEV

Mikhail Gorbachev presents the world with the paradox of a man who rose like a cork from the bottom to the very top of an immense, repressive political system but, once there, adopted policies that brought the system crashing down around his ears. Its downfall had not, however, been his goal. He aimed merely to reform the Soviet Union, not abolish it. On the other hand, he did wish to abolish nuclear weapons. It is one of the ironies of the Cold War that he reached the unintended goal but fell short of the intended one. There remains, as Alan Cranston once commented to me, at least one consistent principle in all his actions: a turn away from violence as a political instrument. If anything about the fall of the Soviet Union surprised the world more than the fall itself, it was the peacefulness with which, under Gorbachev's leadership, it occurred.

As a public speaker, Gorbachev retains some of the woodenness of his Communist predecessors. In person, there is more sparkle in his eyes, more warmth in his smile. Yet he struck me as a solitary figure. As general secretary of the Communist Party and Soviet president, he had been surrounded by colleagues who proved unready to follow him and eventually betrayed him in the coup attempt of August 1991. Even while estranging the Communist Party, however, he did not succeed in retaining the support of the public. To a remarkable degree, he has propelled himself along his tumultuous course on his own steam. Only abroad has his popularity remained high. Now, as president of the Gorbachev Foundation, he tours the world advancing the causes in which he believes. Among them is still the abolition of nuclear weapons.

"When did you first have the idea of proposing the abolition of nuclear weapons?" I asked.

"It was connected with my arrival in the Kremlin," he answered. "The provincial elite, to which I belonged—and even the Moscow establishment—knew little about these weapons. Only when I became a member of the Politburo did I start to become involved in decision-making on matters of defense, and even then there were defense matters that were handled exclusively by the general secretary, the minister of defense, the chairman of the State Security Committee, the minister of foreign affairs, and sometimes the prime minister. It was really a small group. When I saw the monster that we and the United States had created as a result of the arms race, with all its mistakes and accidents with nuclear weapons and nuclear power—when I saw

the terrible amount of force that had been amassed—I finally understood what the consequences, including global winter, would be.

"I can assure you that by the time I became a member of the Politburo, the very tiny group of men who really made the decisions had
a full understanding that nuclear war was impossible. And, frankly,
NATO's strategy of initiating local nuclear war was, I think, bluffing. It
was clear to all that a nuclear war could not be won. So when I went to
London in 1984 as the number-two man in the Party, I said quite a few
things that later made up what I called 'the new thinking.' I said
nuclear war was impossible, and that conclusion was later reflected in
the proposal of January 15, 1986, to abolish nuclear weapons."

"Did you encounter much resistance to this proposal within your
government?" I asked.

"Not to the idea, not to the statement. But I must admit that most
of the military men thought this was just another propaganda bluff,
another deception. What hadn't our government proposed in earlier
days? There had been all sorts of 'peace programs,' 'peace initiatives,'
designed only to put the other side on the spot. My position was: This
plan is one that we should seek to implement. It was linked in my mind
with a proposal that General Secretary Khrushchev had espoused years
before—the idea of a world without weapons, of general and complete
disarmament. It may have been utopian, but it had an impact on the
minds of many people who were afraid of those mountains of weapons,
conventional as well as nuclear. So we seized on that idea, but we introduced it in more pragmatic form, calling for conventional weapons to
be controlled, so that nuclear weapons would not be replaced by all
sorts of new conventional arms.

"At that stage, we didn't encounter the kind of resistance we later
would when we began to discuss specific steps with the Reagan administration. There was, of course, some resistance later—and on the
American side as well. Each side wanted to drive such a hard bargain
that we were afraid to lose a single kopeck or cent. For a person looking
at it from without, this kind of negotiation must have looked ridiculous.
The real watershed was the summit at Reykjavik. It turned things completely upside down. It upset all those decades of calculations and unse-
rious negotiations. Of course, we had had SALT I, the Anti-Ballistic

Missile treaty, and the Non-Proliferation Treaty. Though still minor, they were important. But none of them actually put an end to the nuclear arms race. None of them provided for the actual destruction of nuclear weapons. These things became possible only after Reykjavik. Initially, my partners said on the first evening after the summit that it was a failure, but I said, 'No, it is a breakthrough.' Secretary of State George Shultz took a corresponding line, and the way to real reductions was opened."

"You were one of the few people who have had the unusual experience of possessing the final responsibility for a decision to use nuclear weapons," I observed. "Would you have given the order to use nuclear weapons in retaliation for a nuclear attack?"

"Well, let me tell you right off that this did not concern me, not because I lacked the will or the power, but because I was quite sure that the people in the White House were not idiots. I thought that they definitely knew what any nuclear war would mean, even if the weapons did not actually strike the Soviet Union or America. More likely, I thought, was that nuclear weapons might be used without the political leadership actually wanting this, or deciding on it, owing to some failure in the command and control systems. They say that if there is a gun, one day it will shoot. That fear motivated me to seek an end to the arms race, in spite of my belief that no one would consciously use nuclear weapons.

"I recall that when I was trained in the use of the nuclear button, or the nuclear suitcase, I once was briefed about a situation in which I would be told of an attack from one direction, and then, while I am thinking over what to do about that, new information comes in—during these very minutes—that another nuclear offensive is coming from another direction. And I am supposed to make the decisions!" Gorbachev laughed. "Nevertheless, I never actually pushed the button. Even during training, even though the briefcase was always there with my codes, and sometimes it had to be opened. I never touched the button."

I mentioned Cranston's remark that nonviolence seemed to be a constant theme of his career and invited him to comment.

"We had been through the long experience of the utopian model of society that was imposed on our people by Stalin. It left the country with a hard choice. Despite the fact that the Communists were so consistent—amazingly consistent—in pursuing this line, this policy of building the Communist model of society, and did not hesitate to use force and repression, we saw that force and violence were defeated by the logic of history, by the logic of things. We saw that the country had reached a historical impasse. The gap, which first emerged during the years of the civil war between the socialist system and democracy— the divorce of socialism from democracy, and the resulting attempt to impose a dictatorship—had led to the drastic situation we were now facing. In other words, the most important obstacle we faced was our own experience. Yes, indeed, you can destroy your enemy. You can destroy your ideological foe. You can actually destroy many, many people, or send them to camps, or anything you want. But historically, this does not win. This does not provide victory.

"Marx said that the capitalist system contains within it its own gravedigger, the proletariat. Rephrasing Marx, we can say that our system developed educated people, who were then the gravediggers of the Communist system. The utopian model of Communist, totalitarian dogma was rejected at the cultural level, and cultural rejection is the strongest form of rejection.

"The *shestidesyatniki*—the so-called men of the sixties, and I refer to myself as a *shestidesyatniki*—had a new vision, shaped by the atmosphere of those times. My credo was: We need radical reform without bloodshed, without violence. I arrived at that conclusion for domestic politics, but it was also a conclusion that I drew in the 'new thinking' on international affairs—in the understanding that we lived in an interdependent world and that the presence of nuclear weapons, a colossal threat to humankind, could run out of the control of politicians. So this resulted in an understanding that in the world, too, the use of violence is useless. Yes, you can achieve some temporary successes by using violence. But cooperation, interaction, partnership, trying to harmonize your interests with the interests of others—these are what really work. We cannot reject the interests of others, but instead need to balance our interests with their interests. And of course you cannot do that with war. You can only do it through political methods. So gradually all of this jelled into a certain way of thinking. All of these things are connected. They are links in one chain.

"It was this same belief that led me, right at the beginning, at the funeral of Chernenko [Gorbachev's predecessor as general secretary], to tell the Eastern European leaders, 'Now you are actually independent. You are free. You are responsible for your countries.' They thought this was another propaganda declaration by the general secretary. But I never went back on that declaration. It was a decisive step."

"Let's suppose that there is a treaty to abolish nuclear weapons," I said. "Should it include measures of enforcement? What should they be?"

"That question is very serious. You should not take this whole issue out of context. We will never be able to solve the nuclear question unless at the same time we develop a system of international organizations—unless we develop an effective United Nations, an effective Security Council, and effective systems of regional security—in short, unless we have an active political process. We should act preventively, preemptively. Force is used when a situation is already out of control. Why do we use force? Because we have grown accustomed to it and have failed to develop institutions that will harmonize interests. Of course, we cannot rule out the possibility that there might be some local conflicts in which the situation goes out of control. Therefore the international organization should have certain decision-making powers and mechanisms for enforcement. But the most important thing is to place controls on the whole weapons process. We are moving toward a new world. Yet nothing is being done right now to truly take advantage of the opportunities afforded by the end of the Cold War."

SERGEI KORTUNOV

Sergei Kortunov, who worked in the Foreign Ministry of the Soviet Union and has since worked on Yeltsin's staff, represents an element of continuity in nuclear policy. In his final years under Gorbachev,

Kortunov became a sharp critic of deterrence, and he has remained one. Like many Russians with whom I spoke, he was haunted by a feeling of lost opportunity.

I asked whether, in his opinion, Gorbachev's proposal to eliminate nuclear weapons had been seriously meant.

"It was really serious and honest," he answered. "It was elaborated in 1985 and 1986, in discussions with Marshal Akhromeyev and Defence Minister Sokoloff, and then proposed at the United Nations. It was not just a slogan."

I asked him what changes the end of the Cold War had brought to the shape of the nuclear dilemma.

"The most important point, perhaps, is that the policy of deterrence was a product of the Cold War, the result of a bipolar relationship. For instance, although France and the United States both had nuclear weapons, France obviously was not deterring the United States. In those years, in other words, the nuclear threat became personified: for the United States, it took the form of the Soviet threat, and for the Soviet Union it took the form of the American threat. This state of affairs has of course changed dramatically. The personification of the threat has ended. Russia and the United States began to look on one another as normal countries just as the nuclear danger began to proliferate to a number of other countries. For the first time in the history of the nuclear age, we got the chance to implement really dramatic cuts, and some even began to dream of going beyond the policy of deterrence."

"Whom do you have in mind?" I asked.

"There were proposals, in the late Bush years, to forge a partnership in nuclear matters between the United States and the Soviet Union, but they were not productive. At this point, I think we missed a historic opportunity. I may say that I don't think the fault in this case was entirely Russia's. The idea was received very, very warmly here. This was the result of a kind of euphoria that developed about relations with America. The whole idea of a partnership could be criticized, and it was criticized, both in the United States and in our country. Yet I think it was a noble idea. But our leaders did not address these questions seriously enough.

"Unfortunately, the negotiations were entrusted to military men and diplomats who were veterans of the Cold War. They were unable to escape its stereotypes. When they sat down together, they resorted to the old rules of negotiation.

"At the same time, the usual arms control talks under the START process were continuing. And here, too, of course, the teams were recruited from the negotiators who had been working on the Intermediate Range Forces treaty, the Anti-Ballistic Missile treaty, and so forth. All those treaties, of course, were based on the notion of nuclear deterrence. For instance, the United States was trying to get Russia to give up its heavy missiles, and the Russian negotiators were trying to reduce U.S. sea-launched forces. These considerations—the old logic of the Cold War—remained central.

"And that's why, when, in January 1993, President Bush and President Yeltsin signed START II, it was absolutely clear that we would have a hard time passing it in Parliament. In the eyes of parliamentarians, Russia had given up its most powerful weapons. And yet I remember someone on the Russian negotiating team once telling me that those heavy missiles were unusable. They were really 'political missiles.' Their purpose was to get the United States to take us seriously at the bargaining table."

"Do you think, then," I asked, "that the arms control negotiations became, thanks to their roots in the Cold War, an obstacle to a deeper change in the Russian-American relationship?"

"To some extent, that is correct," he answered. "Of course, politically there was, in fact, a great change; but it was not reflected in the military deployments. I'm not sure, but I still think the opportunity may be open. We'd need to ask ourselves: What would a real and meaningful partnership be? One important area would be not just the traditional area of non-proliferation but counter-proliferation—combining some of the traditional methods of non-proliferation with more active, non-traditional methods, even, possibly, with the use of military force in certain regions.

"Another area would be operational arms control. It is a brilliant idea. Foreign Minister Kozyrev, in 1992, advocated this idea in Geneva and proposed de-targeting. By the way, Kozyrev also mentioned further measures, like the decoupling of warheads and missiles. Some of our military people were very unhappy with this. They said it was absolutely impossible, because you would completely spoil your missile. On the other hand, as it turned out, after negotiations with the United Kingdom and the United States, de-targeting became a mere political declaration, with little technical consequence. As everyone knows, you can very rapidly re-target.

"A third area would be a reconsideration of defense. We believe that at present the Anti-Ballistic Missile treaty is a cornerstone of strategic stability, but it may be that political pressures in your country will force some revision. If the context is one of moving away from nuclear deterrence, then we can even imagine moving toward a defense-dominated model. In this context, the debate on the treaty might be resolved after all. The treaty, too, was a product of the Cold War. We have to address the whole offense-defense relationship.

"Deterrence, in fact, was always crazy and absurd, but now, with the Cold War over, it's even more crazy and absurd. It no longer corresponds to any logic or to common sense."

I summarized the difference between vertical, or numerical, nuclear disarmament and horizontal, or operational, nuclear disarmament and asked for his comments.

"I think that in the post–Cold War environment, operational is more important than numerical disarmament. The preference, at least, should be given to the operational. In the context of deterrence, there is a limit on numerical reductions. There is a contradiction between deterrence and partnership. Therefore, we must go beyond deterrence. Operational disarmament points us in this direction. De-alerting is the most important first step, but we should go farther. One important step would be mutual verification of nuclear weapons and materials— that is, accountability. Another would be to move from mere reduction in delivery vehicles to elimination of actual nuclear warheads. The steps should be irreversible. START I and START II do not provide irreversibility of nuclear disarmament. Still another step would be better joint early warning systems. This, too, is operational arms control. [I spoke to Kortunov before the round of negotiations in which some inspection measures and further reductions in warheads were agreed upon in principle for a future START III treaty.] Such actions are suited to a partnership, because they require a high level of mutual trust."

"Do you think that these steps can be the first along the path to the abolition of nuclear weapons, and do you think that this is a desirable goal to aim at?" I asked.

"It's absolutely clear that the goal is desirable. This is obvious and clear."

I mentioned some of the commonest objections to abolition, including the danger arising from cheating.

"If we are speaking of cheating by Iraq, North Korea, and so forth, we are speaking of first-generation weapons," he said. "A country like the United States, possessing the highest level of technology, could counter such threats quite easily."

I mentioned the argument that nuclear weapons can't be abolished because they can't be disinvented.

"That's one of the most important points," he said, "because even without nuclear weapons, the minds that know how to make them would not disappear, and the technology for building them would still exist, not only in the great countries but in others as well. This is the trend of civilization. They can be 'reinvented.' Yet, given that fact, the question is whether we are safer in a world that sanctions and possesses large nuclear arsenals or one that does not. Of course, we must proceed cautiously, bringing to bear political and diplomatic as well as technical measures. After all, our final goal should be to create a world in which not only does no one reinvent nuclear weapons but there is no need to reinvent them."

GYORGY AND ALEXEI ARBATOV

In the 1970s and 1980s, Gyorgy Arbatov was the director of the U.S.A.-Canada Institute, a prestigious Soviet think tank devoted to the study of the countries that are its namesakes. Arbatov served as an official point of contact for American visitors and also as an apologist for the Soviet regime before Western audiences. In this capacity, he wrote several pejorative books about the United States and appeared frequently on American television. When Gorbachev came to power, Arbatov joined the ranks of his supporters. In his memoir *The System*, Arbatov portrays himself as a liberal reformer struggling for the success of *perestroika* and *glasnost*. In the summer of 1991, when conservative Communists sought to overthrow Gorbachev and Yeltsin, Arbatov threw the support of his institute to their side.

Early in his career, Arbatov took an interest in the nuclear question. The Soviet Union's exploitation of the world peace movement as an instrument of propaganda gave Soviet writers leeway, within certain definite limits, to write in an antinuclear vein. Thus, real opposition to nuclear weapons was able to develop, to a modest extent, with official sanction. When this opposition reached the limits of the officially tolerable, a few people, such as Sakharov, went their individual ways. Many more remained within the fold. Arbatov was one of these.

In *The System*, he recounts a typical episode of official suppression of opposing views. Early in the 1960s, Arbatov joined with others in drafting an "Open Letter," which stated that "the atomic bomb does not hold to the class principle; it destroys everyone who falls within its destructive range." This simple acknowledgment of the power of nuclear arms, however, ran counter to Soviet policy, which held that the socialist bloc would defeat the imperialist bloc in a nuclear war. Therefore, an "editor" added a contradictory sentence, which read: "Of course, it is incontestable that if the imperialist madmen should, nonetheless, start a war, the socialist nations will sweep away and bury capitalism." (In John F. Kennedy's Washington, a similar debate on whether it was possible to win a nuclear war was then under way.)

While Gyorgy Arbatov presided over the U.S.A.-Canada Institute, his son Alexei was getting an academic schooling in the nuclear question at the Institute of World Economy and World Relations. Like his father, Alexei proved an enthusiast of both Gorbachev's internal reforms and his dovish international policy, including his proposal to abolish nuclear arms. After the Soviet Union dissolved, Alexei won a seat in the Russian Parliament, and today he is the deputy chairman of its Committee on Defense. Although father and son are still in broad agreement on nuclear issues, they nevertheless represent two different—

and, to a modest degree, opposed—strains of Russian thinking on nuclear weapons.

Gyorgy represents the tendency by which what once had been mere Communist peace propaganda became, in the hands of Gorbachev, the basis for the radical shift in policy that brought about the end of the Cold War. Gorbachev's resolve to change Soviet society, many observers believe, stemmed as much from his zeal as a sincere Communist as from any doubts about Communism. In the words of the scholar Charles Fairbanks, "One of the elements that produced the collapse of communism in the eighties was the return, in Gorbachev, of the enduring revolutionary desire to re-structure society." In the Soviet Union of the 1980s, taking Communist ideals at face value was a revolutionary program. Something similar appears to have contributed to Gorbachev's revolution in foreign policy. Communist peace propaganda of the 1960s and 1970s became an authentically revolutionary (or counter-revolutionary, if you like) program in the 1980s.

Alexei, on the other hand, may be said to represent the new tendency of Russian nuclear thinking in which the weakness of Russia justifies adoption of the American doctrine of deterrence, which Alexei has thoroughly mastered. Gyorgy remains an abolitionist—if a somewhat weary and unhopeful one—while Alexei favors a posture of minimum deterrence. Alexei's "minimum," however, is very low. He can picture a world in which the United States and Russia each have no more than a few dozen nuclear weapons at the ready.

I talked first with Gyorgy Arbatov. I asked for his opinion regarding abolition.

"I've noticed a funny thing," he commented. "Opinion in favor of abolishing nuclear weapons actually seems to have been much stronger in the past. As early as 1946, you had the American Baruch Plan at the United Nations. Of course, from our point of view, the plan was flawed. It would have left the United States with a monopoly on nuclear technology. But then came a gradual turning away from the idea of abolition. I think it was a consequence of the militarization of our minds that took place during the years of the Cold War.

"Then toward the end of the Cold War, a mood favorable to

abolition grew up again. This was around the time of Gorbachev's proposal in 1985 to abolish nuclear weapons by the year 2000. Of course, he hardly expected that in the year 2000 there would be no nuclear weapons, but he did believe we were going in that direction."

"Then you judge the proposal to have been sincere?" I asked.

"Yes, that was the real goal."

"What has happened to this idea?"

"Today, we face a very peculiar situation," he replied. "The big countries have no policy at all. The United States and Russia do not really act; they only react. There isn't even an agenda. What should be on this agenda? The first item would be to rid ourselves of the legacy of the Cold War, and a great part of that legacy is the mountain of weapons—of all kinds."

"Why, when political relations seem good, is there so little change in nuclear policy?" I asked.

"In my opinion, the situation is not so good, even politically. In the absence of a firm policy, there are forces that push us toward friction. In 1991, there was no anti-American feeling here. We really believed that the Americans were, if not allies, then at least partners. Now the atmosphere has changed. Of course, it hasn't reached the level of Cold War suspicion, but there is already disappointment, some cynical realism. It puts even the ratification of the SALT II treaty in question."

"Where do you think nuclear arms negotiations are headed?"

"The odd thing is that now I don't think people look at these START treaties—even if there were a third or a fourth—as steps toward a complete ban on nuclear weapons. They look on them more as 'arms control,' which means management of the arms race, not ending the arms race. It became a sort of high art and science, which helped to fool the public into thinking that real disarmament was occurring."

"What should be the goal?"

"My own opinion is that we are faced with an alternative: either proliferation or else a complete ban on nuclear weapons. If you say we need only ten weapons to make ourselves secure, it means that everybody can have them—maybe not ten but five, or three, or four. We cannot have a monopoly for ourselves. So we have to make the choice. We can hold the line for a while—maybe with Iraq, maybe with North Korea. Israel and Pakistan and India are over the line already. Japan and Germany could make nuclear weapons any time they chose. Even so-called conventional weapons have become very unconventional and destructive. I believe in fact that war is a luxury we cannot afford— that is, a war bigger, say, than Grenada. Even the war in Chechnya has done great harm to Russia. I think that the period of just wars has ended. The Second World War was a just war. You had some experience with another kind of war in Vietnam. We've had it in Afghanistan and Chechnya.

"War today involves ethnic, national, and religious minorities. We can even add terrorists and criminals. And against none of these can nuclear weapons be used."

"After the First and Second World Wars, serious attempts were made to organize the peace," I observed. "Why do you suppose that nothing like that has been attempted this time?"

"The nations of the world had survived a terrible threat," he said. "And they wanted to prevent such a threat from arising again. At the end of the Cold War, none of this happened. There haven't even been serious discussions about organizing the peace. There was a moment when Gorbachev tried to take the lead in such a process, but then he fell from power. You cannot expect too much from us in Russia nowadays. Now it's your turn—I mean not just America but also some of the other Western countries that are better ordered than we are now. We had a brilliant opportunity to begin right after the Cold War, but we almost missed it. I say 'almost' because if we come to our senses we can still grasp it."

When I visited Gyorgy's son Alexei in his office in the Duma, I asked if *he* believed that a world without nuclear weapons should be the goal of policy.

He answered in the affirmative but added a crucial qualification. "If it's a world that, owing to the elimination of nuclear weapons, has not been made safe for conventional war, then certainly that should be the goal," he said. "By definition, it will be a much more stable world, because all conflicts will be resolved peacefully. But that means a very different organization of the world from what we have today. It basically means world government. There is no other way you can make the world safe from conventional war."

"Why is that?"

"For two basic reasons. First, without world government, all the imbalances alleviated by the presence of nuclear deterrence would once again play a very conspicuous role. So such a world, without world government, would not be stable. Second, in a world without nuclear weapons but with conventional wars, it would be impossible to prevent the reconstruction of nuclear arsenals. Before nuclear weapons were invented, we had conventional wars, world wars, terrible imbalances. After the invention of nuclear weapons, we've had several decades of deterrence and no large-scale conventional war. If we just do away with nuclear weapons, we will return to the pre-1945 era, with all its conventional wars, which led to the conquest of states, the occupation and dismemberment of countries, and so forth. I think the vast majority of people would not claim that nuclear armament is worse than that."

Thus did Alexei Arbatov, a liberal member of the new Russian Parliament, citing the classic arguments against abolition that have been made in the United States for a half-century, take a far more stringent position on nuclear armament than his father Gyorgy Arbatov, the lifelong Communist insider.

He placed such a high hurdle in the way of abolition, I commented, that I was doubtful it would make any sense to place abolition on the political agenda. Wondering whether virtual nuclear arsenals (on which Alexei Arbatov has commented in several articles) might, in his view, offer a way around this impasse, I asked him for his opinion of this proposal.

"If we're talking about big powers, then virtual nuclear arsenals are not adequate deterrence against conventional attack," he answered, "because, as the Persian Gulf War showed, contemporary conventional weapons with their systems of command and control, communication, and intelligence provide a very effective capability to neutralize any reconstitution of nuclear weapons. But we have not defined the various options that are made possible by virtual nuclear arsenals."

"For example?"

"For example, you possibly could provide invulnerability to de-alerted forces, but only if you keep, as insurance, a very, very small number of nuclear weapons on high alert. In that case, it would be possible to rely on the invulnerability of reconstitution, and thus the ability of virtual nuclear forces to deter conventional attacks. But then you are not talking about a de-nuclearized world; you are talking about a world with limited, very small and invulnerable finite deterrent capabilities. The number could be as low as a few dozen weapons."

"Would a world of a few dozen alerted weapons backed up by larger de-alerted or virtual arsenals be your concept of a goal for the nuclear arms negotiations now under way?"

"Yes."

"Why do you require a few dozen alerted weapons?" I asked.

"Because the few dozen would *deter* a nuclear or conventional attack on your reconstitution structure," he answered.

"Are you saying that your 'minimum deterrent' force would be targeted not on the cities of the other side but on its reconstitution capacity?"

"Yes. And in fact we are already inadvertently starting down this path, because our thinking about START is changing. Nobody now is afraid of a surprise attack by the other side, but both sides, for better or worse, are already afraid of the other side's capacity to reconstitute larger arsenals and suddenly revive the arms race. Thus, in thinking about the implementation of START II and START III, we are trying to figure out how to ensure deterrence not against surprise attack but against reconstitution."

"So you are not prepared to advocate an entirely virtual arsenal or even an entirely de-alerted arsenal."

"In fact, I'd love to see that. But the implications are enormous: You would have to deal with all the issues of conventional force balance or imbalance; you would have to deal with defensive missile systems; and you would have to pour more and more resources into the International Atomic Energy Agency in order to keep proliferation under extremely stringent control. Basically, you would have to create an international consortium to deal even with the peaceful suppliers of nuclear energy. And that's already a step toward world government. This is where we reach the quantum jump. Getting from six thousand to fifty is much easier than getting from fifty to zero."

Here, it occurred to me, was another version of the conviction, shared by so many of the proponents of deterrence, that there was a point in the reduction process at which, if you wished to go farther, you required a sudden transformation of the international system into something resembling world government. Different advocates of deterrence, however, placed that point at different levels of disarmament. Advocates of classic deterrence like Richard Perle or James Schlesinger placed the crucial threshold at thousands of weapons. The National Academy of Sciences placed it at hundreds of weapons. Alexei Arbatov placed it at a few dozen. Admiral Turner placed it at several hundred fully de-alerted and partially de-mated arsenals. Each thought that there existed a threshold beyond which you could not go without a quantum change in the international system. Indeed, if, as a group, the advocates of minimum deterrence disagreed with the advocates of virtual arsenals, with whose particular proposals theirs sometimes overlapped, the difference was that the champions of virtual arsenals discovered no such threshold. Although the difference between the two positions might appear narrow and technical, the political difference was great. The first removed nuclear abolition from the political agenda; the second permitted it to be placed there.

I mentioned the objection that Alexei's father had raised to minimum deterrence—that it would encourage proliferation.

"Well, as I understand it, we are discussing not a speech in the United Nations but, in a pragmatic way, strategic and technical paths for the future," he replied. "First, as experience with ratification of the Non-Proliferation Treaty shows, the nonnuclear countries are really not too serious about the linkage between nuclear disarmament by the great powers and proliferation. Second, some—such as Israel, India, and Pakistan—have found a path between the Scylla and Charybdis of possessing and not possessing the bomb, and that is the bomb in the basement. They perhaps do not declare it, or even test it, but they keep it there in the basement."

"Let's suppose, for a moment," I said, "that hostile, nuclear-capable powers are better off with a few nuclear weapons than with none. But do

Russia and the United States now fall into this category? Russians have put an end to Communism and to the Soviet Union. Doesn't this create the foundation for a friendly, not a hostile relationship?"

To my surprise, this Russian liberal produced a version of the "hedging" argument used by nuclear possessionists in the United States. "First," he said, "the victory of Yeltsin doesn't mean the victory of democracy. It means the defeat of Communism. Communism can be defeated either by democracy or by nationalism or fascism. That's why I oppose NATO expansion—it fuels our nationalists. But even if we have democracy here, this in no way means that there will be no geopolitical competition. It is scarcely possible that relations will become like those between the United States and England or among the nations of united Europe. A thoroughly democratic United States and a thoroughly democratic Russia could easily support different clients in a regional conflict. I can easily imagine a democratic Russia supporting Iran while a democratic United States would give preference to Turkey."

He continued with a declaration of allegiance to the doctrine of deterrence, albeit in a strikingly minimalist form: "Some time ago I formulated a rule. It states that the only possible or desirable relationship between two nuclear powers, whoever they are, is mutual nuclear deterrence, unless one of two eventualities can be substituted for it: first, that the two powers are allies against a third nuclear power or, second, that they are out of range of one another and therefore irrelevant to each other's security problems."

"Then, to sum it up, you subscribe to the classic position that in order to have full nuclear disarmament you need world government; ergo, you can't have full nuclear disarmament."

"No," he answered. "The premise is correct. But the conclusion is wrong. True, you cannot have nuclear disarmament without world government. Therefore, if you want nuclear disarmament you have to think about world government. And if you get democracies in the United States and in Russia, why can't you have world government? They are heading toward something like that already in Europe. Besides, building a world government, like moving toward nuclear disarmament, is not a single act but a long process, and the two processes would enhance one another. While reducing arsenals to a few dozen alerted nuclear weapons for each nuclear power, we would have built such a comprehensive system for controlling arms, technology, and the use of force that all of a sudden we would discover: there is no need for the few remaining nukes, either."

V

ABOLITION:
GENERAL
GEORGE LEE
BUTLER

General George Lee Butler was the last commander of the Strategic Air Command before it was folded, in 1992, into the U.S. Strategic Command, of which Butler was also commander until 1994. He joined the Kiewit Energy Group in that year as president. His face is boyish and rosy-cheeked, his manner energetic and precise. His clipped voice would sound right crackling over a military telephone or radio. And Butler was, in fact, from 1991 until 1994, the man to whom the president, if the evil day had come, would have issued the command to launch America's nuclear arsenal, and who, in turn, was charged with delivering that order down the line. He acquired a nuclear education and experience that, in its length, depth, and variety, is possibly unmatched by that of any other American of his generation. He was a professor of nuclear subjects at the Air Force Academy and then was assigned to the Pentagon, where he worked on arms control. He next became the commander of a B-52 wing. He was educated to command nuclear forces, and he did command them, at the highest level. And yet, when that education was done, he decided that nuclear weapons should be abolished.

Butler first publicly announced his dedication to the goal of

nuclear abolition in 1996, at a meeting of the State of the World
Forum, at which Gorbachev also spoke, reaffirming his dedication to
the same goal, and there is a certain analogy to be drawn between the
two men. Both rose to the top of a system that was devoted to high
ideals but relied on terror as the means for achieving them. Each
believed deeply in the system of which he was a part. Each was a man of
outstanding intellect, energy, and vision. And each, after reaching the
apex of his system, turned against it in fundamental ways, for moral as
well as practical reasons. Huge, tottering systems, history suggests, are
in trouble when their best people turn against them. Gorbachev's
change of heart foreshadowed the end of the Soviet Union. Does Butler's change of heart, we may wonder, herald a similar fate for the system of deterrence?

"You have described nuclear policy and deployments as a puzzle
whose pieces did not fit," I remarked when I spoke with him earlier this
year. "Could you say something about the stages of your acquaintance
with this puzzle?"

"My journey through the pieces began in almost the right order, so
to speak," he said. "That is, I began by teaching nuclear subject in the
classroom at the Air Force Academy, from 1969 to 1972. That was my
introduction to the intellectual underpinnings of the nuclear era. My
journey was launched in precisely the way one might embark on a
Ph.D. You begin with the fundamentals. If you were someday going to
be a brain surgeon, you would start, as every other first-year medical
student does, with a picture of the human body, and begin to understand what really makes it tick. A medical student learns the names of
everything in the body, so as to be able to relate them in his mind. It's
the same in becoming an informed expert in this extraordinarily complex nuclear arena, this crazy quilt of forces, histories, and policies that
make up the nuclear puzzle.

"As a professor, I had to come to grips with the arcane issues
of nuclear deterrence theory, the character of offense and defense, the
difference between deterrence and defense. I went through the library
of books being written at the time by learned authors, from Herman
Kahn to Henry Kissinger to Thomas Schelling. As I puzzled through all
this, I became, to some extent, enthralled by it. Here was an intellectual

riddle of the most intricate kind—a puzzle to which there appeared to be no solutions. The wonderful title of Herman Kahn's book *Thinking the Unthinkable* captured the dilemma perfectly: that it is unthinkable to imagine the wholesale slaughter of societies, yet at the same time it appears necessary to do so, in the hope that you will hit upon some formulation that will preclude the act; but then in the process you may wind up amassing forces that engender the very outcome you hoped to avoid. I spent hours at the blackboard, walking my students through those convoluted corridors: flexible response, assured destruction, essential equivalence, the dynamic between strategic offense and defense.

"The second piece of the puzzle that I touched, after I left the academic world, was arms control, at the Pentagon. My assignment was to the staff of the U.S. Air Force. From 1974 to 1977, I became deeply embroiled in the bitter aftermath of the SALT I agreement, in which the Kissingerian bargain of accepting a position of numerical inferiority in delivery systems was ostensibly balanced by our superior MIRV [multiple independent reentry vehicle] technology, which the Soviets, it was assumed, were years from acquiring. The ink was not one year dry on that agreement when they tested their first MIRVed warheads. That's when I came to appreciate the delicious phrase, coined by Kenneth Adelman, that arms control is a holy war.

"In fact, I came to believe ultimately that those negotiations, the anguish, the agonizing, the bureaucratic warfare—euphemistically called arms control—was in many respects a surrogate for the conflict of nuclear battle that never transpired. The stakes were seen as enormous. The bureaucratic infighting and positioning of the players, the skullduggery, the political machinations outstripped anything that I had ever seen in government. It was a morality play that would rival anything Shakespeare ever put on stage. I came away from that experience with the beginnings of an understanding that was quite different from the academic and intellectual constructs I had first formed. I began to see that it was entirely possible for the elements of nuclear policy making and the associated acquisition and posturing of forces to take on a life of their own. For example, when the responsibility for arraying nuclear capabilities was allocated among the three services—

the army, the navy, and the air force—each would then develop an institutional interest that was quite divorced from considerations of the appropriate size of the forces in their totality.

"Even such elemental questions as whether air force or navy systems should be given such and such nuclear targets were decided this way. As it turned out, targets have a caste system all their own. Time-urgent targets, such as missile silos, which had to be hit with devastating effect at the earliest possible moment in a conflict, in order to destroy the missile inside the silo, were assigned to the most modern kind of weapons on our side. It mattered immensely to the air force and the navy whether those weapons were to be land based or sea based. For the service that won the debate, those decisions meant money, power, prestige, forces, resources, and position in the bureaucratic corridors. That rivalry among the services goes back to 1947, '48, and '49 with the B-36 supercarrier controversy, which not only introduced a bitter divide between the air force and the navy that continues to this day but ultimately led to the mental deterioration and collapse of James Forrestal, the secretary of defense at the time. Just the story of air force–navy rivalry would require volumes to tell. The advent of missile-carrying nuclear submarines, for example, was driven by an embittered navy that had lost earlier battles within the nuclear establishment. This same sort of pressure contributed to the decisions to build nuclear warheads by the tens of thousands, to build system after system.

"The truth of the matter was that through the entire Cold War, the United States led the way technologically. What was the impact of that on Soviet thinking? How could they explain it? Imagine the irony if, at some juncture, the Soviets were actually driven to take some action which, in our eyes, appeared incredibly hostile and aggressive but whose motivation was in fact a reaction to a decision of ours that had had little to do with improving our nuclear posture but everything to do with giving one of our services the opportunity to maintain or advance its position against a rival service. That's not fancy. I'm convinced that it happened not just once but time and again. And I'm convinced that everything I'm saying now about the U.S. establishment was mirrored on the Soviet side. We know for a fact that the multiplicity of organizations on their side was a quantum more complex than our own. We know about their breakdowns, lack of communication, and rivalries between parallel agencies like the rocket forces and aviation."

"Your education regarding nuclear weapons has led you to call for the abolition of the object of study," I commented. "The official consensus, however, remains that nuclear weapons are necessary for the indefinite future. Why do you think that view is wrong?"

"Let's start by framing the intellectual context in which the question of abolition is normally placed, for there are some very important underlying assumptions present in it. In the first place, I think that those who say abolition cannot be achieved fall into a very common trap. I've seen it often in my reading of history, and I've seen it operate in my own lifetime. It is the mistake of judging the prospects for future eventualities by today's circumstances. 'General Butler, how can you possibly imagine a world without nuclear weapons? Look, Russia has them by the thousands, and so do other nations.' The answer to that is very simple: The underlying hostility between the United States and the Soviet Union began to collapse with the arrival of Gorbachev, who had the capacity to understand that the society he was leading was a failure and had to be recast. In addition, he knew that its relationship with the United States—and by extension with the rest of the world—had to be transformed. At that point, the game was over. The context was changed forever. We were faced with an array of circumstances left over from a forty-year buildup of systems and beliefs that, in many respects, had been just as murderous as a real war. Consider the history of the intelligence apparatus alone, and the lives that were lost in the decades of labyrinthine schemes.

"I'm always somewhat bemused by people who say that war was avoided. It was not avoided. In a sense, the Cold War was a war in all its aspects. Yet, with a suddenness, a spontaneity entirely unpredicted by the vast majority of the participants, that conflict ended. We were completely unprepared. For example, we have no proper place to store the nuclear weapons that we have removed from deployment under current arms control agreements. We should understand that it will take some considerable time for all of this to recede—for our minds to accept again that we are all human beings with common values and motivations. We're striving to find our way out of this blind corner into which history and fate steered us for almost half a century. We should accept the fact that we begin from a very difficult starting place. But once that's understood, we also need to be aware that change is possible. How many times have you heard it said in the most grave official tones, 'We will never . . .' 'It is impossible that . . .' 'It is inconceivable that . . .' Yet, the next week or the next month or the next year, what was viewed as impossible and unachievable has happened and is now viewed as ordinary and even mundane.

"I give you, for openers, the end of the Cold War. People who say to me that the elimination of nuclear weapons is utopian have somehow managed to completely ignore the fact that the end of the Cold War was a far more utopian prospect than eliminating nuclear weapons is now. Only ten years ago, the Cold War was a given—a seemingly permanent feature on the international landscape. Yet today it is behind us, and we are grappling with its denouement. Therefore, I think that the burden of proof is on anyone who uses 'never' or 'impossible' or 'inconceivable' with respect to what, after all, would only be a further improvement of this already astonishing outcome. Who can fail to be amazed that we are already debating not the next generation of nuclear weapons, not the next nefarious act by the Soviet Union, but whether or not we should cut another thousand weapons from the arsenal? Or whether it is time to take them off alert? Or—in my line of business, the energy business—whether my company should make a thirty-year investment in the Russian energy sector? Who can look at all this and fail to be awestruck by the profundity of the change? And yet even as people witness all this they say that it is impossible to imagine a world without nuclear weapons!

"This seems especially short-sighted when we recall that it has been only a relatively short time since we lived in a world without nuclear weapons, and that the political motivations for their invention and, what is more important, for their acquisition by the tens of thousands are now matters for historical curiosity. So I begin by completely rejecting the assumption that it is impossible to imagine measures that consist of dismantling, reducing, and eliminating elements that were part of a relationship that belongs to a past era.

"That's point number one—the grievous intellectual error of imagining the future solely in terms of the present. Point number two: It is a measure of the pessimism of nations—but especially of the nuclear-weapon states—to assert that a nuclear-weapon-free world is impossible when, in fact, 95 percent of the nations of the world already are nuclear-free. This task is not the elimination of nuclear weapons on a global basis. It is the elimination of nuclear weapons from a handful of states that, owing to peculiar circumstances at the end of the Cold War, inherited nuclear arsenals and from a small number of nations—read three—that clandestinely acquired nuclear arms. Add to these an equal number of aspiring states and that's the size of things. And, in fact, we impute to these states extraordinary capacities that are probably far beyond their real reach. Iraq's nuclear capability we have destroyed, and Iran will need at least a decade to build nuclear weapons—a period giving us ample opportunity to do exactly what we did in Iraq. In a world resolved to be rid of nuclear weapons, it may well be necessary to go in and physically remove the capability, because the states of the world would be resolved that the family of man must not be confronted with this threat ever again. Israel also administered that lesson to Iraq some years ago. We have already bargained North Korea out of the role of nuclear power at the price of two inspectable reactors. If we are holding on to nuclear weapons because we think we can't deal with threats from states the likes of Libya, then the world is making a very bad bargain.

"Point number three: Let's take the words of President Jacques Chirac of France when he explained the rationale for calling off the recent French nuclear testing two tests short of its original program of eight. He made the following, extraordinarily illustrative comment: 'Yes, I can with confidence terminate these tests, knowing they have achieved their objectives, and with the knowledge that France's security is preserved for decades to come.' Now let's parse that message. First, it says that nuclear weapons are irrevocably tied to our security, and that we assure our security by enhancing their safety and operational effectiveness. But, oh, by the way, he in effect adds in the same breath, I am saying that our security matters ever so much more than yours, because, according to the bargain struck in the Non-Proliferation Treaty, you're not allowed to have them. How extraordinarily arrogant for a nation to proclaim that its security fundamentally depends on nuclear capabilities denied to others. Second, with that statement, Chirac gave enormous encouragement to nuclear proliferation. What nation upon hearing his statement would not be tempted to imagine that its security would benefit from a nuclear capability as well? In one breath he denigrated the security concerns of all the nonnuclear states and gave aid and comfort to every state for which the prospects of acquiring a nuclear capability are in the balance, not to speak of new leaders who may wish to aggrandize their perceived power in the world.

"If you believe at all in the sovereign equality of nations, it is untenable that a handful of nations should forever arrogate to themselves the right to nuclear weapons, while denying it to others. One more mistake people make when they imagine that nuclear weapons must be retained indefinitely is in regarding the world as sufficiently static that current circumstances, in which only a handful of nations have these weapons, will endure forever. The assumption is that no new, bitter enmities will develop on the face of the earth. We have a priceless opportunity to put behind us the possibility that we or other nations will be taken hostage by nuclear arms."

I decided to ask Butler—a man who had studied deterrence, taught it, practiced it at every level, and, as the last commander of the Strategic Air Command, presided over it—what his evaluation of the policy now was. "During the Cold War, deterrence, the argument runs, 'worked'—it kept the peace—therefore, we should continue to make it the foundation of policy in the new age," I said. "What is your evaluation of this argument?"

I was rewarded with the most sophisticated, sustained, and knowledgeable rebuttal of the doctrine of deterrence that I had yet heard or read.

"It is fatally flawed as a logical construct in two respects," he said. "First and foremost, deterrence, when raised to its highest level, requires that you make yourself effectively invulnerable to an enemy's attack. In the nuclear age, the requirements are especially high, because the consequences of even one nuclear weapon slipping through your defenses are going to be catastrophic. Yet your perfect invulnerability would spell perfect vulnerability for your opponent, which of course he cannot accept. Consequently, any balance struck is extremely unstable, and each side is led to build larger and larger arsenals, to discover more and more elegant technologies. Yet these never strike the desired balance either—the second logical flaw—because in the history of warfare, from which nuclear war is not immune, neither the offense nor the defense has ever remained dominant for any significant period.

"In addition, deterrence fails at the psychological level, because it requires that you influence the thinking of your enemy in ways that go to the heart of his concern for his security—or, perhaps, his aggressive aims. You must understand every detail and nuance of his motivations, his manner of thinking, and his likely actions under every conceivable condition, from peace to deep crisis. Yet how can that requirement be met? In the archetypal deterrence relationship, between the United States and the Soviet Union during the Cold War, the two antagonists were more deeply isolated and alienated from each other, perhaps, than any rivals in history. The main characteristics of the relationship were lack of dialogue, a conviction that each harbored the most hostile possible motivations toward the other, and, consequently, a set of war plans that were premised on worst-case assumptions and outcomes. These, in turn, easily led to a further profound flaw in the psychology of deterrence: it led the sides to demonize each other, to reduce to caricatures each other's motivations, intentions, and beliefs. Yet all of this flew in the face of the detailed, sophisticated understanding that deterrence requires in order to operate, especially in a crisis.

"What's more, because of its built-in instability, deterrence fails as an analytical guide. There is no limit to the policy sins that can be committed or the weapons that can be rationalized in the name of deterrence. An early example was the crossing of an extraordinarily important line of demarcation when, in the 1950s, the intercontinental ballistic missile was developed and deployed. A feeling of panic spread in the United States when the Soviet Union launched the Sputnik satellite. People recognized that the satellite could just as easily have been an orbiting nuclear weapon, against which we would have lacked any means of defense or capacity to reply in kind.

The introduction of the intercontinental ballistic missile into the operational equation reduced warning time to thirty minutes and decision time to fifteen minutes. In consequence, larger and larger numbers of missiles were brought into the mix—all in the name of deterrence, because deterrence by its nature requires that the threat both be perceived as and in reality *be* utterly devastating, and what better way to make good on that threat than a bomb of megaton capacity that can be delivered at intercontinental range in a time span of thirty minutes? In many respects, it is the perfect weapon for deterrence. Yet if only one side possesses it, this spells fatal vulnerability for the other side, which is then reduced to one or two choices: either to seek to build perfect defenses or else simply to acquire an array of forces of equally devastating power. The latter, of course, is precisely what happened in the 1950s, and thereafter. The nuclear arms race was set in motion. Even higher numbers of weapons of increasingly devastating power were developed in successive generations. The most notable was the multiple independent reentry vehicle, or MIRV, which can carry four, five, eight, ten warheads on a missile—or even twenty, as is the case with the Soviet SS-18. And all were justified in the name of deterrence.

"These developments displayed the ultimate inconsistency of deterrence—a circle that could never be squared. It turned out that the quest to operationalize—to array a force in practice that persuaded the other side that if you attack us you will be unable to stand the destructiveness of our reply—turned the doctrine on its head. It is one thing in theory to have a declaratory policy in which you say, 'I will respond massively if you attack me, therefore you are deterred.' It's quite another thing to give daily, operational reality to that policy in the form of actual systems and actual weapons poised on high states of alert. This operationalization in fact introduced a whole new dynamic into the process—a dynamic that became the motivating, generating force behind the nuclear arms race."

"What do you mean by turning deterrence 'on its head'?" I asked.

"The things that you do in the quest to convey the reality of your retaliatory threat will be seen, through the prism of your enemy's perspective, as a hostile capability to launch a first strike. And that perception forces him, once again, to try to trump your ace. Once you set in motion the genius of technology, once you trigger the inventiveness and dynamism of the industrial bases, once you train the legions of warriors to operate those systems, you build not only a threat that in its operational posture is frightfully real but one that in fact turns deterrence upside down. Thus, your quest for security, by building a highly credible deterrent force, is *unhinged* by your opponent's need to respond in kind. In my view, that paradox is the fundamental problem at an operational level with deterrence."

I mentioned Bruce Blair's conclusion that deterrence had led the two sides, almost against their wills (and certainly against their declared policies), to adopt postures of launch-on-warning and asked if he considered that this, too, might be part of the process by which deterrence undermined itself.

"Part of the insidiousness of the evolution of this system, of this multifaceted, hideously complex, and intricately related set of puzzle pieces—which include the underlying psychology of the actors, their policies, the weapons systems, the intelligence systems, the warning systems—is the unfortunate fact that, whatever might have been *intended* by the policymakers (who, incidentally, had very little insight into the mechanisms that underpinned the simple words that floated onto a blank page at the level of the White House), *in reality*, at the operational level, the requirements of deterrence proved impracticable. It turned out that the efforts to move away from the knee-jerk, spastic, all-out response of massive retaliation in pursuit of increasing flexibility, of more discriminating options, placed whole portions of the force, such as the entire land-based ICBM force, at risk, and this was intellectually unacceptable. The consequence was a move in practice to a system structured to drive the president inevitably toward a decision to launch under attack.

"There's a significant difference, by the way, between launch-on-warning and launch-under-attack. Launch-on-warning covers a gray zone that can include a number of things, including the judgment that the other side is *about* to launch. Launch-on-warning means that when you see your enemy mobilizing you will preempt an attack. Launch-under-attack means that you believe you have incontrovertible proof that warheads actually are on the way."

"But wouldn't launching on the grounds that the other side was *about* to attack be preemption?" I asked.

"Preemption can mean anything from a bolt out of the blue, which is to say, I'm just going to pick a day and a moment when I mean to attack, to launch-on-warning. Pearl Harbor is the quintessential example of preemption. But there are other forms of preemption. It's very much like the levels of severity within the act of murder. Was it cold-blooded and premeditated? Was it involuntary manslaughter? In the case of nuclear attack, it is of overriding importance to make a judgment about these questions. The president needs to know, with as much certainty as his conscience drives him to require, not just that the nation is under nuclear attack but that it is under attack by the nations specified. Further, he needs to know the nature of the attack. What is the target? It turns out that it matters a great deal, in the arcana of parsing a nuclear attack, whether the target is Washington, D.C., or a missile field, or some military installation, or some population center other than Washington. If the attack is on Washington, it is judged to be particularly nefarious, because it means that the effort is to decapitate the president, the only person who can give the order to launch. If you cut the head off the decision authority, you leave the rest of the force helpless.

"This brings us to a set of factors called 'circumstances of war initiation.' The worst circumstance is the famous bolt-from-the-blue attack. Why is that the worst case? Because then there would be a significant fraction of our submarines vulnerable to destruction in port and a significant fraction of our bombers that would be unprepared to make a survival launch—to leap into the air to escape destruction. Let's say—just arbitrarily—that 50 percent of the retaliatory capability is at risk. Or, worse, you might catch the nation essentially shut down—for instance, on a national holiday—or the president might be in ill health. Any of that could cut into the precious minutes supposedly available for a presidential decision and for conveying the message to the forces, to have it coded and decoded. Several minutes are required actually to act upon a presidential direction.

"Now, as it happens, we are dealing here with precisely the sort of calculations that drove the uncontrolled expansion of the force. If you conclude that a bolt out of the blue is a reasonable likelihood, then your military advisers will recommend forces so large that the surviving forces will be sufficient to attain the minimum objectives of deterrence, which are to destroy X percent—let's say, 80 percent—of the leadership, forces, conventional forces, and military-industrial complex of the adversary.

"One of the cornerstones of deterrence against surprise nuclear attack is the so-called triad of forces—on land, in the air, and in the sea. I say 'so-called' because the triad is not a construct that was first conceived, and then underwritten with forces. We developed forces in somewhat arbitrary fashion—for instance, owing to service rivalries—and then described them as a triad. These forces had independent characteristics yet were complementary in such a way that, when arrayed in various stages of alert, they confronted a prospective enemy with an unsolvable attack problem. For example, even after a bolt-out-of-the-blue attack, alert bombers and submarines at sea were likely to survive and would still confront your opponent with a prospective reply that he could not stand. Thus, with the triad in place, your opponent cannot plan for both simultaneous launch of his forces and simultaneous arrival of their warheads to achieve a hundred percent effective surprise attack. A full-scale attack gives too much warning, and partial attack achieves too little damage to avoid a devastating retaliation. In theory, this calculated redundancy gave the United States the flexibility to introduce two very important elements into its retaliatory calculus. The first was a move away from massive retaliation to a war plan with a variety of response options. Presumably, this allowed a response tailored to some fine-grained judgment about the nature and intent of the attack—i.e., its scope and targets. For example, an attack focused solely on U.S. military forces might suggest that we spare nonmilitary targets in our retaliation, or even, if we thought the attack was limited, to spare selected countries in the Warsaw Pact. The second key consideration is that a triad of survivable forces gave the president the option of 'riding out' the initial wave of the attack, whether to better assess its motives or even to ensure that the attack was real and not simply a faulty warning from computer systems gone haywire.

"Such are the considerations one faces when weighing the various scenarios of war initiation and retribution. These matters are especially important when you are assessing your war plans as presumptively a second-strike nation, which is what the United States professes itself to be. Our policy was premised on being able to accept the first wave of attacks. We never said publicly that we were committed to launch-on-warning or launch-under-attack. Yet at the operational level it was never accepted that if the presidential decisions went to a certain tick of the clock, we would lose a major portion of our forces. That is, the U.S. would lose part of the target coverage designed to limit damage or to destroy the Soviet Union. You see the difficulties that arise out of this. Notwithstanding the intention of deterrence as it is expressed at the *policy* level—as it is declared and written down—at the level of *operations* those intentions got turned on their head, as the people who are responsible for actually devising the war plan faced the dilemmas and blind alleys of concrete practice. Those mattered absolutely to the people who had to sit down and try to frame the detailed guidance to exact destruction of 80 percent of the adversary's nuclear forces. When they realized that they could not in fact assure those levels of damage if the president chose to ride out an attack, what then did they do? They built a construct that powerfully biased the president's decision process toward launch *before* the arrival of the first enemy warhead. And at that point, all the elements, all the nuances of limited response just went out the window. The consequences of deterrence built on massive arsenals made up of a triad of forces now simply ensured that neither nation would survive the ensuing holocaust."

"Permit me to be a devil's advocate for a moment," I responded. "Doesn't it stand to reason that, had it not been for the sobering effect of the nuclear arsenals, the two great powers of the Cold War might have gone to war? Isn't there common sense in that idea?"

General Butler was unyielding in his rejection of the idea. "The bumper-sticker version of that—the short version—would be 'Nuclear weapons prevented World War III.' But step back and take a look at the assumptions that underlie this seemingly reasonable assertion. The real circumstances were much more complicated. I discussed what happened when you tried to make deterrence operational. But we need to ask what was happening on the other side as well. For the statement that nuclear weapons prevented World War III to be true, it would first have to be the case that the Soviet Union had a compelling urge to

launch an aggressive war against the West. At this moment, we have yet
to find the evidence for that. There's no question that the entire era
during which Joseph Stalin rose to power and held sway over the Soviet
Union was one of the most monstrous periods in history. One evening
on TV-Moscow, when I was there, I heard a Russian commentator state
that by Russian calculations Stalin and his regime killed fifty million
of their countrymen—far more than the twenty million lost in World
War II. No one can possibly be an apologist for Stalin. It's nevertheless
true that serious historians such as John Lewis Gaddis, with access to
Soviet archives, are beginning to make different findings—that in
operational terms the Soviet Union was more circumspect. Galling as
the enslavement of the Eastern European nations was, it appears that
the Soviet motivation may have been chiefly to create a cordon sani-
taire as a defensive perimeter. They may have sincerely seen themselves
as the likely victim of aggression, given their weakness and the emer-
gence of the United States as a superpower virtually unchallenged on
the world stage. At the same time, it's perfectly understandable that,
thanks to such Russian actions as the Berlin blockade, the breaking of
agreements made at the end of World War II, and the refusal to withdraw from Eastern Europe, American policymakers came to believe
that here was a Russia set upon global domination. I accept that. Yet
the pernicious outcome, which had very real meaning for millions of
people around the world, was that the United States abandoned the
difficult intellectual work of trying to understand the motivations of
this enemy in favor of a simple demonization of him. We saw this in
the McCarthy era, during which thousands of careers and lives were
ruined through the Machiavellian posturing of one man. You see what
was set in motion here. I'm responding to your question whether deterrence really did spare us conventional world war. So point number one
is that we really don't know to what extent the Soviets were inspired to
confront us. Some day perhaps we will.

"There's a second important point about Soviet policy to consider.
The Soviet military never understood deterrence as it was formulated
by the West. Our view of nuclear deterrence was embodied in the ex-
cruciating expression 'mutual assured destruction.' The Soviets never
accepted this—never accepted that it was an unavoidable aspect of

nuclear confrontation that their country would be destroyed and all would be lost. Their view, until the 1980s—until Chernobyl—was that nuclear war must not be lost, and therefore they never operated according to the intellectual construct we preferred. Deterrence was really a uniquely Western construct. Therefore, those who insist that deterrence prevented World War III are seeing that proposition through a Western lens."

"It would be hard to say where deterrence came in at all, except on the theoretical level," I commented, "if, as you say, the United States never succeeded in making deterrence operational and the Soviet Union did not adopt it at all."

"I don't say that the Soviets were unmindful of the destructiveness of nuclear war," Butler answered. "But, in contrast to the United States, which paid mere lip-service to protecting command and control and population, the Russians raised that to an art form. Why did they go to such lengths to bury their command centers at depths that we could never reach with our nuclear weapons? Why did they put whole cities underground? Why did they so widely disperse their military infrastructure? How do you square that with our view of deterrence? Their view was, if war comes, we're going to win it. What it says to me is that nuclear weapons did not prevent or deter World War III. Let me give you another illustration. Declared U.S. policy, which was driven by a belief in deterrence, began to move in the direction of supposedly greater flexibility and response. What did the Russians do? They introduced an automatic feature into their command and control system—the dead hand—through which their forces would be launched automatically if their command and control was decapitated. Where's the deterrence in that?

"What I'm suggesting to you, then—after years of observation and reflection—is that I cannot accept the simple premise that deterrence is what stood between us and nuclear conflict. In the same breath, however, I will add that I cannot sit here and explain to you definitively why there was no nuclear conflict between the two nations. I can only tell what I *believe* to be the case, historically.

"You could argue that it is impossible to deal with the issue intellectually without tracing the forces that, since the rise of the nation-state in the fifteenth century, have brought us to this point. But let's just look at one little snapshot of this era, the year 1945.

"It's crucially important to understand that the Cold War presented the world of 1945 with a set of circumstances that it was completely unprepared to deal with. The world was exhausted by a global conflict of unprecedented proportions. You survey the carnage on that landscape, and try to imagine a world that was just beginning to apprehend the reality of the Holocaust, which was something quite different from the millions who had died in combat. And picture that suddenly statesmen are confronted with a challenge that, even in the best of times and circumstances, would have strained their imaginations, namely, what to do about the atomic bombs.

"Interestingly, it didn't have to be that way. Nothing at the outset, except perhaps the capriciousness of the gods, dictated that simultaneous with the arrival of the East-West confrontation would come a weapon whose destructive capacities *perfectly mirrored* the ideological enmity. Total ideological warfare was underwritten by total destructive capacity. What an historic coupling! Absent the atom bomb, there still would have been the bitter enmity between East and West. Europe still would have been divided. The Soviet Union still would have confronted the West at a multiplicity of points around the world. These things alone would have constituted a challenge of unprecedented proportions for American policymakers. When you consider that all this was overlaid with the unlimited destructive power of nuclear arms, it boggles the mind to realize that, somehow, we got through it.

"It's remarkable, in retrospect, that there was even the suggestion, put forward in the Baruch Plan, to put the genie back in the bottle by internationalizing the technology. I don't know if there was an inevitability about the Cold War; in retrospect, it appears to me that there was. There definitely was going to be some form of hostility, some East-West divide. But what I also know is that the nuclear component rapidly closed off the prospects for traditional methods of diplomacy. To decide whether or not nuclear deterrence prevented World War III, you would have to go back literally minute by minute, day by day, year by year, to reconstruct the U.S.-Soviet relationship. For instance, when did deterrence become an operational concept in the United States? In

1945? No. In 1950? No. In 1954? No. Only when the Soviet Union began to achieve parity with the United States were we forced to confront the incredible nature of a nuclear policy premised on massive retaliation.

"*If*, up to that point, you were viewing the nuclear relationship through Soviet eyes, what were you seeing? A very aggressive and bellicose policy: 'Look, if we don't like what you're doing, if we don't like the way you got up this morning and looked at us across the breakfast table, watch out!' I jest, but the truth of the matter is that massive retaliation was to be carried out at a time and place of our choosing—*we* will measure and judge. There's great irony in the fact that, today, Russia is adopting some form of the policy of massive retaliation. Its leaders fail to recognize that no neighbor credibly threatened by Russia will long endure lacking nuclear forces of its own, at which point the same thing will happen to Russia that happened to us in the early years of the Cold War. Their ace will be trumped. Their nuclear force will be rendered useless by the opposing nuclear threat, and not only that but they will have no adequate conventional forces to protect themselves from attack. So where's the bargain? If 'deterrence fails,' they will lose utterly. We've been through that.

"When asked why there has been no third world war, I answer, first, that the trauma of the Cuban missile crisis was so great that both sides came to accept certain unwritten rules of the game that had already been taking shape. They boiled down ultimately to respect for spheres of hegemony, or influence. It was unwritten that there were certain things you did not do. We set a very important ground rule even prior to the missile crisis when we did not intervene in the revolution in Hungary, in 1956. Now why was that? Was it because we feared that a nuclear war might ensue? Was it because we believed that militarily, on the ground, we were not really in any position to impose our will successfully—to send troops into Hungary and secure it, to forcibly evict the Russians who were there? Was the decision complicated by the fact that the French and the British had just invaded Egypt and the Suez, and therefore we felt we were in a poor position to ask for the kind of international support we would have needed to launch yet another intervention? You see, it's very difficult to judge.

"Whether you are looking at Hungary and Suez, or Lebanon, or the U-2 incident, or the Cuban missile crisis, or a whole succession of breakdowns in warning systems, you have to look at the totality of circumstances. Within that totality, though, it is absolutely fair to conclude that the presence of nuclear weapons introduced great caution. It is equally true, however, to say that deterrence had this further peculiar quality: it worked best when you needed it least. In periods of relative calm, you could point with pride to deterrence and say, 'Look, how splendidly it's working!' It was in moments of deep crisis that not only did it become irrelevant but all the baggage that came with it—the buildup of forces, the high states of alert—turned the picture absolutely upside down. As you entered the crisis, thoughts of deterrence vanished, and you were simply trying to deal with the classic imponderables of crises. Now what had deterrence brought you? I will tell you that in the Cuban missile crisis, the fact that we did not go to war had nothing to do with deterrence. Talk to Robert McNamara and others. They will tell you that there was no real talk of deterrence in those critical thirteen days. What you had was two small groups of men in two small rooms, groping frantically in an intellectual fog, in the dark, to deal with a crisis that had spun out of control. That was the quality of the relationship: total alienation and isolation from one another.

"That is why in my public statements I have resorted to saying that I think it is miraculous that we escaped this period without a nuclear conflict. Deterrence, in a word, never operated the way that we imagined or envisioned it would. It was never the construct supported by exquisite insights into mutual motivations and intentions that we thought it was. It led to an open-ended arms race—at that level, it failed utterly."

I noted that among those who now favored abolition there were many who had been in the line of command, and now were recoiling against it. "I would like to ask you," I said, "to reflect on the very singular human experience of being engaged in decisions that could have led to nuclear war."

"I'm speaking for myself here and for others who have uniquely borne those responsibilities, such as nuclear advisers to the president, who would have had to utter the fateful words, 'And, therefore,

Mr. President, I recommend that you implement major attack option four,' which would have sounded the death knell for an entire nation—for tens of millions of people—but, what is more important, would have called into question literally the survival of the planet. One response is to become inured to it—to reduce it all to a dispassionate reading of options, to a request for a decision that is then carried out with surgical precision through orders passed to young men and women trained and disciplined to obey without question. For, in fact, deterrence depends on that. It depends on arraying the credible threat implicit in deterrence—the fighting edge that transmits a message of implacable commitment. Never in my entire experience in the nuclear arena, however, did I permit myself to fall into the trap of forgetting for a single instant the consequences of what was at stake.

"Let me tell you how central this question of deterrence is. (Incidentally, it poses a terrible dilemma for me personally.) I have come to the conclusion that this historical assessment would not matter much if it were not for the fact that, as I've said, others have been listening and they have been learning the lessons we've been teaching. And those lessons have been that nuclear weapons matter, that deterrence is the foundation of relationships between nuclear-capable states, and that this is what keeps us from war. Unless we introduce serious new questions about the underpinnings of these arguments and demonstrate the practical risks that flow from acceptance of the premises of deterrence—which is the basic rationale for acquiring and maintaining nuclear weapons—then we have little chance of eliminating them in the near term, or at all.

"Now here's the dilemma for me. To the degree that I am successful in conveying my own judgments and my reservations about deterrence, I am by the same token depreciating the sense of service and sacrifice of the people who have spent their lives in service of deterrence and believe that its success is what justifies their service. It's a terrible dilemma. That's why well-meaning friends have counseled me that the goal of elimination leaves me prey to cynics and disbelievers who say I've set the bar too high.

"My colleagues at CISAC," Butler went on, referring to the National

Academy of Sciences committee on which he had served, "refused, steadfastly, to accept my almost unbridled insistence that we have something in our report that would at least plant the seed of the idea that somehow deterrence could not be accepted without question as having been the linchpin of the absence of nuclear war in the Cold War years. All that we managed to get done, as you have seen, was to say that deterrence has now been reduced to a core function, which is to prevent attack by nuclear weapons. But, you see, that still gives it away. That, I think, is the Achilles' heel of our report. By allowing even that single, reduced rationale for deterrence, what we've said is that the United States had it right during the entire period of the Cold War."

Butler's analysis of deterrence, if it did not put in place the final piece of the puzzle of this labyrinthine, conscience-twisting doctrine, did, it seemed to me, at last offer a resolution of one of the most vexing conundrums. The riddle was whether nuclear deterrence "worked," as the possessionists and the virtual arsenaleers said, or whether it did not work, as the traditional abolitionists claimed.

Butler acknowledged that the bare fact of nuclear arsenals could produce "caution" on the part of those possessing them or menaced by them. In doing so, it seemed that they might also produce a certain "stability." Why then did he so vigorously rebut the contention that deterrence worked? The answer was that the *operationalization* of the threat, as he called it, unleashed a host of counterpressures that tended to destroy the very stability deterrence was meant to produce. The goal—the *wish*, really—might be to prevent nuclear war, but the operational *plan* had to be to wage war. After all, actual nuclear "deterrence"—which is to say a mental state of restraint brought about by terror of annihilation—was nothing that we could bring about by ourselves. In the last analysis, it was up to the enemy whether he would be deterred or not. What both sides had to *do* in the meantime was plan for nuclear war. Wish and plan collided at every point—psychologically, intellectually, but, above all, operationally.

Citizens did not have to ponder these riddles often or very deeply, for the nuclear dilemma was largely out of the public eye. It was otherwise for military people and their civilian overseers—especially men like General Butler and Secretary of Defense McNamara, on whose shoulders the responsibility fell for giving tangible life to the doctrinal tenets.

Butler's revelation of the demons that, unnoted by deterrence theory, operationalization unleashed, it seemed to me, pointed to a lesson: the farther you got from full operationalization—which, in the Cold War, meant tens of thousands of nuclear weapons on full alert, holding the human species hostage on a hair trigger—the quieter and more distant the demons became. The paradoxes, though still present, became less and less acute, the psychology less and less hysterical, the influence on mutual relations less and less poisonous. In the last analysis, there was no contradiction between the proposition that nuclear weapons had finally and completely stymied war between great powers and the proposition that fully operational "deterrence" (something so filled with contradiction that the military leaders of both sides quietly gave up trying to produce it in practice) was a reckless, irresponsible, and untenable policy. Abolition, in the last analysis, was nothing but de-operationalization (which would be another name for disarmament along the horizontal path) carried to the farthest extent.

"I'd like to ask for your responses," I said, "to some of the specific arguments made against abolition: that getting rid of nuclear weapons will unleash conventional wars, that the weapons cannot be disinvented, that breakout will occur, giving the violator an unacceptable advantage."

"Michael Quinlan [a former British Defense Ministry official] recently stated the argument regarding conventional war at the end of a long piece in one of the strategic journals," he began. "He says—and this was surprising for a man of his erudition—that he would rather live in a world with nuclear weapons but without the prospect of major conventional war. His argument was that in a world without nuclear weapons we once again would be vulnerable to the wholesale destruction of global war. Any professor of Logic 101 would quickly give him a failing grade for having fallen into one of the most fundamental traps of logic—the faulty dilemma or the false dichotomy. As if those were the only two possible outcomes! In truth, in the world of nuclear weapons we have seen some of the most murderous wars in history: Iraq and

Iran—over 100,000 casualties; the Korean War; the war in Vietnam. What did nuclear weapons do to prevent, contain, or constrain those conflicts?

"So the notion that nuclear weapons prevent major conventional war is false on the face of it. Would you argue, for example, that the Korean War was not a major war? We lost over fifty thousand soldiers in that war. We lost about the same number in Vietnam. But the penalties of Vietnam went far beyond the casualties. For the United States they were something akin to those of fighting and losing a global conventional war. What was that price? It was the breakdown of the very political fabric of our society. Lyndon Johnson decided not to run for reelection because of the price of his misjudgments in Vietnam; Richard Nixon was so diverted from the duties and responsibilities of his office that he became involved in Watergate. How can we measure the impact on his mental state, his emotional stability, a man already prone to paranoia? How much else does it take to put him in the state of mind that leads him to the egregious misjudgments that led to Watergate? It's very difficult to measure the full price that we paid. There was also the sharp, sharp wedge that was driven between the American people and their armed forces in the aftermath of Vietnam.

"Now the next argument: nuclear weapons cannot be uninvented. Again, I think any professor of freshman logic would take this argument apart in a second. Because the response to that question is, 'And so?' Are you suggesting that because the knowledge cannot be eradicated from the books and the files, from the histories, from the minds, that somehow we're powerless to construct systems of enforcement, agreements specifying collective action, capacities for intervention? Are you suggesting that we cannot establish norms of behavior that not only will powerfully act against building such weapons in the future but will make virtually automatic a response, in the event of violation, by the family of civilized nations, as occurred when Iraq invaded Kuwait— norms that state to potential violators that the moment we understand that you are bent on this course of action, you will be brought to the bar of justice? How could anyone not understand what we did in Iraq? And we must reflect that in a world that had agreed to eliminate nuclear weapons the commitment to do that would be a hundred times stronger than it is today. Recall that the United States was in most difficult circumstances when Saddam Hussein invaded Kuwait. George Bush did not hesitate to make that decision. Even when so august a figure as Sam Nunn recommended against it, George Bush saw immediately what was at stake. I happen to have been immediately involved in presenting the pros and cons of a decision on whether to intervene or not.

"And what was our first and foremost motive there? I know that arguably it was to maintain access to the oil reserves, but in fact the single most important motivation was to destroy the infrastructure for the production of weapons of mass destruction. The point is that we have already seen convincing evidence that the world stands ready to do whatever is necessary to act against any leader who presumes to take such an egregious step outside a certain norm of behavior.

"Now what of the argument that a nation might cheat on an agreement and suddenly reveal that it had a cache of nuclear weapons? South Africa, for instance, had six before it dismantled them.

"Here again, the answer is, 'So what?' We have had that circumstance already, with nuclear weapons present in the world. Saddam Hussein took no mind of the nuclear capabilities of the United States as he pursued his program of building nuclear weapons. Why? First, because he was basing his calculations on propositions of a kind that we would not view as rational. But, second, he was simply taking a lesson from our book. But what if we conveyed a new message: that the world should not accept as a norm the proposition that nuclear weapons will be used to intimidate or to influence the actions of other states, that this is simply an unacceptable basis of behavior for a nation-state because of the threat it poses to all nation-states?

"Now, let's imagine an even worse circumstance—that one of these weapons is actually exploded. What at that juncture would be the right response, in a world in which the elimination of nuclear weapons had been agreed upon? It would be an immediate and unconditional intervention, which, if necessary, goes in and physically removes the leadership of the state, puts the country under occupation subject to a global mandate, for whatever period of time is deemed necessary, just as we did at the end of World War II with Japan and Germany. It would be done according to a law that was put in place to authorize just that, with forces and plans and—most important—commitments that were firmly in place beforehand. If what opponents of abolition are searching for is a perfect world in which threats of that kind will be forever eliminated, then they have made the classic error making the perfect the enemy of the good."

I asked General Butler where he stood on the question of the horizontal path.

"One of the penalties of arms control as it came to be practiced during the Cold War is that its patterns and routines have become so embedded that today we continue to bargain as if we were still in that context. The result is low-expectation negotiations that are highly formalistic, mechanistic, and numbers driven—in which modestly shrinking numbers are viewed as adequate progress. But the issues are now much larger. They have to do with the manner in which the forces are arrayed. One can almost be content with the proposition that, considering the restraints on dismantling warheads owing to the lack of facilities, we're going to have to live with large numbers of these weapons for some years to come. If the assumption is that we're not willing to invest the money in dismantlement facilities, even though this would require only a fraction of the cost of any weapon system of the Cold War, we can nevertheless achieve the immediate needs of arms control in large part simply by taking the weapons off alert. We should do this not so much because we fear the risk of accidental, inadvertent, or unauthorized launch as because the two sides must cease sending each other the message that not only do we not trust each other but we are still of a mind to destroy each other and millions of people in a nuclear exchange. What possibly warrants, validates, justifies sending that message? It continues to profoundly chill the Russian-American relationship. Why do we still have so-called tactical nuclear weapons in Europe? It's absurd to imagine that in a Europe that has been totally transformed, these weapons have any conceivable role. And not only that, they arguably are the most dysfunctional, menacing, and generally counterproductive element in the current relationship—one that, for example, greatly feeds Russia's fear of the expansion of NATO. Why is it that, showing a singular failure of vision and willingness to begin afresh, we are hell-bent to expand NATO? We could easily have proposed working for a few years, on a collegial basis with our former adversaries, to rewrite the rulebook regarding how the world proceeds at this point. This shouldn't be just a dialogue between the United States and the former Soviet Union. It should be 1945 afresh—starting again, with a whole new construct."

"I was surprised how little feeling of celebration the end of the Cold War produced," I remarked. "Do you think that a part of the reason is that people are aware, perhaps unconsciously, that we have yet to deal with the underlying question of nuclear weapons? Perhaps, for the United States, the Cold War cannot truly be over until we face up to the nuclear question."

"I think that at some level there is a very real understanding that the bulk of the work is ahead of us," Butler replied. "We have been unable so far to do better than just sort of go on intellectual autopilot. No one has been prepared to come to grips with all that is required."

"Was the element of surprise at the end of the Cold War a part of that?"

"It was huge. We were not prepared. Let's imagine, for example, that we *had* prepared for this moment with the intellectual equivalent of the Manhattan Project. Let's suppose that the capricious gods had sent down a message to us in March 1985, when Gorbachev came to power, saying, 'Pay attention! This is important. In five or six years, there will be no more Warsaw Pact or Soviet Union. We're giving you a heads-up, so that you can begin preparing.' We would have answered, at first, 'What? Are you guys joking?' And then, on the offhand chance that the message was serious, that we weren't sure it was long enough to begin to deal with such a new situation, we would have answered, 'Can we have ten years to think this through? We have some problems. If you look at nuclear weapons alone, we don't have any place to store them even if we wanted to take them all off alert.' Imagine, then, that we had set about considering the matter in a systematic and orderly way. The president would undoubtedly have called a national blue-ribbon commission on the adaptation of national security strategy to a post–Cold War era."

"Why did nothing like that happen?"

"Remember that the final whimsical act of the gods was to drive George Bush from office and force us to go through a presidential transition at the most critical juncture. Policy positions sat vacant for months. Then the next administration was caught up in the controversy over Clinton's desire to address homosexuality in the armed forces. Remember? The priceless opportunity got stepped all over.

"We need to reflect on how revolutionary ideas get implemented and become evolutionary realities. The first and foremost test is whether, at its very core, the idea makes sense. And I believe that the idea of abolishing nuclear weapons passes that test with flying colors. Today, we are left with the spectacle of democratic societies clinging to the proposition that threats to the lives of tens of millions of people can be reconciled with the underlying tenets of our political philosophy. Why should we accept a bargain whose contractual terms take as commonplace forms of retribution that hold at risk the lives of so many people and threaten the viability of life on the planet? Who can argue that this is the best to which we can aspire?

"There's a terrible price to be paid, I believe, for accepting these terms. What is the measure of civilization? What is the test of morality? What are the qualities and capacities of human thought? What are the scales on which, ultimately, the capacities of mankind to live in peace on this planet will be measured? Isn't it, in fact, not only highly to be desired but also likely that someday we will come truly to understand that the distinctions upon which, until now, we have based our assessments and calculations regarding the prospects of peace—considerations of culture, religion, color of skin—have been entirely superficial, and simply recognize that fundamentally we are all of us of a piece? That, at the level of our DNA, we are indistinguishable, and that, given the opportunity, we all aspire to common values, including the right to live in peace and harmony, free from fear, and with the opportunity to realize all of the talents with which our creator endows us? Why would we cut off these prospects, which are set forth in the founding documents of our democracy, by embracing a creed that, given certain provocations, we will resort to methods that will extinguish the lives of tens of millions of people? That's barbaric. In fact, it is more barbaric than, perhaps, any measures for survival that you'll find in the animal kingdom. I have arrived at the conclusion that it is simply wrong, morally speaking, for any mortal to be invested with the authority to call into question the survival of the planet. That is an untenable allocation of authority, and yet it has become the central feature of the nuclear age.

"Nuclear weapons are irrational devices. They were rationalized and accepted as a desperate measure in the face of circumstances that were unimaginable. Now as the world evolves rapidly, I think that the vast majority of people on the face of this earth will endorse the proposition that such weapons have no place among us. There is no security to be found in nuclear weapons. It's a fool's game."

VI

EPILOGUE

The people I had interviewed were many things—statesmen, soldiers, scientists, cabinet officers, legislators, scholars, activists. But at this historical moment they were above all, it seemed to me, bearers of a wonderful piece of news: that it is possible, if only we can muster the political will, to free the world of nuclear danger. The immediate reason for their confidence is, of course, that great windfall handed to us by history, the end of the Cold War. To say that history has done something, though, obviously is only a manner of speaking. History does not act. Men and women do—in the case at hand, chiefly the millions of men and women in Eastern Europe, Russia, and the other republics of the Soviet Union who, at exorbitant personal cost, resisted and finally defeated the totalitarian system under which they were forced to live. They included, in Russia, Alexander Solzhenitsyn and Andrei Sakharov; in Poland, Lech Walesa and Adam Michnik; in Czechoslovakia, Jan Palach and Vaclav Havel, to name just a few of the better known. The battles in that war—which at the time seemed quixotic gestures, and only now can be understood as stages along the path to the Soviet empire's final defeat—included the rebellion in East Germany of 1953, the Hungarian revolution of 1956, the "Prague spring" of 1968, the Solidarity movement in Poland in 1980, the Baltic revolts of the late 1980s, and, finally, the successful resistance by democratic forces in Russia to the hardline Communist putsch attempt against Gorbachev and Yeltsin in August of 1991.

It was not, in most cases, the intention of these activists to advance the cause of nuclear disarmament, but that, as it turned out, was one of their achievements. It is a pleasant paradox of our current situation that the antitotalitarian movements within the Soviet empire have done more for nuclear disarmament than those of us in the West who directly resisted nuclear arms. (This is not to overlook the contribution of the Western antinuclear movement, which played an important role in moderating American and NATO policies throughout the period. The campaign against Pershing missiles in Europe and the nuclear freeze campaign in the United States, to give just two examples, unquestionably made a major contribution to the complex series of events, as yet incompletely understood, that led to the Reagan-Gorbachev rapprochement of the late eighties, and to the reversal of the arms race.) The paradox, however, is only apparent, for there is a deep inner logic connecting the two causes, inasmuch as both have been rebellions against vast and closely linked systems based on terror. Western hawks as well as doves are prone to underestimate the achievement of their anti-Communist brethren in the East. While some doves imagine that they reversed the arms race by their own efforts, some hawks imagine that they "won" the Cold War. In truth, it was chiefly the peoples of the East who, through their efforts in their own countries, won the main victory—in consequence of which the Cold War disappeared. This is not to deny the Western governments credit for their steadfastness in resisting the Soviet Union—especially, perhaps, in the years immediately following the end of the Second World War—any more than it is to deny the Western peace movement credit for ending the arms race. It is only to acknowledge that the main drama of the period—the drama that led directly to the dramatic, unforeseen collapse of the Soviet Union in 1991—was the struggle in the East.

The point in the present context is not to apportion historical credit or blame but only to observe that those, mainly in the West, who now seek to abolish nuclear weapons stand on the shoulders of those in the East who won the fight for freedom. Important consequences flow from this realization. If we suppose that the most important task before us today is to dismantle the unprecedented systems of indiscriminate mass terror that in our century fastened themselves, in the form of totalitarian rule, upon whole nations and, later, in the form of the system of mutual assured destruction, upon the entire world, then the antinuclear cause must be seen as the second stage of a process whose first stage was the overthrow from within of the Soviet Union. Although the West did not "win" the Cold War, there is no doubt that the modern Western system—characterized by democracy in politics, capitalism in economics, and reliance on the fruits of advanced technology and science—has in fact spread throughout world, very much including the territories of its former adversaries. It is no secret to anyone, however, that this dominant system has profound flaws. And chief among them is the surpassingly strange fact that it holds a loaded, cocked pistol to its head and threatens to blow its brains out—that it has a pronounced suicidal bent. At least as strange is the fact that a cottage industry of experts declares that it is in principle impossible to desist from threatening self-destruction. As long as the Western countries were engaged in an epic, global struggle with a rival bloc, it was possible to believe that the suicide danger was an unavoidable product of that struggle. But now that the former adversary is no more, we are compelled—as long as we insist on holding on to nuclear arsenals—to suspect that the suicidal tendency may be a symptom of our own civilization.

Just as the peoples of the East found the way to dismantle the system of totalitarian terror under which they lived, so now it is the responsibility of the peoples of the West to lead the way in dismantling the system of nuclear terror under which we all have been living. In acknowledging our indebtedness to the peoples of the East, however, it would be self-serving to imagine that our circumstances are as difficult as theirs were. They accomplished by far the most arduous part of our common task. It was their ambition, in the face of ferocious repression, to establish freedom. We begin with freedom. All the instruments of democracy—a free press, the right to vote, an intact bill of rights, a rich array of civic associations—are at our fingertips. It may in fact be the comparative luxury and ease of our circumstances that is the chief obstacle to the fulfillment of our responsibility. What is more, precisely because our global rival has evaporated, we do not even possess an external foe to goad us to action. Our effort therefore must, in unusually high degree, be self-starting. It must be action in its purest form, not *reaction*. (The events for which we would wait in order to be able to *react*—the use again of nuclear weapons—are not something to await, they are something to prevent.) Such an effort, though difficult, would be of a piece with our goal, the preservation of life, which, after all, arrives unbidden and unconditionally from the hand of God, not by invitation, or in reaction to something or other.

REVOLUTION FROM THE SIDE

Historians distinguish between revolutions that proceed from the top down and those that proceed from the bottom up. The movement to abolish nuclear weapons has, so far, been what you might call a revolution from the side inward. It has begun with groups in civil society— the nongovernmental organizations that founded Abolition 2000 and several of the braver think tanks in Washington, including the Stimson Center. They have been supported by a considerable number of retired military officers and civilian officials. This class of retired persons is well suited to play an important role. Retired soldiers and statesmen often retain much of the prestige of office, but without the constraints. They can provide an early indication of deep but invisible changes of heart among those in power and also serve as a bridge to their incumbent colleagues. Of course, once the unretired are ready to join the cause, the battle is all but won.

This revolution-from-the-side against the nuclear system now is expanding both "upward" to the policymakers—seeking above all to bend the ear of a president of the United States—and "downward" to the public, whose response to the project will in the last analysis be decisive. It also continues its sideways motion—seeking, for example, to establish itself in professional organizations, including the medical and the legal ones, which would provide the movement with depth and, what is especially important, staying power. If the large professional associations were to establish committees to keep track of the issue, lobby in its favor, and report back regularly to the memberships, the cause would be hugely strengthened. Street protests and demonstrations, of the kind so useful in bringing the Vietnam War to an end, seem, for now, unlikely. Nevertheless, it's possible to imagine that, if public awareness of the issues were to increase, a single immense, peaceful demonstration in favor of abolition might be possible. Million-person demonstrations are the fashion these days. The first of these—although not so named—was the one in favor of the nuclear freeze in New York in June of 1982. Abolition is an incomparably more important goal than a freeze and deserves a larger crowd—let us say, in various cities around the country, ten million.

The path to abolition is by no means unobstructed. As my conversations made clear, even if the political will were present, there still would be many questions to be answered and hurdles to cross. The most difficult and contentious issue, certainly, is the question of breakout, about which, as Robert McNamara pointed out, no full-scale, detailed study has yet been done—perhaps because no government has yet taken the goal of abolition seriously enough to feel that it needs to know the results. Still, in the absence of such a study, many of those I talked with presented convincing reasons for thinking that the problem would be manageable. Joseph Rotblat pointed out the benefits of "social verification" for an inspection regime, especially over the long run; Generals Butler and Horner set forth the world's power of collective action to restrain or punish a violator, as had been done in the Gulf War; Michael Mazarr outlined the power of "virtual arsenals" to deter a violation; George Perkovich cast serious doubt on the benefits of such a violation in the first place; Molander and Wilson in their war games demonstrated the dubious utility of possessing nuclear weapons if violation *did* occur. Especially telling, perhaps, was Robert O'Neill's recital of all the occasions on which a power possessing a nuclear monopoly failed to find any way of turning it to military or political advantage. If in the years of the Cold War great nuclear powers—the United States in Vietnam, Russia in Afghanistan—could not intimidate small nonnuclear powers, then how, in a world that had agreed to abolish nuclear

weapons, could small nuclear powers intimidate great nonnuclear powers? Deterrence theory teaches that nations without nuclear weapons
are helpless in the face of nations that have them. Fifty years of history
have taught a different lesson. History has suggested, in fact, that
the advantages, if any, of possessing nuclear arsenals are far smaller
than theory predicts. What McGeorge Bundy has called "the tradition
of non-use" has proved surprisingly durable. And wouldn't that tradition—the product of a half-century of experience, not of theory and
supposition—be incomparably strengthened if it were embodied in a
solemn treaty backed by the collective voice and will of mankind?

WHAT IS ZERO?

All of these arguments are reasons for believing, as McNamara did, that
if the study of breakout were done its conclusions would be reassuring.
There was one question, however, that had long vexed me and that,
during my conversations, continued to trouble me. It was the question
I had discussed at length with Harald Müller: What, in specific terms,
does "zero" nuclear weapons mean? In the early eighties, when the
Cold War appeared to have gained a new lease on life (its final chapter,
as it turned out), I had written two articles on the nuclear question for
The New Yorker. In the first, "The Fate of the Earth," which appeared in
1982, I described the effects, insofar as these could be known, of a full-
scale nuclear holocaust, and I concluded that human extinction was a
real possibility. At that time, the article's readers often asked me the
very natural question, "What, then, shall we do about this peril?" Two
years later, in an article called "The Abolition," I advanced what I
thought might be the beginning of an answer, which I called "weaponless deterrence." It amounted to an elementary version of the horizontal path of disarmament. My fundamental point was that in a world
that had agreed to abolish nuclear weapons the knowledge of how to
build them, backed up by a certain amount of technical equipment,
would serve as a deterrent against breakout. Just as the unlosable
knowledge, in the hands of rogues, could threaten any agreement, I
suggested, so, in the hands of law-abiding nations, it could shore up the

agreement. My hope was that the proposal would provide an alternative to the unpalatable all-or-nothing choice between eternal deterrence and world government. Abolition, I concluded, did not have to await the establishment of a world government to protect us against cheaters and rogues—we could proceed to it directly.

Even during the Cold War, however, I was aware of a strong ethical objection to the idea of weaponless deterrence—especially for someone like myself, whose opposition to the use of nuclear weapons in any circumstances was absolute. I opposed a second strike as much as I opposed a first strike. Indeed, I opposed any nuclear strike whatsoever—first, second, third, or thirty-third. How, then, could I be proposing any form of deterrence, with or without the hardware? Why would I introduce deterrence, of all things, into a nuclear-weapon-free world?

I was sharply, even painfully, reminded of this objection when Joseph Rotblat told me he opposed the idea of virtual arsenals, and when Harald Müller referred to this idea as a symptom of the "sickness" of the mind induced by nuclear arms. I had to admit, to begin with, that I found the doctrine of nuclear deterrence to be one of the most diabolical riddles ever set before the mind of man. Faust's dilemma, it has sometimes seemed to me, was pleasant and easy by comparison. Deterrence is an abstract doctrine, yet it risks the most drastic conceivable material consequences. It's a product of pure thought whose centerpiece, nuclear annihilation, is commonly called "unthinkable." Seen in one light, it's a doctrine of limitless intricacy, shot through with conundrum and paradox. Seen in another light, it expresses the simplest schoolyard maxim: If you touch me, I'll knock you flat. It's a system of terror that purports to hold terror at bay. Naturally, we'd like to escape it—to go "beyond" deterrence—yet as soon as we try to do so, it seems to overtake us again. We seem to escape it by considering the wholesale destruction of nuclear arms, only to find it rising up again in "virtual" form. And yet if we accept the doctrine we implicate ourselves in the willingness, in some circumstance or another, to kill millions of people, and no amount of casuistry can free us from that complicity.

At issue, broadly speaking, is the role, in our nuclear-capable world, to be played by nuclear terror. Must we rely on it—in one form or another—for our safety? Must its use be immediate and overwhelming or can it somehow be attenuated, or rolled back? In a world that has acquired the fateful know-how, can nuclear terror be eliminated from military and political calculation?

The distinction between technical zero and political zero, though apparently arcane, leads into both the moral and the practical center of this question. My conversations made clear that defining technical zero is not easy. But difficulty is not impossibility. There is clearly a difference, as Morton Halperin has suggested, between scattered nuclear "materials" and nuclear "weapons." Perhaps the line between the two is crossed, as he also suggests, when the plutonium cores are removed from warheads. But whether we choose this point or another point farther along the horizontal path of disarmament, it is unquestionably possible, through technical means, to turn something that is a nuclear weapon into a collection of materials that plainly is not. It therefore would be perfectly accurate to say that when every nuclear weapon has been dismantled to a certain extent, abolition has occurred. And this word, it seems to me, remains fitting whether or not a nation still intends, in the event that another nation builds nuclear weapons, to rebuild them itself.

The definition of political zero requires an entirely different set of calculations, having to do with human will, not with technical equipment. It is theoretically possible, for instance, to reduce one's society technically to the Stone Age while still not ruling out the intention of building nuclear weapons and using them one day. It would also be possible (though senseless) to possess nuclear arsenals while having no intention of using them. Britain and the United States are, insofar as their nuclear relations with each other are concerned, at political zero, even though each has a nuclear arsenal with which it could devastate the other. The defining feature of political zero, which can exist independently of any existing nuclear materials, is a complete disavowal by political authorities of the intention to use nuclear weapons, in any circumstances. Britain and the United States feel no need to go to a mutual technical zero because their confidence in their political zero is so strong.

Political will, admittedly, is a less tangible thing than nuclear technology, but it too can be embodied in institutions. A no-first-use policy, for instance, is a declaration of intention that would have both technical and legal consequences. The technical consequences would be a shift in the composition of military forces to provide defense without using nuclear weapons first. The legal consequences would be adherence to a treaty agreeing on no-first-use. However, the great—the transforming—step along the path to political zero would certainly be the renunciation of the retaliatory strike, for only this step would render renunciation of nuclear weapons complete. The consequences would of course be profound. In the first place, the path then would be clear to declaring both possession and use of nuclear weapons crimes against humanity. (This would not be possible if nations reserved the right to reconstitute nuclear weapons. Then, only first use, or first possession, would be a crime.) In addition, a far deeper reconfiguration of military forces as well as international alliance would be required. In the third place, the "social verification"—the universal whistleblowing—of nuclear disarmament could be established in both international and national law.

To designate political zero, we might borrow a leaf from the National Academy of Sciences committee and press the word *prohibition* into use. However, we would not be using the word as they did, to indicate a step that fell short of abolition—which to the academy's ear meant a final, theoretically irreversible, and therefore unattainable riddance of all nuclear weapons. It seems to me that the word *prohibition* would be better used to describe the more thoroughgoing and difficult step. We say that something is prohibited when it has been legally banned. But a true legal ban on nuclear weapons requires a renunciation not just of the technical devices but of any intention ever to rebuild them. Therefore, the prohibition—the illegalization—of nuclear weapons would rule out virtual arsenals. Prohibition would mean no-second-use as well as no-first-use, and no-second-possession as well as no-first-possession. Prohibition would embody the will of the world to break its reliance on nuclear weapons without qualification or reservation, and to depend entirely on other means for its security.

I said at the beginning of this book that only nuclear abolition solves the essential moral dilemma posed by nuclear weapons because only abolition delivers us from complicity in historically unprecedented mass slaughter. Strictly speaking, however, I should have said that only the form of abolition that embraces political as well as technical zero releases us, finally, from this complicity.

The goal of reaching weaponless deterrence or virtual arsenals, then, emerges, as Harald Müller remarked, as a stage along the way to the further—the truly final—goal of abolition that is prohibition. Of the intermediate stage of virtual arsenals we can say what Bruce Blair said of de-alerting: It allows the technical-military arrangements to keep pace in an unbroken continuum with the political arrangements. It assures that for every political step forward, there is a technical one to match. It thereby breaks the stranglehold that the present deterrence system, with its requirement for an ever ready, overwhelming threat of mutual nuclear destruction, has over us, and releases us from the absurd situation of menacing, and being menaced by, countries like Russia with which we have friendly relations.

Lee Butler's observations, based on a lifetime of experience with deterrence, were consistent with this conclusion. It was true, as Butler said, that the presence of nuclear danger produced caution among policymakers. However, the more they tried to make the nuclear threat operational, the more they undermined the very stability they were trying to create. A reasonable conclusion was that while nuclear weapons could not be disinvented, safety from nuclear danger would steadily increase as the world proceeded along the path from fully alert to fully disassembled arsenals.

Let us turn the familiar image of nuclear escalation upside down and picture the path to nuclear safety as a de-escalatory ladder, leading, at its end, to the prohibition of nuclear weapons. If we picture this ladder as suspended from the high and dangerous precipice on which we now sit, we would like to know, before we start climbing down, that it reaches all the way to the ground. According to current deterrence theory, many of the lower rungs are missing. According to the advocates of virtual arsenals, all the rungs are present. The ladder proceeds step by descendable step to safety. The way to abolition—and beyond abolition to prohibition—lies open.

If that destination were reached, would the infernal paradoxes of nuclear deterrence then at last be dissolved once and for all? They would. No "side," in that world, would threaten "the other side" with nuclear weapons, whether credibly or incredibly, thinkably or unthinkably. No citizen would be drawn into the barbarism of threatening to kill millions of innocent people. All political efforts would truly bend toward preventing such acts, which would unambiguously be named as crimes. However, this answer requires a qualification. Although nuclear threats would be gone, nuclear danger would remain—far, far in the background of our affairs, perhaps, but present nevertheless. Moreover, everyone would know this. If the world returned to anarchy, nuclear weapons could reappear. This is the truly ineradicable political consequence of the fact that nuclear weapons cannot be disinvented. There is, in the last analysis, no turning back to a prenuclear age. In that sense, you could even say that a kind of nuclear deterrence would persist. The fear of returning to a nuclear-armed world would always stand guard over the treaty by which the world had eliminated such weapons. The difference from the present would be that rather than one nation deterring another, all would jointly deter all from starting back up the path to the nuclear abyss. If, in a last gasp of the paradoxical language of deterrence, we wished to assign a "use" to nuclear danger in that world, we would say that the purpose of nuclear danger is to prevent ourselves from ever again possessing—not to speak of using—nuclear weapons. This would be deterrence that truly works.

A VIEW OF MOUNTAINS

On August 9, 1945, the day the atomic bomb was dropped on Nagasaki, Yosuke Yamahata, a photographer serving in the Japanese army, was dispatched to the destroyed city. The hundred or so pictures he took the next day constitute the fullest photographic record of nuclear destruction in existence. Hiroshima, destroyed three days earlier, had largely escaped the camera's lens in the first days after the bombing. It was therefore left to Yamahata to record, methodically—and, as it happens, with a great and simple artistry—the effects on a human population of a nuclear weapon only hours after it had been used. Some of Yamahata's pictures show corpses charred in the peculiar way in which a nuclear fireball chars its victims. They have been burned by light—technically speaking, by the "thermal pulse"—and their bodies are often branded with the patterns of their clothes, whose colors absorb light in different degrees. One photograph shows a horse twisted under the cart it had been pulling. Another shows a heap of something that once was a human being hanging over a ledge into a ditch. A third shows a girl who has somehow survived unwounded standing in the open mouth of a bomb shelter and smiling an unearthly smile, shocking us with the sight of ordinary life, which otherwise seems to have been left behind for good in the scenes we are witnessing. Stretching into the distance on all sides are fields of rubble dotted with fires, and, in the background, a view of mountains. We can see the mountains because the city is gone. That absence, even more than the wreckage, contains the heart of the matter. The true measure of the event lies not in what remains but in all that has disappeared.

It took a few seconds for the United States to destroy Nagasaki with the world's second atomic bomb, but it took fifty years for Yamahata's pictures of the event to make the journey back from Nagasaki to the United States. They were shown for the first time in this country in 1995, at the International Center for Photography in New York. Arriving a half-century late, they are still news. The photographs display the fate of a single city, but their meaning is universal, since, in our nuclear-armed world, what happened to Nagasaki can, in a flash, happen to any city in the world. In the photographs, Nagasaki comes into its own. Nagasaki has always been in the shadow of Hiroshima, as if the human imagination had stumbled to exhaustion in the wreckage of the first ruined city without reaching even the outskirts of the second. Yet the bombing of Nagasaki is in certain respects the fitter symbol of the nuclear danger that still hangs over us. It is proof that, having once used nuclear weapons, we can use them again. It introduces the idea of a series—the series that, with tens of thousands of nuclear weapons remaining in existence, continues to threaten everyone. (The unpredictable, open-ended character of this series is suggested by the fact that the second bomb originally was to be dropped on the city of Kokura, which was spared Nagasaki's fate only because bad weather protected it from view.) Each picture therefore seemed not so much an image of something that happened a half-century ago as a window cut into the wall of the photography center showing what soon could easily happen to New York. Wherever the exhibit might travel, moreover, the view of the threatened future from these "windows" would be roughly accurate, since, although every intact city is different from every other, all cities that suffer nuclear destruction will look much the same.

Yamahata's pictures afford a glimpse of the end of the world. Yet in our day, when the challenge is not just to apprehend the nuclear peril but to seize a God-given opportunity to dispel it once and for all, we seem to need, in addition, some other picture to counterpoise against ruined Nagasaki—one showing not what we would lose through our failure but what we would gain by our success. What might that picture be, though? How do you show the opposite of the end of the world? Should it be Nagasaki, intact and alive, before the bomb was dropped—or perhaps the spared city of Kokura? Should it be a child, or a mother and child, or perhaps the Earth itself? None seems adequate, for how can we give a definite form to that which can assume infinite forms, namely, the lives of all human beings, now and in the future? Imagination, faced with either the end of the world or its continuation, must remain incomplete. Only action can satisfy.

Once, the arrival in the world of new generations took care of itself. Now, they can come into existence only if, through an act of faith and collective will, we ensure their right to exist. Performing that act is the greatest of the responsibilities of the generations now alive. The gift of time is the gift of life, forever, if we know how to receive it.

ACKNOWLEDGMENTS

This book originated in a conversation in the fall of 1995 with Victor Navasky, the publisher and editorial director of *The Nation*. The magazine, he said, occasionally invited a guest editor to put together a special issue of the magazine on a single topic. Did I have any ideas? I did. I suggested that the time was ripe to revisit the nuclear question. Now that the Cold War was over, wasn't it possible to eliminate nuclear weapons? I proposed the idea to the magazine's editor, Katrina vanden Heuvel, and she was enthusiastic. I suggested a series of interviews—a kind of conversation on the printed page—mostly with people who had been involved at high levels in framing Cold War policies and now were rethinking their support for nuclear arms. A few— among them General Charles Horner and Robert McNamara—had already spoken up in favor of abolition. I felt sure that more could be found, or would step forward of their own accord, as in fact happened.

The Nation project received support from several quarters. I wish to thank the Ploughshares Fund for its help to me in launching the project. The MacArthur Foundation, the Samuel Rubin Foundation, the Public Concern Foundation, Rockefeller Financial Services, and the

Investigative Fund of the Nation Institute enabled *The Nation* to complete this ambitious project, which included printing an issue about twice the normal size of the magazine. The W. Alton Jones Foundation gave its support to a program to publicize the calls for abolition contained in the special issue. I wish to express my gratitude to all of them.

I am grateful for the editorial help at *The Nation* of Art Winslow and Roane Carey, and for research assistance from Jonathan Taylor, Philip Connors, and Philip Higgs.

Special thanks are due to Tom Engelhardt, who gave indispensable editorial advice throughout and managed the arduous task of simultaneously editing the manuscript for the magazine and the far longer manuscript for the book. Thanks, too, to my agent, Lynn Nesbit, who expertly shepherded a project that at first was not intended to be a book but gradually became one. I also wish to express my warm appreciation to Augusto Lopez-Claros for his hospitality, help, and advice during several trips to Moscow.

I wish also to thank all of those whom I interviewed. They each not only gave me hours of their time but agreed to read over and correct the edited versions of the interviews. I wish to express my particular gratitude to Senator Alan Cranston, who guided me to many of the people I interviewed and, throughout, gave me the great benefit of his wisdom, acquired over a lifetime of work for peace.

Finally, I want to thank my daughter Phoebe, for proposing the title for this book.

INDEX